Alberta's Camelot

Culture & the Arts in the Lougheed Years

Fil Fraser

To Dolores Ewen

Best Wishes

Lone Pine Publishing

The Publisher: Lone Pine Publishing

10145 – 81 Avenue	1808 B Street NW, Suite 140
Edmonton, AB	Auburn, WA
Canada T6E 1W9	USA 98001

Website: www.lonepinepublishing.com

National Library of Canada Cataloguing in Publication Data
Fraser, Fil, 1932–
  Alberta's Camelot: Culture & the Arts in the Lougheed Years

  Includes index.

  ISBN 1-55105-393-4

Editorial Director: Nancy Foulds
Editorial: Eva Radford
Illustrations Coordinator: Carol Woo
Production Manager: Gene Longson
Text Design & Production: Heather Markham
Cover Design: Gerry Dotto
Scanning, Separations & Film: Elite Lithographers Co.

Cover painting, *The Buskers* by Toti

The photographs in this book are reproduced with the generous permission of their copyright holders.

We acknowledge the financial support of the Government of Canada through the Book Publishing Industry Development Program (BPIDP) for our publishing activities.

PC: 01

To my parents,

Marguerite Enid Wiles

&

Felix Paul Blache-Fraser,

on whose shoulders I stand.

Acknowledgements

There are many people to thank. First, Jeanne and Peter Lougheed and Horst Schmid, who opened their personal archives and gave generously of their time. Les Usher, Dennis Anderson (who first described the 1970s to me as Alberta's Camelot years), Grant Kennedy, Senator Tommy Banks, Jim DeFelice, Tom Peacocke, Mary Glenfield, Brian Paisley, Jim Edwards, Dick Wong and many others. Mel Hurtig gave me encouragement just when I needed it and steered me to my intuitive and talented editor, Eva Radford. Thanks also to Shane Kennedy, Nancy Foulds, Lee Craig and Heather Markham for their help from the early stages of this book. My extended family and especially my wife, Gladys, have been supportive in ways I can never fully describe. In addition to those I've named, there are literally thousands of Albertans who helped to make this great province my spiritual home. I am grateful to them all.

This book was written with generous support from the Alberta Foundation for the Arts.

Contents

*If the Kennedy years were America's Camelot,
the Lougheed years brought the same magic
to Alberta.*

—Dennis Anderson, Minister of Culture, 1986–87

Foreword

by David Leighton

A memoir is defined in *Webster's Dictionary* as "an account of something deemed worthy of record" and "the reminiscences of a person, either general or dating to a particular period." And that is exactly what *Alberta's Camelot: Culture and the Arts in the Lougheed Years* is— a deeply personal, first-hand account of what can happen when a talented arts community, a prosperous economy and an imaginatively led, supportive government converge, as they did in the province of Alberta during the Lougheed years from 1971 to 1985.

Those years were Camelot for the arts in Alberta. Building on modest foundations put slowly and painstakingly in place through decades of settlement, drought and world wars, the arts did explode with the coming to power of Peter Lougheed and his Conservative

Party in 1971. Suddenly, there was an activist government with a strategy and funds to create new and exciting theatre and dance companies, festivals, concert halls and art galleries. Alberta, and particularly Banff, became a magnet for many of the world's greatest artists. Filmmaking and book publishing took root in the prairie landscape. These years were exciting times to be an Albertan.

Fil Fraser was a significant player in Alberta's "Camelot years"; in this book he shows that he was a perceptive observer as well. A radio and television host, feature film producer, cultural commentator, board member and social activist, he was a key part of it all. As a partner of his on several of these fronts, I can vouch for his creative participation, for the accuracy of his observations and, above all, for his personal integrity and leadership. It is hard to imagine anyone better positioned to write about this period.

The result is decidedly not a stuffy academic history, but a lively and engrossing labour of love, full of fascinating insights, personal stories and often-provocative commentary. As the author acknowledges, others with different backgrounds will undoubtedly write quite different accounts—particularly expanding the coverage of the development of music and the visual arts, activities in which he was not directly involved, or no doubt taking issue with the emphasis he, as an Edmontonian, gives to Edmonton's leading role.

He is a particular admirer of Peter Lougheed and his wife, Jeanne. Peter told many people that "the greatest supporter of the arts in Alberta is the lady who sits across the breakfast table from me," and in this account, Jeanne finally gets the credit that is her due. As does Horst Schmid, the dynamic German-born immigrant who became a hard-driving Minister of Culture, who had the job of implementing the government's arts strategy, and did so with a vengeance.

The Lougheed years were parallelled by growth in the arts in the rest of the country too, but it is not an overstatement to claim, as this book does, that Alberta's was "Canada's Most Extraordinary Explosion in the Arts." Much of the development in central Canada came following the 1951 Massey Report and the subsequent creation of the Canada Council. For a number of reasons, mostly political priorities, Alberta had been slow to gain from what was happening elsewhere in the country. When the "explosion" did come, it was all the more dramatic, indeed revolutionary. This book makes it clear that the explosion was not because of any one cause, or any individual, but because of an incredible, once-in-a-lifetime confluence of dynamic individuals and circumstances, led by Peter Lougheed's desire to shed the image of "redneck Alberta."

These circumstances may never be repeated. But they have left a legacy of individuals, institutions, facilities and memories that make Alberta a major centre of creativity to this day—one that is still not fully appreciated in the rest of the country. If there is one message that can be taken from this account, it is that it takes leadership at many levels to "make it happen." Fil Fraser has amply demonstrated his leadership in adding to our understanding of an important era in Canada's history.

—Dr. David S.R. Leighton, O.C.,
is chair of the Board of Trustees of the National Arts Centre.
He was president of the Banff Centre from 1970 to 1983.

Pound for pound, when I lived in Edmonton it was the most vibrant, artistic city in Canada, even more than Toronto.

—Paul Gross, Canadian actor[1]

Introduction

An Explosion of the Arts

This memoir is a view of an extraordinary period in the life of Alberta, and of a time in my own life that still astonishes me. When I look back through the lens of the political and economic realities of the early 21st century, it is hard for me to believe that for a decade and a half, in the 1970s and early 1980s, the Government of Alberta supported culture in ways unmatched, with the possible exception of Québec, anywhere, anytime in Canada. Premier Peter Lougheed, with the active encouragement of his wife, Jeanne, supported the arts with strongly positive attitudes and with generous, well-placed funding. The government treated culture as if it really mattered. And, in the process, it changed the way that many Albertans, myself included, saw themselves and their communities.

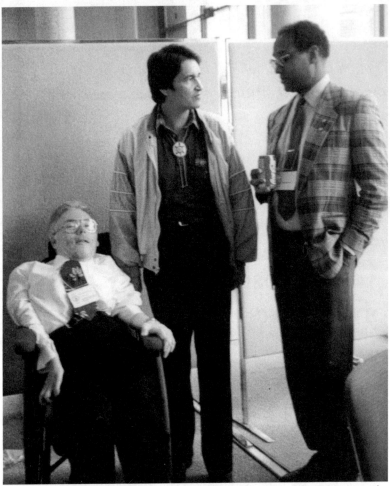

Me with Ovide Mercredi (centre), then-Chief of the Assembly of First Nations, and Gary McPherson, chair of the Premier's Committee on the Status of Persons with Disabilities, at a human rights conference in Lloydminster. *Photo: Fil Fraser*

If this book has any purpose, it is to demonstrate to Canadians, and to their governments, the significant impact that progressive support of the arts can have on the life of a province and a country. I may be guilty of overstating the case, but I point to the legacy of that magnificent era. The Banff Centre, the Banff International

Television Festival, the Citadel Theatre, the music, theatre and other arts festivals that enrich communities across the province, did not just happen. They took place because the government of the day created a supportive environment for its creative citizens. Make no mistake, these events and facilities could not have developed without the support of an enlightened government.

This is not a political book; it is a celebration of the people who, during a time that in hindsight seems almost magical, created a legacy that includes some of Canada's most important cultural institutions. Few outside of Alberta think of the province as a fountain of culture. Too many see only our almost embarrassing wealth, our abundance of oil and natural gas. They are aware of the macho celebration surrounding the Calgary Stampede and the spectacular beauty of the Rockies. Some chuckle derisively at the largest temple to consumerism in the world, West Edmonton Mall, appropriately, they think, located in Alberta. Many think of Alberta as the Bible Belt province that elected Social Credit governments for three and a half decades and the redneck territory that spawned Holocaust denier James Keegstra and the Reform and Alliance parties. Alberta is known as the home of the Ralph Klein government that showed Ontario and British Columbia how to really cut deficits. The right-wing label sticks uncomfortably tight.

But during the 1970s and into the mid-1980s, Alberta had a progressive red Tory government that believed the province's wealth had to offer something for the spirit. Culture and the arts achieved a rare level of respectability and success with the creation of such institutions as the internationally recognized Banff Centre for the Arts, a leading destination for young artists from around the world. The annual Banff International Television Festival is now one of the most important events on the international calendar for television executives and creators. The Edmonton Fringe Theatre Festival is the largest and most successful event of its kind in North America. *The Canadian Encyclopedia,* the greatest publishing feat in Canadian history, was a gift to all of Canada from Alberta in celebration of the province's 75th anniversary. The Citadel Theatre complex is one of the finest facilities for the presentation of stage drama in the country. Edmonton's Heritage Days, the nation's and probably the continent's largest multicultural festival, showcases the art and crafts, the music and the food of as many as 70 cultures. And throughout Alberta, the era saw the launch of a sparkling constellation of annual festivals celebrating the visual arts, film, jazz, folk, blues and country music, and every kind of theatre.

Even sports flourished. Don't laugh. When the head of The Sports Network (TSN) appeared before the 1985 Federal Task Force on Broadcasting Policy, his first words to us were, "Ladies and gentlemen, sport is culture."[2] The Edmonton Eskimos won five Grey Cups in a row. The Edmonton Oilers, led by the greatest hockey player in the world, won five Stanley Cups in seven years. Edmonton declared itself the City of Champions.

This may not be a political book, as I said, but part of its purpose is to demonstrate how culture and the arts, when properly supported, can change the life of a community and a province. I feel lucky that the trajectory of my life, which has so frequently put me in the right place at the right time, allowed me to play an active role during what some have described as Alberta's Camelot years. So the book is also my story.

I was born in Montréal in August 1932 and grew up in a mixed immigrant and French Canadian community in the city's east end. In high school, I was spellbound by radio, especially after appearing as a student disc jockey on radio station CJAD's afternoon teen program, "Club 800." I wanted, more than anything, to be a radio announcer. So after high school, I hitchhiked all over western Québec and eastern Ontario, stopping at every small-town radio station to tell them what a "swell" job I could do for them as a DJ. Many, many stops later, after waiting around for several days in Woodstock, Ontario, for a job that looked promising but didn't materialize, I ran out of money. Very early one morning, before the town came to life, I skipped out of the local hotel and hit the road for Toronto. Putting my broadcasting ambitions on hold, I went to work as a shipper in the original Coles Book Store at Charles and Yonge streets, mailing *Coles Notes* to students across the country.

In 1951, broadcasting legend Foster ("He shoots! He scores!") Hewitt gave me my first job in radio as an operator at his Toronto radio station, CKFH. The man who had the job had quit just before

Sports director, radio station CKBB, Barrie, Ontario, 1952. *Photo: Pete Ward*

I walked in, and the station needed someone to cover the overnight shift. I, never having done it before, told Hewitt, "Sure I can run a control board." That led to a real disc jockey job in Timmins, the CKBB play-by-play hockey voice of the Barrie (Ontario) Flyers, and then back home to Montréal, where I became a news reporter at CFCF (Canada's First, Canada's Finest), the Marconi station that had been on the air since 1919. I left Montréal for Regina in 1958 with an assignment to produce a "sound biography" of Saskatchewan Premier Tommy Douglas for the CBC. I was quickly caught up in the greatest Canadian story of the time, the introduction of Medicare. In what seemed like no time flat, I was offered a public-relations job in Regina and stayed in the city for seven years, later founding and publishing the *Regina Weekly Mirror,* and still later, becoming supervisor of education for the Saskatchewan Bureau on Alcoholism.

An offer to do the same job for more money brought me to Edmonton in 1965 as director of education for the provincial alcoholism

Me at the controls doing the morning show on radio station CKXM, circa 1982.
Photo: Gordon Karam

and addictions program. I was often its radio and television spokesperson. In 1969, I returned to full-time broadcasting as program manager of Canada's first on-air educational television station, the forerunner of ACCESS-TV. Over the next two decades, my broadcasting career ranged from co-anchoring the CBC's supper-hour public-affairs show to hosting the daily *Fil Fraser Show* on ITV, to stints as an open-line radio and morning show host. During the same period, I produced more than 20 documentary films for television and three feature movies.[3] In 1989, I found myself assuming the role of Chief Commissioner of the Alberta Human Rights Commission, followed by teaching a course on the evolution of human rights to third-year law students at the University of Alberta.

Thirty years after moving to the province, I left Alberta for a sojourn in Toronto as president and CEO of Vision TV, a national multifaith and multicultural television network. There's more—not for this book—but you get the idea. My Saskatchewan-born wife Gladys Odegard and I never intended our move to Toronto to be permanent. And so, after I retired from Vision TV, we came home to Alberta in January 2001.

We were surprised at the number of our eastern friends who wondered why, after six years in the Mega City—the "world class, most multicultural city in the world," as Toronto brands itself in its advertising—we would want to return to Edmonton. "What's in Alberta?" they asked. Some were surprised to learn that we had not sold our Edmonton home, that we had planned all along to return. "Culture," they advised us patiently when we told them that Edmonton's cultural life was a major reason for our return, "is to be found in Toronto and Ottawa and Montréal, where *all* of the important national institutions are centred."[4] So, another reason for this book is to tell them, and the rest of Canada, the story of why a disproportionate amount of our country's cultural creativity is centred in Alberta. During the halcyon years of the 1970s, Edmonton became a bubbling centre of creative innovation. For example, in one wonderful flight of whimsy, the city created a waterfall from the High Level Bridge over the North Saskatchewan River. On special occasions, water cascades for several hours in a block-wide curtain. Imagined by artist and designer Peter Lewis, the waterfall is higher than Niagara Falls by 7.3 metres (24 feet).

I will show you a different side of Peter Lougheed, premier of Alberta from 1971 to 1985. He is the man many Canadians think of as the Blue-eyed Sheik of Calgary, the man who fought Pierre Trudeau over the National Energy Program in the early 1980s. But from the time he swept into office in 1971 until his retirement party on October 11, 1985, Lougheed's Alberta experienced an unprecedented mushrooming of cultural and multicultural activity. With oil revenues flowing copiously, the province became a patron of the arts. Editorial writer Rosemary McCracken, writing in the *Calgary Herald* in the mid-80s, when deficits had already begun to erode cultural spending, noted that Alberta and Québec had the only two provincial ministries in Canada devoted exclusively to culture. "Alberta," she wrote, "has the highest per capita expenditure on culture in Canada, and is second only to Québec and Ontario in total amount."[5]

What you will read in the pages ahead is by no means intended to be the complete story of this remarkable era. There are many arts disciplines in which I had little involvement—music, dance, opera—and many other events that were significant achievements in the cultural life of Alberta then. Rather, this volume is a tribute to some of the people with whom I crossed paths—innovative leaders who helped to create the most exciting cultural period in the province's history. One of the era's most endearing characters was Horst A. Schmid, the Minister of Culture during the 1970s. I first knew him toward the end of the 1960s when he was a leader of the Edmonton German Canadian Business Association. The rise of an immigrant who arrived in Canada in 1952 with no money and no English to become a provincial Cabinet minister is a good story. But the better story—the one that will give him a special place in the history of Alberta—is how he used his position to help foster a veritable Golden Age of the Arts.

But if Horst Schmid was the angel who delivered support to Alberta's arts and cultural communities, he could not have done it without the enthusiastic support of Peter Lougheed, and especially of Peter's wife Jeanne, an artist in her own right. She had studied voice, music and dance and could have gone on to a professional career in ballet or in opera. She insisted that Alberta's prosperity would lose its lustre if it satisfied just the material wants and needs of an increasingly affluent community. She knew, and her husband agreed, that the province's wealth wouldn't mean much in the long term if it did not also nurture the spirit of its people. The Lougheeds *went* to theatre and ballet and opera and symphony, not to score political points, but because they had a real appreciation, a genuine love, of the arts. Because they went, it *became* the thing to do for thousands of other Albertans who, often to their surprise, found themselves becoming enthusiastic patrons of the arts.

I may be accused of short-changing Calgary and perhaps other parts of Alberta in this book. I'll do my best to explain the Edmonton–Calgary conundrum (there's enough material for a doctoral dissertation to document and analyse the striking differences between the two cities), but there is little argument that the arts have found a more receptive environment in Edmonton. As recently as

With publisher Grant Kennedy. *Photo: Fil Fraser*

the summer of 2002, when an art installation that looks and acts like a giant pan flute when the wind is right, was installed at a major Edmonton intersection, the artist, Tony Leong, noted the difference. Leong, a Calgary designer who with his business partners Marc Boutin and Dave Goulden had won a commission to create the sculpture, told the *Edmonton Journal* that the city was a better place for it than Calgary. Edmonton, he said, "has a greater appreciation for the arts and culture."[6] Many Calgarians confirm the perception, telling me that their city came late to the cultural table, that the blossoming of the arts in the province's undisputed financial power centre did not really begin until well into the 1980s and never reached the heights achieved by Edmonton. It is sadly illustrative that the

October 25, 1992. Preparing to interview Prime Minister Brian Mulroney the night before the referendum for the Charlottetown Accord. *Photo: Government of Canada*

Calgary Philharmonic Orchestra was forced to declare bankruptcy early in 2003.

The book begins with an overview of the culture shock Albertans experienced when they threw off the narrow world of the Social Credit government that had ruled the province for three and a half decades. It ends with an attempt to understand the culture shock that took on stark reality when deficit fighting dominated—some would say hijacked—the political and economic agendas. Now, early in the 21st century, Albertans are enjoying huge budgetary surpluses from another boom in the price of oil. I hope this book will help to persuade their provincial government to invest some of that wealth in culture and the arts.

*The Social Credit government had
spanned two generations … an electoral
defeat was unthinkable.*

—T.C. Byrne, *Alberta's Revolutionary Leaders* [7]

Chapter 1

Culture Shock:
The Changing of the Guard

In December 1965 when I moved from Regina to Edmonton, it was almost like moving to a different country. Alberta was rich. Saskatchewan was poor. But even as a have-not province, subject to capricious weather and yoyo bounces in the price of grain, Saskatchewan was one of the most politically interesting places in North America. The province had elected the Co-operative Commonwealth Federation (CCF) party in 1944, the first socialist government on the continent. The whole country was fascinated by Premier Tommy Douglas's plan to introduce Medicare. In Saskatchewan almost everyone talked about, argued about, got involved in politics; it was, along with football and curling, their favourite sport.

Not in Alberta. It was as if the subject embarrassed people in my new province. Alberta's Social Credit was as much a prairie populist movement as the CCF, but it was at the other end of the political spectrum. The Socreds, founded by William Aberhart, burst into power in 1935. Under his leadership, and that of Ernest Manning who took over in 1943, the party won election after election by landslides. Yet it was an inside joke that you could hardly find anyone who admitted to voting Social Credit. Coffee talk seemed to be about anything but provincial politics. When the subject did come up, there were elbow-to-the-ribs nudges, winks and behind-the-hand whispers about "funny money." One of the principal pledges of early platforms of the Socreds had been to wrest the perceived control of the economy from the (eastern) banks by creating their own currency. The Social Credit governments, like their successors the Reform and Alliance parties, saw economic issues in an "East vs. West" frame. During the 1930s, Alberta made several legislative attempts to create a form of currency. The government in Ottawa disallowed each attempt. So-called Prosperity Certificates worth one dollar when issued in 1936 have long since become collectors' items.[8] Cheque-like Citizen Royalty Dividend Certificates issued in 20-dollar denominations during the 1950s, "being dividend for 1957 in accordance with the Oil and Gas Royalties Dividend Act," have suffered the same fate.

Orvis Kennedy, a member of the party's inner circle, summed up the Social Credit mindset in a 1951 pamphlet. Elected to the original board of the party in 1934, he was described by the *Edmonton Journal*'s Karen Sornberger as "the organizational czar of the party." In *Principles and Policies of Social Credit—A Free Individual Enterprise Movement Opposed to Socialist and all Other Forms of Statism*, Kennedy proclaimed,

> Social Creditors believe that whenever goods and services are produced there should automatically be brought into existence sufficient purchasing power or medium of exchange, to at all times deliver those goods and services to the people…It is the sovereign right of the people to demand that their government

> create this medium of exchange in sufficient amounts,
> and only in sufficient amounts, to distribute this
> wealth to the people, the rightful owners. Anything
> short of this is the betrayal of the people's rights.[9]

So, instead of discussing provincial politics, Albertans (especially those who worked for or whose jobs depended on the government) chuckled at the malapropisms of the national Social Credit leader, Robert Thompson, an American-born chiropractor who, through the 1950s and most of the 1960s, led the federal wing of the party from a base in Red Deer. He once complained from his seat in the House of Commons that, "Parliament is being turned into a political arena," and declared, "The Americans are our best friends, whether we like it or not."[10] Thompson seemed to be on a different wavelength from the provincial party upon which he was financially dependent. He resigned in 1967 when the Alberta party, whose funds were tightly controlled by Orvis Kennedy, cut him off. After Thompson, the federal party provided new grist for the banter with the equally entertaining Québec Creditiste leader Réal Caouette.

No one chuckled at the leadership of Ernest Manning. He and his government had an earned reputation for being nit-pickingly meticulous and almost insufferably honest in their management of the province's affairs. And that, not Social Credit's debatable economic theories, is what produced majorities through nine successive elections.

My move from Saskatchewan, a province of political free thinkers, to Alberta's tight-lipped, straight-laced environment required adjustment. The deep-rooted differences between the western neighbours developed early and ran deep. Saskatchewan was the province where, in 1960, Tommy Douglas, facing down the frenzied rage of the medical establishment, had introduced universal health care. The storied Roman Catholic priest Père Athol Murray, founder of Notre Dame College in Wilcox, Saskatchewan,[11] was temporarily banished from the province by the Regina archbishop during the Medicare crisis of the early 1960s. Murray's scathing attacks on socialized medicine led to accusations that his pronouncements were close to an incitement to riot. Thirty years later, in 1990 and 1991, I travelled the country as a member of the Citizen's Forum on Canada's Future, also known as the Spicer Commission, which was attempting to discover how Canadians felt about their country. It is one of our great national ironies that people invariably told me that, for them, the most important thing about being Canadian was our health-care system. Many who were prepared to fight to keep Medicare in the 1990s were the children of those who had fought bitterly against its introduction in the 1960s.

The Alberta government saw itself as anything but socialist and was, with equal irony, the place where old (left-wing) Depression war cries such as "The People versus the [eastern] Banks"[12] echoed loudly. To counter their power, the Aberhart government had created its own (near) bank, the Alberta Treasury Branches, in 1938.[13] There was shocked disbelief in his party when, after his retirement, former Premier Manning accepted membership on the board of directors of one of those "damned eastern banks." The reaction from the old guard was swift and bitter. A.J. (Alf) Hooke, one of the original Social Crediters who had come into government with Aberhart and Manning, wrote the following:

> In February 1969, the papers carried a story which I am sure surprised every Social Creditor...the Honourable E.C. Manning, who throughout his career has condemned in every way orthodox banking, has been appointed as a Director of the Board of the Canadian Imperial Bank of Commerce. I was only one of thousands who could not believe what I read.[14]

I have always found it fascinating that the two provinces, with similar agricultural economies (until the discovery of oil at Leduc in 1947), should choose such divergent political directions. During the early 1970s, I tried hard to put together a television special that would have brought Ernest Manning and Tommy Douglas together. As a journalist, at the time co-anchoring[15] the CBC supperhour news and public affairs program in Edmonton, I came to know Manning as well as a journalist could expect to. I knew Tommy Douglas even better, having had many conversations with him during my time in Saskatchewan.[16] I thought that an open discussion might have provided valuable insights into why men with such similar backgrounds chose such different paths; why the politics of Saskatchewan and Alberta are so diametrically opposed. The rules, as I proposed them, were that the discussion was to focus on the early days of their respective movements, and that there was to be no discussion of contemporary politics. The objective was to look back on the years when Social Credit founder and Premier William Aberhart in Alberta and CCF[17] founder J.S. Woodsworth in Saskatchewan were trying, in the midst of the Great Depression, to find ways to improve the lives of their people. Manning and Douglas were contemporaries, born four years apart. Manning was from small-town Saskatchewan, and Douglas emigrated from Scotland to Canada at the age of 15. Both became prairie preachers, powerful orators and honest, effective administrators. Each was heir to a political movement created by an idealistic, charismatic leader; each was deeply devout in his Christian beliefs. Each led successful, long-term governments; Manning from 1943 to 1968, Douglas from 1944 to 1961, when he entered federal politics. Yet these men, who had come to maturity in the same era, in the same region, who developed parallel political careers, saw the world through dramatically different lenses.

Douglas was enthusiastic about the television project from the beginning and offered to turn up virtually anytime, anywhere, for the discussion. But Manning, who gave me what I thought was provisional agreement, hedged for many months about a suitable time and place. He never really said no. Years later, after I had abandoned the project, I encountered his son, Preston, on Edmonton's Jasper Avenue. He told me, lowering his voice to a near whisper, that maybe it was because his father simply couldn't stand to be in the same room with "that socialist."

By the time Manning stepped down after 25 years as premier, people in the province, especially in the cities and most especially in Edmonton, were becoming restless. It was the '60s. The western world was trying to lighten up (remember teach-ins, Rochdale,

Free University North[18] and "turn on, tune in, drop out"?). But many in Alberta's old guard government still displayed a defensive, if not openly skeptical, view of culture and the arts. Some who had struggled to survive through the Depression saw them as, at best a harmless but unessential frill, less charitably as a waste of time and money, and at worst as a potential threat to their (Christian) way of life.

Canada's current poet laureate, George Bowering, while at the University of Alberta in the late 1960s, described the province as "a cultural desert, a province inhabited mainly by ungrammatical pro-Socred letter writers, stupid newspaper editors, fiery eyed fundamentalists and right-wing politics."[19] The narrow Socred view of the world also included a distinct bias against minorities. In her 2001 book, *Mavericks,* Alberta author Aritha van Herk recalled that the government

> exercised considerable bias against pacifist sects like Mennonites, Hutterites and Doukhabors, who were exempt from conscription, especially Hutterites, perceived as increasing their land holdings at the expense of regular farmers who were off fighting in the war. Hearings after the war reflected a pervasive hostility to Hutterites, leading Manning to implement the Communal Property Act, which stayed in force until 1972 when Peter Lougheed's government repealed the measure.[20]

Two huge complexes most visibly symbolized the Manning government's commitment to the arts, one in Edmonton and one in Calgary. The Jubilee Auditoria were erected in 1955 to celebrate the province's 50th anniversary. The nearly identical, utilitarian buildings, each capable of seating 2750 people, were used for local symphony, opera and ballet performances. Major uses came from university convocations, high school graduation ceremonies, the Kiwanis Music Festivals and such other cultural events as the Scottish Society's "White Heather" shows. Touring extravaganzas starring popular entertainers such as Harry Belafonte, Victor Borge and the World Adventure Tour slide shows and movies filled the buildings from time to time. The Australian hypnotist/entertainer Reveen was a frequent and popular visitor. The buildings were kept absolutely free of any form of alcohol.

It was difficult to imagine the Alberta of the '60s as a place where the arts could flourish. The province's Lord's Day Act was a kind of "Thou God see'est me" checklist for what people could do, and could not do, on Sundays, and it set the behavioural tone for the rest of the week. Manning was diligent in separating the opinions and values expressed on his Sunday *Back to the Bible Hour* radio broadcasts from his role as premier. But those values permeated the way that official Alberta did its business and lived its life. You could not get a glass of wine with a meal on Sundays, even in the finest restaurants—at least not openly. Some establishments turned a blind eye when patrons brought their own bottles in brown paper bags and hid them under the table. At the drinking establishments that were allowed to exist, there were still separate entrances, one for men, one for "Ladies and Escorts." Unattached men and women were not to be trusted around the demon rum. Beer parlours were required to close between 6:00 p.m. and 7:00 p.m., to make sure that husbands who had stopped for a quick one after work went home for dinner. The only place you could see a movie on Sunday was at a drive-in, and the province's Film Censor Board was still busy excising the naughty bits from Hollywood's latest, increasingly risqué productions.

Open calls for a change from the old Social Credit ways began to surface soon after Manning's retirement. The unfortunate Harry Strom was elected to succeed him at a party convention in December 1968. A decent man, Strom tried mightily to transform the old party. He brought in young Social Credit thinkers such as Erik Schmidt, Owen Anderson and John Barr. Preston Manning got his political feet wet as a member of the group, which the *Edmonton Journal* dubbed the "whiz kids."[21] Barr and Anderson wrote *The Unfinished Revolt*, published by McClelland and Stewart in 1971. The book tried to give the party and its ideas a new lease on life. It was the first of several attempts, which continue to this day, to reinvent the party.[22]

Strom promoted some of the younger MLAs such as Bob Clark and Ray Speaker and fired Cabinet stalwarts such as the unhappy Alf Hooke, the most outspoken of the originals who had served in the Cabinet for 26 years. In his book, *30 + 5: Those Incredible Years of Social Credit*, Hooke described his first meeting with Strom after the latter became premier. As the conversation dragged on, he gradually realized that the new leader had no intention of inviting him back into the Cabinet. "I could not do to a dog what you are doing to me," Hooke raged, but nevertheless pledged his grudging support, saying, "I am concerned with getting the government back on the Social Credit track much more than I am with personalities." "Someone has to speak out," Hooke declared in a personal note to me in 1970, "and, God willing, I intend to do so." One of the last of the "real" Social Creditors, he continued to fight for his principles until his death in 1992.

Strom was quiet and mild mannered, a strict teetotaller who affected a casual air by driving with one finger on the wheel, his right arm draped across the back of the passenger seat.[23] In his well-meaning attempts to modernize the party, he set up Canada's first provincial Department of the Environment. He brought the province into Medicare. He changed the law to allow 18-year-olds to vote. He put a plebiscite on daylight savings time, which had been defeated in the 1967 election, back on the ballot. He allowed Sunday movies for the first time, and to the horror of many Social Credit stalwarts, allowed people to order a drink with their meals in restaurants—even on Sunday. He set up a well-funded Commission on the Future of Education, chaired by Professor Walter Worth. *The Worth Report* endorsed the establishment of what was to become Athabasca University and the expansion of the Banff School of Fine Arts into a year-round institution. On March 1, 1970, the Strom government launched Canada's first over-the-air educational television station, operated by the Metropolitan Edmonton Educational Television Association (MEETA). The station was the pilot project for ACCESS, the provincial educational television network, which was privatised by the Klein government in 1995.

But Strom's attempts to modernize the party set the old guard on edge. He had to fight the coming election without much support from the party's aging establishment—and without much of the money that they controlled.

Early in 1971, with an election on his mind, Strom changed the name of the Department of Youth to the Department of Culture, Youth and Recreation. The department had been established by Manning in 1966 to deal with the challenges presented by youth in the 1960s and to support the province's popular, rural-based 4-H Clubs.[24]

In July 1971, with an August election looming, Strom ran the Alberta Multicultural Conference, and on July 16 published a white paper titled *A New Cultural Policy for the Province of Alberta*. But Peter Lougheed had put his response on the record two days earlier. In a July 14 news release, he committed his future government to the development of a "mosaic" approach: "We believe that the promotion of different cultures, if handled properly, would not lead to the fragmentation of our society but would provide Albertans with the opportunity of being exposed to and experiencing many cultures and traditions."[25]

In the end, Strom could not change the Manning–Kennedy image of Social Credit, now seen by voters as old and tired. He was too modern for the doctrinaire old guard and not modern enough for the new Alberta. A letter to the editor of the *Edmonton Journal* from a self-described "charter Social Creditor,"[26] chastised both Strom and Manning (who late in the campaign had offered token support for Strom) for not being "real" Social Creditors. Alf Hooke, who over a span of 14 years had been acting premier whenever Manning was away, was considerably more than upset with Strom. Hooke released his book just before the election to champion the "real" Social Credit agenda and to oppose what he saw as Strom's deviant approach. Bitterly, Hooke declined to run and in fact showed up at a Lougheed rally at the Edmonton Jubilee Auditorium, which had packed the hall to overcapacity with some 4000 supporters. Someone pinned a "For Pete's Sake—Vote Now" button on his lapel. Hooke said he would keep it.

Like Woodrow Lloyd who took over the Saskatchewan government after Tommy Douglas moved to the federal arena, Harry Strom had the bad fortune to come to power at the end of an era. Political sensibilities were changing everywhere. The mood was "out with the old," whatever the old was—a left-wing government in Saskatchewan, a right-wing one in Alberta. *Time Magazine*[27] noted, "Since 1969 there have been eight provincial elections, in which six incumbent governments have been thrown out. ...None of the defeated governments were singularly incompetent, corrupt or uncaring." Their great sin—they "looked tired."[28]

When the change came, it was massive and unexpected. Lougheed himself was caught by surprise. At noon on election day, he told *Edmonton Journal* reporter John Hopkins, "I don't think we're going to do it."[29] But in the end, the growing stream of desire for change became a flood. Lougheed, young, energetic and telegenic, had bounded from taking over the leadership of the virtually non-existent provincial Progressive Conservative party in 1965, to becoming Leader of the Opposition with a rump of six members following the 1967 election, to winning 49 of the province's 75 seats on August 30, 1971.

"People didn't vote against Social Credit," Lougheed argued. "They hadn't done anything wrong. They voted *for* us."[30]

In an editorial titled "A Farewell Tribute" following the Social Credit's defeat, the *Calgary Herald* said the party "has maintained old-fashioned complexes in the face of altering social concepts in such spheres as liquor consumption, blue laws and censorship. It has maintained an observable sense of authoritarianism which, at times, has seemed scarcely indistinguishable from the outmoded concept of divine right."[31]

The average age of the Alberta Cabinet dropped by nine years, from 52.4 to 43.2.

The extraordinary impact of the change is difficult to appreciate without an understanding of how deeply entrenched the Social Credit party had been through more than 35 years in power. It was a true culture shock—a dramatic and unexpected change from Social Credit's doctrinaire, ideology-driven regime to Lougheed's relatively open and pragmatic approach to government. For Alberta's creative community, it presented, as Tree Frog Press publisher Allan Shute told me in an interview, "one of those once-in-a-lifetime opportunities."

From my own perspective, the change was every bit as noteworthy, though less noticeable on the national stage, as Québec's Quiet Revolution, which fundamentally changed the way that province saw and felt about itself. In Alberta, with Peter Lougheed's active support, with Jeanne Lougheed's unwavering and enthusiastic encouragement, and with Horst Schmid's "Energizer Bunny" activism, culture and the arts rose from the bottom rung on the ladder of government priorities to a place much closer to the top.

And so the stage was set for what can only be described as a cultural revolution. The decade and a half from 1971 to 1985 saw a profuse flowering of the performing and literary arts. With recognition of the arts came official recognition of Alberta's multicultural reality. The 1971 census showed that 47.4 percent of Albertans were of neither British (46.8 percent) nor French (5.8 percent) descent. In Edmonton, in contrast to Calgary, the non-British population was considerably larger than the provincial average. Soon after the election, the premier and his wife made a point of hosting delegates in ethnic dress from a variety of cultural communities at a gala reception at Government House in Edmonton. The occasion launched the Alberta Cultural Heritage Council. The government's *Position Paper No. 7,* subtitled *New Directions Position Paper on Alberta's Cultural Heritage,* was issued in November 1972. One policy objective was "to stimulate the living arts—painting, dancing, music, handicrafts and the human drama."[32]

In telling any story about Alberta, however, it is important to recognize that there are really three major and quite distinct constituencies within the province. Edmonton, Calgary and the "rest-of-Alberta" represent three different political and cultural realities. Edmonton has, since its earliest days, been more ethnically diverse, more cosmopolitan. That may have been both the cause and the result of the fact that the city is the location of both the provincial capital and its first university. Calgary, the financial capital, had a larger Anglo-Saxon base, and so many Americans lived there that it was called the largest American city outside of the US. Calgary was about cattle, oil and money. The city, as I will show, came late to the development of a full cultural life.

The rest-of-Alberta, like rural Canada everywhere, was losing population and economic power. Its people, older, with less formal education, are more monocultural within their communities. While there is some diversity in heritages across the province, individual communities tend to reflect, in some cases overwhelmingly, a single ethnicity —Ukrainian, German, Scandinavian or some other, usually European, culture. They, in large part, embrace ultra-conservative political and religious values. Rural Alberta was the source of Social Credit's strength from the 1930s through the 1960s and of the Reform and Alliance parties in contemporary times. An electoral system in need of repair gives them more voting power than urbanites in Edmonton and Calgary. Prior to the most recent reorganization in 2003, the smallest rural constituency, Chinook, had 15,642 voters while the largest, Edmonton Rutherford, had 38,262.[33] The new 2003 reorganization redressed some of the imbalances but still left rural Albertans with more voting power than urbanites. The new rules allow for a 25 percent variance above or below the average number of voters: 35,951.

But the demand for change by the urban majority would not be denied. Harry Strom unlocked the door to change, but Peter Lougheed and his team swung it wide open. Alberta entered a new world. In my essay "Our Best Years," published in *Farewell to the 70s,* edited by Anna Porter and Marjorie Harris,[34] I described the decade as "our yeastiest years…the world is waking to Edmonton—dare I say it?—the new Athens of North America." A bit over the top, perhaps, but indicative of the creative high so many Albertans enjoyed during that astonishing decade.

The most critical area of human need now lies within man himself; in terms of his self respect, his rights and dignity, his spiritual malaise, his search for meaning in an age of increasing automation and anonymity.[35]

—C. Les Usher, Deputy Minister, Alberta Culture, Youth and Recreation, 1971–80

Chapter 2

From Agricultural Fairs to Arts Festivals

In the fall of 1955, Walter Kaasa was teaching drama at Victoria Composite High School in Edmonton, when government officials approached him with an offer to head up a cultural development division.[36] He declined. He was under contract to the Edmonton Public School Board and, having been on a sabbatical at the Central School of Drama in London, England, the previous year, was obligated to teach for at least another year. To his astonishment, a few days later, he was summoned from the classroom for a "very important" call. He rushed to the school office to find the premier himself, Ernest Manning, waiting on the telephone. The premier wanted to know why he had turned down the job. Kaasa told him it would be dishonourable for him to break a contract signed in good faith. Kaasa remembers the

Walter Kaasa as Ebenezer Scrooge in a 1991 Chinook Theatre production of
A Christmas Carol. Photo: courtesy of Walter Kaasa

premier saying. "Good, that's the right thing to do. When does the
contract end?"

"Next June."

"Would you take the job if we held it open until then?"

"Yes. Yes!"

Premier Ernest Manning personally hired Walter Kaasa to
develop cultural programs within his Department of the Provincial
Secretary. Kaasa, already a respected actor and teacher, became the
Alberta government's first cultural bureaucrat. On a limited budget,
he did what he could to build programs that would support theatre
and writing and music and dance.

In the 1960s, the attention and support of the Social Credit government, and of many Albertans, focused more intently on events that
celebrated the province's pioneering agricultural spirit—the famous
Calgary Stampede, Edmonton's Klondike days, rodeos, and agricultural fairs in scores of smaller communities. Alberta's mostly rural
youth worked for success within the framework of the farm-oriented
4-H clubs. Team sports were also an acceptable and important outlet.

Alberta had already made its mark on the national scene with the Edmonton Eskimos and the Calgary Stampeders. Tens of thousands of eastern football fans and I were stunned on Saturday, November 27, 1954, to see the Edmonton Eskimos steal the Grey Cup from my home town Montréal Alouettes with a heart-stopping 26 to 25 win. I was then the play-by-play hockey announcer on Barrie radio station CKBB, the voice of the Barrie Flyers. We were having a great, raucous time at the traditional Grey Cup party in one of those wood-panelled basement rumpus rooms, already celebrating the expected win of East over West. We were barely paying attention to the dying minutes of the game on the brand new 17-inch black and white television set when a shout brought the revelry to a halt. "Look at that bugger run!" We all turned to the set just in time to see Jackie "Spaghetti Legs" Parker running down the field like a wild man, tying the game with a last-minute touchdown. Bob Dean put the convert through the uprights to give the Eskimos what we thought was a shocking one-point win.

The official view of the arts was still narrow, although the Jubilee Auditoria in both Calgary and Edmonton did good business through the 1960s. A touring British theatrical company, according to Ron Wigmore, then the general manager of the Edmonton Jubilee, had to remove one of the plays from its repertoire because some government officials thought it was too risqué. The company starred Sir Laurence Olivier in a pair of light-hearted comedies and farces. It was a special treat for everyone there that night to be in the audience when Sir Laurence graced the stage of the Edmonton Jubilee Auditorium in productions of *Love for Love*, an English comedy of manners by William Congreve, and a famous French farce, *A Flea in Her Ear* by Georges Feydeau. The plays featured fancy, lace-trimmed velvet costumes and exaggerated, foppish gestures. Seeing Sir Laurence cavorting across the stage, obviously having a great time, was one of the memorable events of my early years in Edmonton.

In the late 1960s, a personally memorable result of Kaasa's support of artists was my "discovery" of the late Marek Jablonski[37] in a high school gymnasium at Grand Centre, Alberta. An immigrant who became one of Canada's most respected concert pianists and an internationally famous interpreter of Chopin, Jablonski was in Grand Centre as part of a touring artists program created by Walter Kaasa, travelling around the province to bring culture to smaller communities. I was in town in my role as director of education for Alberta Health's Division of Alcoholism, giving a series of talks to students and teachers. Staying overnight, I asked if there was anything going on in town. "There's some piano player gonna be at the high school tonight," someone told me. And there, on an Alberta-cold winter night, I listened to Jablonski, still in his mid-20s, transport his audience to a new appreciation of classical music. Jablonski's piano travelled in the back of a truck and had to be set up and tuned at each location. Years later, when he was a master teacher at the Banff Centre, Marek and I enjoyed remembering how and where we had first met.

During those years Alberta, like the rest of Canada, began experiencing the long, slow demise of the old-fashioned family farm. The farm, where the majority of Albertans lived from the '20s into the '60s, provided both home and employment for families who had worked hard to survive the Great Depression, the caprices of weather and the price of grain. Today's industrial size farms, even when they are still owned by families, are huge, mechanized enterprises, requiring $250,000 tractors and expensive, patented fertilizers, weed-control systems and seed stocks. By the 1970s, the move to the cities had turned the demographic, which had most Albertans living in the country, on its head.

Time had run out on the restrictive, moralistic, rural-based Social Credit era. The new urbanites, bolstered by immigration, had access to new information, new ideas and new opportunities. It was time to step away from a world in which everything had to be narrowly useful, had to have a specific purpose; a world in which anything that was not productive work or worship was dismissed as a frill, at best useless and suspect, at worst dangerous, perhaps even subversive. Writers and thinkers through the ages have written that without art, we stand in danger of being trapped in spiritual poverty.[38] Life without singing and dancing, without the gasps and the tears and the laughter of drama, without the potentially life-altering inspiration of literature, is no life at all.

As Social Credit's time on the provincial stage approached its finale, the embers of a cultural revolution were already aglow in Alberta. When Lougheed and his team took power, they fanned the embers into a bright fire that would raise the province into the ranks of the most culturally active in Canada. The genius of the Lougheed government was its ability, like a spring cleaning, to throw open the doors and windows of the province to let in the fresh, invigorating air of the new, more relaxed lifestyles that were gaining acceptance and momentum as we entered the 1970s. The focus on agricultural fairs, with their determinedly purposeful 4-H Clubs, fruit pies and bull sales, began to take a back seat to urban festivals celebrating life through the arts. As oil replaced agriculture as the engine of the provincial economy, the money to support culture and the arts was there—and there was plenty of it.

The wave started in Edmonton. (In Chapter 10, I outline some of the reasons why Edmonton's commitment to culture was so strong, and why Calgary came so late to the party.) The provincial capital was bubbling with an increasingly diverse population, poised to unleash a cultural revolution as the restrictive attitudes of the Social Credit era faded. Even a partial list of the festivals that got their start during the era is impressive.

The Edmonton Heritage Festival, launched in 1974, still bills itself as the World's Largest Celebration of Cultural Diversity and Ethnic Harmony. Held for three days on the first weekend in August, it has attracted as many as half a million attendees. People revel in the attractions of the more than 70 cultures represented in 50 colourful pavilions, set up for the occasion in Edmonton's river valley in Hawrelak Park. Each pavilion offers performances, crafts and food from Africa to Wales.

Since 1982, the Edmonton Fringe Theatre Festival has grown to become the largest theatrical event in North America. Every August, the festival plays host to more than 150 groups of artists presenting live shows in street venues, intimate theatres and customized performance spaces in Edmonton's Old Strathcona district. As many as half a million people take part in the festival.

The Edmonton Folk Music Festival began in 1980 with the vision of Don Whelan and the energy of more than 300 volunteers.

It has matured to become one of the leading folk festivals in the world.

There are many others, including the Jazz City International Festival, the Edmonton International Street Performers Festival, Dreamspeaker, the Aboriginal Film Festival, the Edmonton International Film Festival and The Works visual arts festival.

While the festivals movement gained its early momentum in Edmonton, in a wonderful chain reaction, Calgary and many of Alberta's smaller communities have caught the wave with festivals of their own. There are arts festivals in Drumheller, Okotoks, Fort Macleod, Lesser Slave Lake, Sylvan Lake and in scores of other communities. Rosebud, nestled in the Rosebud River valley an hour's drive northeast of Calgary, presents the Rosebud Dinner Theatre. It has three major productions each year, including the increasingly popular Christmas favourite, *The Passion Play*. The theatre is a key contributor to the town's economy. A visit to the Web sites of most major, and some minor, municipalities will reveal a variety of festivals that have become part of life in Alberta.

In 1985, Alberta Culture and Economic Development commissioned a study, *The Economic Impact of the Arts in Alberta*. The study estimated the economic impact of the arts and culture at between $454 and $555 million. "The estimates produced by this study," it said, "indicate that a relatively low level of support or subsidy is required relative to the number of jobs and the economic impact produced."[39]

The culture shock that came with the transfer of power from Social Credit to Lougheed's Conservatives had a profound effect on the way Albertans behaved and saw themselves. The success of the 1970s was built on a foundation created by dedicated artists who had worked throughout the 1960s with little government support. By the time Lougheed became premier in 1971, Joe Shoctor had already launched Edmonton's first Citadel Theatre in an old Salvation Army Hall on 102 Street. Mel Hurtig had already opened what became Canada's largest bookstore. Canada's first on-air educational television station had been broadcasting for a year and a half. CKUA, the country's oldest public broadcaster, had been on the air since it was licensed as the University of Alberta station in

1927. The Banff Summer School for the Arts, like CKUA, a creature of the University of Alberta Department of Extension, had been around since 1933. In 1961, Larry Matanski produced the first made-in-Alberta-by-Albertans feature film, *Wings of Chance.* Amateur or little theatre groups, with great support from the University of Alberta drama program, had been active in Edmonton, Calgary and a few smaller centres since the 1930s.

There had always been a strong nucleus of people in Alberta who were committed to the arts. Despite being criticized as a cultural wasteland, the province had bright islands of artistic activity that rewarded those who sought them out.

No more appealing couple will grace the Canadian political scene.

—*The Lethbridge Herald,* March 25, 1965

Chapter 3

The Lougheeds

There was an obvious star quality about Peter and Jeanne Lougheed. While Peter's political life captured most of the headlines, Alberta media also paid attention to the woman the *Edmonton Journal* later described as the province's "beautiful First Lady."[40] She, beautiful and talented, was a dancer and singer with an operatic voice. He, handsome and athletic, had played halfback for the storied Edmonton Eskimos in the days when football was as big as hockey and Grey Cup parties were national rituals. People loved to share space with the premier and his wife. A public reception following the Lougheed government's first Speech from the Throne saw the Edmonton Jubilee Auditorium filled to overflowing with some 4000 crowding the 2750-seat facility.

There was a sparkling aura of modernity about them. Albertans, like Canadians under Trudeau, had a leader who transcended political ideologies and who was, in the vernacular of the time, "with it." *Time Magazine*, praising Peter Lougheed's "Trudeau-like firmness" (a description Lougheed grudgingly appreciated), wrote, "It's not often that Canadian politicians are given movie star treatment."[41] Had there been some tragedy in their relationship or in their lives, they might well, like the Trudeaus and the Kennedys, have been subject matter for tabloids, television and movies. Pierre and Margaret's Camelot, like Jack and Jackie's, was short-lived and star-crossed. Peter and Jeanne Lougheed, dignified but far from regal in their behaviour, inspired Albertans to be their best selves for nearly two decades.

They met at the University of Alberta, he studying law, she completing a degree in philosophy with a Fine Arts major. He was smitten the moment he saw her. He asked a friend, Duncan Stockwell, if he knew that "good-looking girl." He did. Peter organized his courtship like a political campaign, first getting Stockwell to find out if Jeanne would go out with him on a blind date. She turned him down flat. So he persuaded Stockwell to invite Jeanne for coffee at the Tuck Shop on campus. Lougheed just happened to accidentally drop by, whereupon Stockwell suddenly remembered that he had to be somewhere else. "He's always been resourceful," said Jeanne. She allowed Peter's campaign to go on until she was sure she wanted him as her life partner. In the process, he found himself attending events at which many of his athletic buddies wouldn't be caught dead. But if Peter wanted to be with Jeanne, he had to go to where she was, either to watch her perform on stage, singing or dancing, or to join her in the audience applauding ballet, opera or symphony. He just *had* to like it. And in the end he, confessed that even though he was a jock he honestly grew to enjoy the performances.

Jeanne Estelle Rogers, born in October 1928, in Forestburg, Alberta, is the daughter of the late Dr. Lawrence Rogers and Estelle Christena Gunston. Jeanne grew up in Camrose where her father practised medicine. When she was in her teens, he moved the family to Edmonton, where he became a medical health officer. She

Jeanne Lougheed at Alberta's first grand piano, brought to the province by Sir James Lougheed. *Photo: Fil Fraser*

completed grade 10 in piano and attended University High School in what is now Corbett Hall at the University of Alberta. The school achieved a kind of legendary status between 1942 and 1955, when it closed, with graduates such as jazz musician (now Senator) Tommy Banks, flute player Harlan Green, Ottawa mandarin Ivan Head, former Alberta Solicitor General Graham Harle, football coach and manager Norm Kimball and composer Roger Deegan.

Jeanne could dance. When she was 12, her Camrose ballet teacher urged her to train with a professional company such as the Royal Winnipeg Ballet. At university, she became vice-president of the Campus Ballet Club. But Jeanne wasn't ready to leave home. She says her parents wanted her to have a normal childhood. Anyone who knows about ballet will tell you that children who enter its rigorous training programs lead anything but a normal childhood. It is among the most demanding of artistic disciplines. People in the audience don't hear the thumps, the grunts or the heavy breathing, nor do they see or smell the sweat that goes into a performance that, from the other side of the footlights, seems magically, effortlessly light. Dancers not only needed to be superb athletes, but the endless training leaves little room in their lives for anything else.[42]

Jeanne could sing. She was blessed with a rich coloratura soprano voice and was encouraged by her teachers, including the founder of the Richard Eaton Singers, to go on to a professional career. She performed in the University Mixed Chorus under Eaton's direction and appeared frequently in shows ranging from a production of *Guys and Dolls*, to Mozart's *The Magic Flute,* along with future stars Bernard Turgeon and Robert Goulet.

"If I had been more career-oriented…," she answered when I asked about her choice not to pursue a professional career on stage. Her friends confirm that the truth about Jeanne is that she is unswervingly family-oriented; for her, family is always the first priority.

Edgar Peter Lougheed was born in Calgary in July 1928, the grandson of Sir James Lougheed, one of Calgary's first lawyers and a founder of the Law Society of Alberta. Sir James was, in an illustrious career, a successful real-estate developer, a founding member of Calgary's Ranchmen's Club, a federal Cabinet minister and Alberta's first senator. His legacy includes Beaulieu, one of Calgary's finest houses, now a National Historic Site, being restored for the 100th anniversary of Alberta in 2005.[43] Peter Lougheed was profoundly influenced by his almost mythic grandfather, though they never met. It was a central part of his life's ambition to uphold the name his ancestor had so solidly engraved on Alberta's honour roll.

You could cite Peter Lougheed as a classic representation of the term *goal oriented.* Few people I've met had a more clear idea of what they wanted to do in life. Playing professional football between 1948 and 1950, he more than made up for his lack of bulk with energy and gutsy determination as the team's punt return specialist.[44] Peter demonstrated a talent for leadership and organization early in life. He became president of his high school student union. But first, as it happened, he had to create and organize the union before he could run to lead it. At the University of Alberta, he ran for the presidency of the Students' Union against Ivan Head, later a key advisor to Pierre Trudeau, and won. Lougheed did well in law school, and, after their graduation, Peter and Jeanne were married in a candlelight ceremony at Metropolitan United Church in Edmonton on June 21, 1952. Then, it was on to Boston, where Peter completed a Harvard MBA.

Jeanne learned to type so that she could help Peter with his assignments. But the *quid pro quo* was his attendance at shows that she wanted to see. Wives of students usually had to go to performances on their own. But Jeanne's bargain was that she would go to his football games if he came to her concerts. Boston was a major out-of-town tryout venue for Broadway shows and other performances destined for the Big Apple. Jeanne, who remembers it as an idyllic time in their lives, recalled that they enjoyed scores of first-rate shows at student prices. She kept up with her music, among other things singing with a string quartet. The couple bought a turntable with a 10-record changer, a luxury for them at the time, she recalls. They listened to Benny Goodman and other big bands, but Jeanne made sure that every third record in the stack was Brahms, Mozart, Bach or another of the great classical composers.

After Peter's graduation, the couple spent a honeymoon summer in Europe. "It was a great time. We had no job, no mortgage and no baby," Jeanne told me. She thought she just might have lost her husband as a lover of the arts when she took him to a heavy Wagner opera in London. Peter fell fast asleep. But later, in Italy, she managed to get him to an open-air performance of *Aida*, complete with elephants, camels and all of the trappings of one of the grandest of grand operas. "Now, that's more like it," he said, and never complained about opera again.

Law degree and MBA completed, the Lougheeds returned to Calgary to build a base and start a family. Peter did his articling with William McGillivray, later to become a provincial judge, and then joined a local law firm, Fenerty and Fenerty, before accepting a job with the powerful Mannix family enterprise, first as a junior lawyer, but quickly rising to become vice-president, administration. Jeanne took a university course in design, which gave her grounding in the foundations of art and painting. She put her artistic talent to use decorating and supervising additions to their home as their family grew.[45]

Jeanne, a bit tongue in cheek, told me she hadn't anticipated a political career. Peter came home from the office one day, she said, and wanted to discuss her philosophy of life. She talked for some time, about her sense of responsibility and her commitment to family, about values. After all, she had a degree in philosophy. When she had finished, he exclaimed, "Oh, good, you're a Conservative!" And he told her he was thinking about a life in politics. How long? "Twenty years," he promised. No longer.

In 1964, the prospects of the Alberta Progressive Conservative Party, without a leader, without a seat in the Legislature, without a constituency organization, were worse than dim. Lougheed, always a pragmatist, decided that the party would provide the ideal base from which to launch a campaign that would lead him to the premiership. The Liberals, a party within whose ranks he might have felt just as comfortable, already had a leader, Mike Macagno. The ruling Social Credit party, Peter was almost alone in believing at the time, was tired and nearing the end of its run. Besides, his grandfather had been a Conservative, and those who know Lougheed well believe that the memory of his grandfather's role in politics was never far from his mind.

His run for the leadership was so well organized that in March 1965, 91 percent of the delegates to the party convention gave him their votes. In the 1967 election, the party went from zero to six seats in the Legislature, and Lougheed became leader of the official Opposition. By the time the election of August 1971 was called, the party's legislative numbers, through by-elections and defections, had expanded to 10 seats. Lougheed, who always kept himself in good physical shape, built on an approach that he had successfully used in the 1967 campaign, and literally ran from door to door in constituencies all over the province. He was comfortable on television, and *Time Magazine* described him as "a tireless mainstreeter and a polished TV performer."[46]

"We're going to Edmonton!" he said from his Calgary constituency headquarters, when victory became apparent. The party had won every seat in the provincial capital. An overflow crowd came to Lou Hyndman's[47] Edmonton party headquarters to celebrate, and the *Edmonton Journal* sent a reporter to write a feature about Alberta's new first lady.[48]

The Lougheeds worked together as a couple. At Easter time in 1971, well before the election was called, the couple went to Jasper for a short holiday. Sitting in front of a warming fire, they also took time to develop a list of who might be in the Cabinet, "just in case." "I haven't heard *culture*," Jeanne pointed out, emphasizing the word. There was no resistance from the future premier. For both of them, Horst Schmid was the clear choice. Jeanne liked his energy and commitment. Peter wanted non-Anglo-Saxons to feel comfortable in Alberta. It was typical of the way the couple planned ahead and worked together.

Rooting through his papers long after his retirement, Lougheed found the report of an old aptitude test he had taken when he was about 19. "I didn't score very well in mechanical skills," he said as he handed it to me. But when I looked at it I saw that he was off the scale in persuasiveness, above the 100 percentile. He scored almost as high in social studies. Just don't ask him to fix a leaky faucet. He has a way of talking to people that convinces them that, at that moment, they are the absolute centre of his attention. While in office he kept in touch by telephone with a large cross-Canada network. The phone would ring, usually between 7:30 and 8:00 in the morning, and it would be Peter Lougheed wondering what you thought about this policy or that initiative.

The Cabinet was a reflection of Lougheed's persuasive powers. He convinced a very talented group of people to give up secure businesses or professions to run for office. They had no doctrinaire ideology. They were small-*c* conservatives who saw themselves, pragmatically, in the centre of the political spectrum. They came into office with a series of ambitious position papers that really added up to the following: "Alberta is the greatest darned province in the world, let's just make it a better one." Lougheed's goal, in politics as in sports, was to win, to be the best he could be, and that goal included his government and his province.

"It is just possible," wrote columnist William Gold in the *Calgary Herald* on May 18, 1972, "that Alberta now has, man for man, the best collection of provincial government ministers in the country." With the exception of Dr. Hugh Horner, who had served in the federal Parliament, none was a professional politician. All had enjoyed successful careers in "real" life. There was an architect, a pharmacist, educators, businessmen and one woman, Helen Hunley, who had been mayor of Rocky Mountain House, a small central Alberta foothills town. She was quite emphatic when she once told me that she was *not* a professional politician. She later became the province's first woman lieutenant-governor.

Lougheed took a hands-on approach to everything he did. It was one of the reasons that people appointed to various boards and commissions were not the most politically expedient, but those he believed to be the best, most appropriate people for the job. He spent a lot of time on appointments, not waiting for them to percolate through the political process. He told me, with some emphasis, that he didn't follow party lines. "I always looked for the right skill sets, and that put community over party." Eighty percent of major appointments, he told me, came from his office.[49]

One of the ways in which the Lougheeds influenced the way Albertans saw the arts was by becoming true patrons, attending and taking part in scores of events, large and small. It was obvious that they genuinely enjoyed themselves doing it, but it was also true that Jeanne was determined to show personal and public support for the arts. They lived in Edmonton throughout their time in office, and Jeanne would sometimes invite as many as 50 people to an early buffet dinner at their home, on the understanding that everyone would then proceed to the opera, or the ballet or whatever performance was being held. A neighbour who attended some of the dinners was asked if he liked opera. "I do now," he affirmed. Albertans found it hard to resist an invitation from the premier and his wife, or to duck out of going to performances that might have kept them away from hockey or football. Many of them came to enjoy the arts and some became patrons.

It was important to Jeanne Lougheed that they create a positive climate for the arts. "I wanted my province to be a great province in Canada," she said. And actions followed words. The couple raised many thousands of dollars by offering their services at fund-raising auctions. People bid serious money that went to charities to have the premier and his wife act as butler and maid at a fancy dinner or cook a pancake breakfast for a dozen or more. It was a dramatic change from the days, before or since, when political leaders were not only rarely seen at arts events, but who left the impression they considered such frivolities to be of only peripheral importance.

The Lougheeds' sense of humour was lost on those who saw only Peter's sterner side as, holding a tight rein on the government, he fought the energy wars with Trudeau.[50] But people in the arts and cultural communities knew better. Jeanne tells the following story. When the National Press Club Jazz Band, on an annual fund-raising tour around the country, came to Edmonton with the likes of journalists Charlie Lynch, Bruce Phillips and Geoffrey Scott, they played passable jazz and entertained audiences with often hilarious skits about the politicians of the day. Scott, a talented mimic, had many of the leading politicians of the day down cold, including Pierre Trudeau and Robert Stanfield, the federal Conservative Party leader. But the centrepiece of their sold-out April 1976 performance at the Edmonton Jubilee Auditorium was "The Sheik of Calgary," sung by Lynch, decked out in an outlandish, vaguely Arabian costume.[51]

The performance was followed by a reception at the Chateau Lacombe hotel, perched atop the riverbank overlooking the North Saskatchewan. The party was in full swing, with members of the local media and the band whooping it up about the evening's great success, when someone said that the Lougheeds had entered the room. Everyone knew they had been at the performance. The place went deadly quiet until we absorbed the reality that Peter was wearing an Arab sheik's burnoose, and Jeanne was attired in something that looked like a harem dancer's outfit. Jeanne had heard that there would be some ribbing of Peter over his oil battles with Trudeau, and she was prepared, getting the costumes and composing their own song, which they proceeded to sing to the assembled throng. When the hooting and the applause settled down, Jeanne summoned Charlie Lynch to bare his stomach. From her purse, she produced a largish rhinestone and proceeded to plant it squarely in Lynch's also largish bellybutton. Lynch later wrote the following in his April 13, 1976 column in the *Edmonton Journal:*

"Bare your navel," she commanded, an order that no red-blooded Canadian boy could refuse. No sooner was the desired exposure achieved, amid boos and cheers, than she produced an exquisite little jewel box from which she took this walloping great rhinestone, and plunked it in, setting me to frenzies of bumping and grinding. The closing quote came from Premier Lougheed: "If we can just get the country laughing and keep it laughing, we just might hold the place together." Now my problem is I can't find the ruddy rhinestone—I know it's in there someplace.

"That was fun," Jeanne said, laughing as she went on to tell me the following story.

Peter and Jeanne offered their services as butler and maid at a celebrity auction to raise money for the arts held by the Edmonton Effort Auctions, which raised thousands of dollars for Edmonton's symphony, theatres and art gallery. The winning Edmonton couple were upset when the premier of Alberta and his wife insisted on coming in through the back door, she in a maid's uniform, he in a butler's tuxedo. They would have preferred to welcome them at the front door, but Peter and Jeanne were determined to stay in character as servants.

As the evening progressed, Peter welcomed the guests and poured the drinks; Jeanne served the meal on the family's heirloom dinnerware. When the plates from the first course were cleared and Jeanne and Peter had retired to the kitchen, the guests heard the ominous clatter of dishes crashing on the floor. The matron, although worried about her fine china, restrained herself. The noise continued unabated, but still she held back, on the one hand fearing the complete loss of her fine set of china, on the other, worried about embarrassing her very important "servants." The cacophony of smashing continued. Long-time Edmonton arts supporter Barbara Poole, who was among the dinner guests, said they couldn't believe their ears. Just at the point when the matron and her guests could stand it no longer, the Lougheeds appeared, gleefully carrying a box full of smashed dishes. There was relief and near hysterical laughter as the hosts realized that the debris was not their heirloom china: Jeanne had bought a box full of dishes at a local discount store and sneaked it in the back door. It was the sense of fun the Lougheeds displayed everywhere they went. This Peter Lougheed was a far cry from the tough, no-compromise fighter for provincial rights, battling Ottawa's gunslinger over the control of oil prices.

Jeanne's energetic volunteerism helped to animate Alberta's cultural landscape. And while the Alberta Ballet became her "baby," she was generous in giving her time and energy to many organizations, not all of them directly connected to the arts. She was an advisor to the Canadian Association for Community Living, which supports the integration of disabled Canadians into mainstream life. She chaired the provincial Heart Fund for two terms (1976–77), years during which Albertans donated the highest per capita amount in the country. To help these and other causes, she showed up regularly at scores of receptions, at schools and at fund-raisers.

But her heart was with the arts. Jeanne was, at various times, on the board of directors of Edmonton's Northern Light Theatre and the Edmonton Opera Society, and when we created the Banff International Television Foundation, Jeanne was a committed member of that board. She was an active participant in the campaign for the highly successful Tri-Bach Festival, organized by Alberta College president Sherburne McCurdy to celebrate the 300-year anniversary of the birth of Johann Sebastian Bach. She was a director, later a governor, of the National Ballet of Canada; a director of the Calgary Philharmonic Orchestra; and an honorary director of the Institute for Modern and Contemporary Art in Calgary. After Peter retired from politics, she accepted an appointment as a member of the Canada Council. John Poole,[52] one of Alberta's great patrons of the arts, wrote her in June 1983, saying, "In my opinion, you have personally done more for the arts in this province than possibly anyone."

Jeanne Lougheed's only public brush with controversy had to do with the selection of art for Government House, once the residence of Alberta's lieutenant-governors, which sits close to the banks of the North Saskatchewan River west of downtown Edmonton. The stately residence, opened in 1913 by then-Lieutenant-Governor

G.H.V. Bulyea, was the site of many grand receptions for hundreds of guests. It became a favourite of visiting royalty and other notables until it was closed in 1938. After a varied career that included several years as a residence for ailing World War II veterans, the house took on a new life after the Provincial Museum and Archives of Alberta building opened next door in 1967.

In 1976, when Edmonton was planning for the 1978 Commonwealth Games, there was speculation that if the Queen came to the city, she might stay at the residence. Government House underwent a complete refurbishing. The establishment of a Government House Foundation with a mandate to advise on the preservation of the house and "to inform the public of its architectural and historical development" was Jeanne's idea, and she recruited its first chairman, the late broadcasting pioneer and philanthropist Dr. G.R.A. Rice.

There are several versions of the story of how the art that now decorates the building was selected. In the official version,[53] a committee of three artists had been established, with a budget of $70,000, to select from the works of Alberta artists. After the selections were made and the winning artists advised, the budget was summarily cut in half by the then-Minister of Housing and Public Works Bill Yurko. A new committee was appointed to select works that would fit within the slashed budget. Jeanne Lougheed, putting herself in what she knew was a "touchy spot," agreed to chair a committee that included Carolyn Tavender, a member of the Alberta Art Foundation (and later chair of the Banff Centre Board of Governors) and two government architects.

There was a public furore when the artists whose work had originally been selected found out that they would not be represented in the Government House collection.[54] They complained, loudly and publicly, that their work had been subjected to a second evaluation without their consent. A member of the original selection committee stated, "I was assured that our adjudication was final." A group of about eight artists threatened to launch a class action lawsuit against the government, contending that the original committee's endorsement was tantamount to a commitment to purchase their works. The headlines were, in the context of the times, brutal and greatly upsetting to Jeanne. "Experts' art choices rejected by premier's wife," shouted the *Edmonton Journal*. "Mrs. Lougheed wields the art budget axe as two provincial departments [Culture and Housing] squabble," proclaimed the *Edmonton Report*.

The unofficial version of the story[55] suggests that the work selected by the original committee included a number of large abstracts. Someone, whose identity is shrouded in mystery, thought the paintings were inappropriate for the stately old building. A further judgement, its author(s) masked by bureaucracy, determined that the members of the original committee were too intimately involved to make the cuts.

There is a letter from the premier in the files appointing Mrs. Lougheed to chair the committee on the recommendation of Minister Yurko, who insisted she take on the task because of her familiarity with the house's history and décor.[56] But I also found a hand-written note from Jeanne, who first heard about the controversy on a car radio, saying that, had she been informed that the committee's decision would be reviewed, "I would never have agreed to chair that committee."[57]

In the end, all of the artists whose work had been originally selected were paid for their work (by Horst Schmid's Department of Culture) and given a commitment that their work would be displayed in other government buildings. "Alberta artists see green...like in cash," announced the *Calgary Herald*.[58] Today, works from a collection that includes Walter Phillips, William Kurelek, Nicholas de Grandmaison and Harry Savage decorate the walls of Government House.

That same year, another great Canadian artist, the world-famous photographer Yousuf Karsh, agreed to bring an exhibit of his work to Alberta. The exhibit, "Men Who Make Our World," opened at the Glenbow-Alberta Institute in Calgary. It was, according to a memo from Horst Schmid to the premier on November 18, 1976, "a culmination of negotiations begun in 1974 for the acquisition of 125 photographs from Mr. Yousuf Karsh's company 'Little Wings, Ltd.' for an amount of $50,000."[59] The memo continued, "It is planned to exhibit 'Men Who Make Our World' after the closing in Calgary [January 2, 1977] either at the Art Gallery or the Jubilee Auditorium in Edmonton. Subsequently, through careful planning, in communities, since it is our desire to make this collection, in whole or in part, available throughout Alberta. ..."60 The memo, a lengthy justification of the acquisition, was a response, Schmid recalls, to concerns raised by Lougheed of a perceived conflict because of the friendship among Jeanne, Karsh and he. And possibly to the furore over the Government House art selection. But Horst prevailed, and it was Jeanne who cut the ribbon to open the first showing of the Karsh collection.

The Lougheeds had indeed come to know and like Yousuf Karsh.61 The friendship between Jeanne and Yousuf was so close that she "adopted" the great man. She still cherishes a number of letters from him and an official-looking document that playfully commemorates their relationship. The document was sworn before then-Alberta Cabinet member Lou Hyndman. "A Commissioner for taking Affidavits within the Blue and Orange Province," and accompanied by two Polaroid photographs, one showing the couple being sworn into uncle-dom and niece-dom by Hyndman, a second showing Uncle Yousuf giving his niece a very gentlemanly kiss.

But Jeanne's heart was with ballet. The ballet was "almost like my child," she told me in an interview.62 Her crowning public achievement was the support she gave the Alberta Ballet.

The Alberta Ballet was the dream and the child of Margaret Ruth Pringle Carse, born in Edmonton where she began Scottish dancing as girl. Her talent (choreographer Brian MacDonald called her "small, quite fast and quite, quite gutsy") took her to an international career. But an injury forced her premature retirement and brought her home to Edmonton where she formed Dance Interlude in 1958, renaming it the Edmonton Ballet in 1961 and touring small communities throughout Alberta. The Alberta Ballet became a professional company in 1966. Ruth Carse retired as artistic director in 1975.

Jeanne sat on the Alberta Ballet's advisory committee and was their most constant patron. She advised, she encouraged, she helped raise many thousands of dollars, among other things supporting a fundraising cookbook called *Repas de Deux*. Over the years, her interest never waning, she developed relationships with ballet companies across the country, including the nationally recognized ones in

Winnipeg, Toronto and Montréal. If professional ballet has succeeded in Alberta, it is more than partly because of Jeanne Lougheed's determined efforts.

DATED: May 5, 1975

IN THE SUPREME COURT
OF THE BLUE AND ORANGE PROVINCE

IN THE MATTER OF THE
"ADOPTION ACT"

AND IN THE MATTER OF
THE ADOPTION OF
YOUSUF KARSH (UNCLE)
by
JEANNE LOUGHEED (NIECE)

AGREEMENT TO ADOPT

Baker and van Kampen
Banishers--Solitaries--Notorieties

OUR FILE: Confidential
YOUR FILE: Lost

A copy of the cover of the original "adoption" document. *Photo: Jeanne Lougheed*

Her first publicly visible initiative was the inauguration of the Tea Dances on April 22, 1978. The invitation read as follows:

The Alberta Ballet Company
and
Jeanne Lougheed
Cordially invite you to take a Sentimental Journey

Imagine gathering on a Sunday afternoon in April in a luxurious ballroom for tea and dancing to a big band orchestra. We men were in tails; the women wore their most beautiful gowns. The decorations in the room gave the impression that you had entered a fairyland of gossamer beauty. Upon entering, each of us was issued a dance card. Every song the band would play had a number, and you filled in your card with the names of the ladies or gentlemen you wished to dance with through the afternoon. I remember having to compete with sculptor Roy Leadbeater and many others to get Jeanne's name on my card. She danced every dance. Cocktails were served at 3:00 p.m. The Alberta Ballet performed at 4:00 p.m. There was a light supper and we left, always reluctantly, at about 7:00 p.m. The tea dance cost $50, of which $35 was a tax-deductible donation to the ballet. Horst Schmid's Department of Culture matched the donations dollar for dollar. Rarely have so many people had so much fun supporting the arts.

But it was the 15th Anniversary Gala Benefit Performance held in mid-November 1981 that really gave the Alberta Ballet the national and international recognition it enjoys today. The company was struggling financially, and Jeanne, with some friends, decided to put on the greatest gala in support of ballet that Alberta, and the country, has seen, before or since. To celebrate the anniversary, the event honoured the four grande dames of Canadian ballet: Dr. Gweneth Lloyd and Betty Farrally, co-founders of the Royal Winnipeg Ballet in 1939; Celia Franca, founder of the National Ballet of Canada in 1951; and Ludmilla Chiriaeff, founder of Les Grands Ballets Canadiens de Montréal in 1957.

Jeanne accepted the role of honorary chairperson of the event. She approached two Calgary industrialists, John Scrymgeour and

Standing, Betty Farrally; *seated, left to right,* Celia Franca, Dr. Gweneth Lloyd and Ludmilla Chiriaeff. *Photo: Jeanne Lougheed*

Dancing with Jeanne Lougheed at the Banff Centre Ball. She is the best dancer I've jived with since I used to win jitterbug contests at the east-end Montreal YMCA. *Photo: Banff Centre*

Robert Borden,[63] who owned a Boeing jetliner that they had refurbished as a corporate aircraft. Could they, Jeanne asked, arrange to have the aircraft pick up the four ballet founders, and, by the way, a New York critic, and bring them to Alberta? And make it, of course, a donation?

I found a briefing note in Jeanne's files that read, "Aircraft to depart New York, Montréal and Toronto November 17th and to return November 19th." The four great ladies had, of course, known each other, but they had never spent much time in each other's company. The flight to Alberta gave them an opportunity for uninterrupted hours of conversation. The briefing notes also set out the seating arrangements for a Government House dinner party. Table one: Premier Peter and Mrs. Jeanne Lougheed, Madame Celia Franca, Dr. Gweneth Lloyd, Madame Betty Farrally, Ms. Ludmilla Chiriaeff, Tom and Ida Banks.

It was a GALA. It started with an invitation to a black-tie reception and dinner at Government House "in honour of the Four Founding Ladies of Canadian Ballet." A local fur company provided full-length coats for them to wear for the occasion, and they were welcomed under a storm of confetti. The following day they were presented to the Alberta Legislature, and that evening some of the best ballet dancers in the world participated in a dazzling performance at the Edmonton Jubilee Auditorium. There were guest artists from Germany's renowned Stuttgart Ballet, the Royal Winnipeg Ballet, the National Ballet of Canada, and Les Grands Ballets Canadiens, all performing under the direction of artistic director Brydon Paige. Boris Brott conducted the Edmonton Symphony Orchestra.

Performances were also mounted at the Jubilee Auditorium in Calgary. Carolyn Heiman of the *Edmonton Journal* reported, "At first it seemed cheeky of the Alberta Ballet Company to mount an extravagant gala for its 15th anniversary. …After an almost three-hour performance before a nearly full house it could be said that the company did it, and did it with fanfare."

Stephen Godfrey, writing in the *Globe and Mail* on November 20, 1981, said,

> One of the most gratifying developments of the last decade is the success with which the country's three largest ballet companies—the Royal Winnipeg Ballet, the National Ballet of Canada and Les Grands Ballets Canadiens—have continued to grow and win new audiences for the ballet. It was high time for someone to pay tribute to those who started it all, and it is to the great credit of the Alberta Ballet that it had the initiative to do so.

And, as always during those years, Jeanne made sure that every dancer had a red rose. The gala was one of the last great cultural events of the era.

Peter Lougheed retired in 1985. An economic downturn, which had begun in 1981, was taking hold. When a reporter asked Jeanne when he had told her he was going to retire, she replied, "Twenty years ago." His retirement party was, for many, a nostalgic tribute to some of the best years Alberta had ever lived. I had the honour of being the master of ceremonies before an audience of 4000 at

Edmonton Northlands on Friday, October 11, 1985. The highlight of the evening was a video tribute created by Jeanne and the four Lougheed children, which caught the premier totally by surprise and brought tears to his eyes. People in the hall knew that we had come to the end of an era. Peter said, "Thanks for the memories." But columnist Don Braid summed up the event by noting "the Alberta Tories [had] lost their security blanket."[64]

What I remember is how the Lougheeds, in their public and private lives, created an environment that encouraged thousands of Albertans to develop and celebrate their creativity. The Lougheeds are now in active retirement in Calgary. One of their major projects is the restoration of Beaulieu, the house built by Sir James Lougheed, and its establishment as an archive of their time and contribution to Alberta. Both continue to support the arts.

Few political couples have had such a profound and positive impact on their times. Alberta's "Golden Age of the Arts" might not have happened without Horst Schmid or Les Usher, whom you will meet in the next chapter. It might not have happened just because Alberta had a rich community of artists. But it certainly would not have happened without the active endorsement of Peter and Jeanne Lougheed. Because the Lougheeds, Schmid and Usher provided the leadership and helped shape a receptive environment, Alberta artists and innovators were able to create one of the most vibrant cultural landscapes in Canadian history.

Horst was rough-hewn, but no one doubted the diamond within.

—Grant Kennedy, Lone Pine Publishing

Chapter 4

Mr. Alberta Culture: Horst Schmid

A fellow Cabinet minister[65] once said, "Horst talks faster than I can listen." Even today, Horst Schmid speaks so rapidly that you often have to ask him to repeat himself. When he says his own name, he barely skirts the scatological mispronunciation he laughingly cautions others not to make. "Be careful how you say my name," he says, his eyes twinkling. "It's a good thing they didn't make me Minister of Agriculture."

He was born in Munich, Germany, on April 23, 1933, and christened Horst Adolph Louis Charles Schmid. When he was four, his parents would stand him on the dining-room table while he sang his favourite Bavarian tune, a folk song about why there were no more *weisswurst*, or white sausages. He was no boy soprano; even as a child his voice was lower than average, foreshadowing the rich bass of his adulthood. His mother and grandparents loved opera, and their Munich house was filled with the sound of arias, later overridden by the wail of World War II air-raid sirens in a war the child Horst could not comprehend. All he knew was that his father, a service station owner, was away, first on military service in the German army, then as a prisoner of war.

Horst attended a liberal arts language school in Munich where he picked up Latin, Greek and a little French. His qualities of leadership were recognized early. He became his school's air-raid warden. "The best thing you could say about it was, when we had air raids after midnight," he said, characteristically finding the bright side, "we didn't have to go to school the next day." His high school work placement was in a machinery design training program, about which the most significant thing was a foreman who wrote poetry and inspired his young charge to develop an appreciation for literature in general and poetry in particular. He received his postwar education in a Jesuit school and joined a movement of Young Christian Workers that fought for workers' rights. He was soon its executive secretary for Munich and upper Bavaria, organizing the first postwar exchange camp between French and German youth worker organizations. He joined a student opera association, and with his now grown-up, *basso profundo* voice, sang in choirs performing classical works. By the end of the 1940s, he had acquired a working knowledge of Italian.

In 1951, at age 19, he decided that his future was not in Bavaria. He applied to immigrate to both the United States and Canada; friends had moved both countries. He sold almost everything he owned, including a prized bicycle, and packed what was left—clothes, some books and a few favourite 78-rpm opera records—into two suitcases. Canadian immigration came through first, and on May 7, 1952, he disembarked at Québec City. He spoke no English. After a long cross-country ride, he stepped off the train at the old CNR station in Edmonton and, with a friend, went thirstily into the beer parlour of the old Ritz Hotel. They were, to their surprise (not understanding what they were being told), forcibly ejected from the premises. They had entered the Ladies and Escorts section. In the

1950s, Alberta's unattached males who wanted to buy themselves drink could do so only in the "men's beer parlour." And furthermore, under Alberta's liquor laws, he was still too young to drink.

At the Edmonton immigration centre, an officer made him understand that he had the choice of work on a farm in northern Alberta for about $50 a month plus room and board, or a job in the gold mines in Yellowknife. Yellowknife paid $1.25 an hour. "That was five marks in Germany," he said, "a lot of money." So he went to work in the gold-mining camps of Yellowknife. He saw the inside of an airplane for the first time on his flight to Yellowknife in an old DC-3. He was terrified. When the stewardess, as they were then called, offered him breakfast, he thought she was talking about a barf bag and, sucking up his pride and fear, declined. He still hates flying. He began work, first as a ditch digger, then on a mucking machine, then as a cage tender watching men begin their descent 3000 feet (914 metres) into the Precambrian Shield to dig, drill and blast for gold.

Settling into Yellowknife, Horst learned one of his first and, he says, most important lessons about Canada. Workers at the mine, many of them immigrants, were treated equally, no matter where they came from, no matter what their history or culture or religion. In an era when Germans were still often vilified, it was a huge lesson. But that only begins to explain Horst Schmid's colour- and culture-blindness, unusual for a man of his era and background. Some of his eagerness to embrace people of all faiths and heritages, he says, comes from an early appreciation of the ideals of what were then called North American Indians.

Many young Germans were enthralled by a series of romantic travel and adventure books for young people by Karl Friedrich May, who wrote idealistically about Indians and about nomadic desert Arabs. May is not widely known in North America, but his books have been international best sellers, with especially high sales in Germany. Young Germans often looked beyond their culture, so badly tarnished by the Nazis, to the romanticism and high ideals of the Indians heroically portrayed by May. May's Indians always had magnificent battles, always treated their enemies as honoured adversaries, their prisoners with dignity. Nature was, for them, beautiful, benign and sacred. German youngsters were told that if they didn't behave, they would not grow up to be like Indians. "When we played cowboys and Indians," Horst told me, "the Indians always won."

In Yellowknife he quickly began to pick up English, beginning, as is almost always the case, with the well-known expletives used by the rough men who worked the mines—words that got him into trouble when he innocently used them in more polite society. They threw him out of the local Hudson's Bay store when, after carefully checking his dictionary, and, casually adding what be believed was a commonly accepted prefix, asked where he could find some "fucking underwear."

At the end of six months, possibly with his English-German dictionary under his pillow, Schmid says he began to dream in English. His energetic approach to life was already apparent: he organized a barbershop quartet, volunteered at the local radio station, and began to sing and to appear in little theatre productions, once, incredibly, playing an Englishman in a Noel Coward play. He struck up a friendly relationship with the local Indians, at one point learning to sing "Nearer My God to Thee" in Dogrib. At the same time, he began taking University of Toronto correspondence courses in business finance, administration and business psychology.

In 1956, Schmid decided it was time to move to Edmonton and go into business. His first venture foreshadowed later roles when he worked in the areas of multiculturalism and international trade. With an East Indian partner based in Vancouver, he set up Eastec Development Corporation, which exported Alberta fertilizer and sulphur to India and Taiwan. The business grew into a profitable import/export enterprise, at one time sending Alberta honey to Switzerland and importing Swiss hair clippers.

Schmid continued his business development with a restaurant, the Hofbräuhaus, with partners that included the well-known Edmonton entertainer, Gaby Haas. In his spare time he took up dancing, organizing a German *schuhplattler*, or folk dance group, which performed on weekends at the Hofbräuhaus. The group, with the future Minister of Culture in *lederhosen* and the now-famous Shumka Dancers, under the musical direction of Eugene Zwozdesky, a future Minister of Community Development (also responsible for Culture), was invited to perform at Canada's greatest-ever party, Expo 67.

Schmid became a jazz fan. Senator Tommy Banks, then and now a bandleader of renown and one of Canada's best jazz pianists, said that Schmid was the "right guy, right place, right time." Banks told me about some of Horst's early inclinations in the following note:

5 a.m. Breakfasts with Horst and the beboppers

The Yardbird Suite, Edmonton's musician-established and volunteer-operated jazz club, had been founded in about 1956. In about 1956 or 1957, we began to notice that at the end of the weekly Saturday night jam sessions (which started sometime around 1:00 a.m., when the musicians arrived at the Suite from their commercial engagements), after most of the hardiest civilians had finally gone home, there was, among the jazz stragglers listening to every last note of every last player, this nice little German guy whose attention was riveted on the music at least as much as it was upon the invariably stunning girl who he had brought to the club.

After the first few months, it became his habit to accompany the last remaining players to an all-night restaurant on 104th Street for big, hot breakfasts, usually at about 5:00 a.m. or so. That's how the beboppers met and came to know Horst. Then we began to notice that he was also at the symphony concerts, and the ballet and the opera. He was, in fact, ubiquitous at anything to do with the performing (and probably all the other) arts.

By 1960 Schmid was also selling insurance, driving a red 1952 Meteor convertible to small towns in northern and central Alberta. In Rimbey to settle a claim, Horst met the daughter of one of the claimants, Arleen Farnham. He wooed her with top-down drives in his convertible. "I knew quite a lot about astronomy in those days," he said. "I used to show her the constellations." They were married in 1961.

At the same time, Horst was becoming more deeply involved in community affairs, becoming host, from 1956 to 1966, of *Music from the German-speaking Countries of Europe* on CKUA. The program made him a kind of informal ambassador for Edmonton's substantial German immigrant community, and that led him to teaching English to immigrants in church halls.

When budget cuts resulted in the loss of the studio operator for Horst's radio program, future federal Cabinet minister Jim Edwards,[66] then a news broadcaster at CKUA, taught Horst how to operate the control board and cue his own records. Edwards was then a member of the Edmonton Opera board and co-chair of its fund-raising committee. It wasn't long before he recruited Schmid. Together, they convened a fund-raising bee in the wine cellar of the Hofbräuhaus. Schmid played host in the *lederhosen* that were to become one of his trademarks. Edwards rigged a roll of Saran Wrap and used it with an overhead projector to display a list of prospects with a marker pen. "I think Horst raised more money than any of us," Edwards recalls.

Sometime in 1965 Schmid recalls going to a gathering in Bill Skoreyko's basement. Skoreyko, a Member of Parliament for the Conservatives, was introducing an "interesting" young man to people in Edmonton. The youthful Peter Lougheed, who was organizing his drive for the leadership of the Alberta Progressive Conservative Party, more than impressed Horst. Jim Edwards, recruited by Lougheed as a communications advisor for northern Alberta, recalled the following in an interview with me:

> Peter wanted a linkage to first-generation immigrants. Edmonton was the centre of that immigration, and German speakers were the largest component. I invited Horst to the Palliser Hotel in Calgary for his first meeting with Peter. Horst and I arranged to meet at the Riviera Hotel on the Calgary Trail. He pulled up in his Buick, folded himself into my VW Beetle, and off we went [it was probably a lot easier for Schmid than for Edwards, who is well over six feet tall, to fit into the Beetle]. Horst and Peter turned out to be a political marriage made in heaven.

In the run-up to the 1971 election, the two potential candidates were discussing which of them should run, each offering to support the other, almost, according to Schmid, in the manner of *après vous Alphonse*. Edwards, who later had his own electoral success in the federal arena, urged Horst to go for it. Schmid decided to run in Edmonton–Avonmore, mainly because the constituency had a heavy concentration of German immigrants. But he quickly learned to his disappointment, that most of the Germans could not vote in Canada. They were hanging on to their German citizenship because as long as they remained citizens of that country, wherever they were in the world, they could still collect German government pensions. Knowing his work was cut out for him, Schmid, in a tradition established by Peter Lougheed in the 1967 election, hit the pavement, with a plan to knock on every door.

But he was concerned about his German immigrant status. "If a hundred people tell me to go back to where I came from," he promised himself, "I will withdraw my nomination." His command of English was by then more than acceptable, but his accent was still pretty thick. He taught himself to say, slowly and very carefully, without accent: "My name is Horst (short pause) Schmid. I am Peter Lougheed's candidate. I would app-rec-i-ate your vote." He knocked on 5746 doors. No one told him to go anywhere.

Schmid was the first post-WWII immigrant elected to the Legislature. When he phoned his mother in Munich with the news, she didn't believe him. "Impossible!" she said. "What would you say if I told you that, here in Germany, we had elected a Turk to the government? You're crazy." She was just as incredulous when, 10 days later, he called to tell her that he was a minister in the Cabinet. It wasn't until she actually saw the newspaper clippings that she accepted the truth: her son had become the first post-World War II immigrant to be appointed a Cabinet minister in Canada.

"Yes," was the way he always answered the telephone. A fellow Cabinet minister joked that every time Horst Schmid answered the phone that way he gave up his negotiating position. It wasn't long into his tenure that people in the arts community knew that he could often be found alone in his office late at night, cleaning up the odds and ends of the day's usually frenetic activities.

"Yes," he would say, with rising inflection.

"Thank you for agreeing, Minister, for your generous support of my project," the person on the other end of the line would say.

"What have I agreed to?" Schmid would retort in mock shock—and they would have a good laugh.

It was characteristic of the easy and trusting relationship he came to develop with leaders in Alberta's feisty arts community. Between 1971 and 1979, Schmid would say an emphatic "yes" to a dazzling variety of projects that made momentous contributions to an era during which Alberta led the country in support for cultural development. He rarely said "no." His most frequent response was "How can we do this?"

To this day, he retains his man-of-the-people touch, turning up at cultural events on a regular basis. We both love to tell the story of his participation in a television series on multicultural issues I was producing and hosting on Canada's first on-air educational television station.[67] Horst was a guest on three consecutive programs during the summer and fall of 1971. On the first I introduced him as Horst Schmid, representative of the German-Canadian Business Association. A week later he was Horst Schmid, member of the Alberta Legislative Assembly. And on the third program I found myself addressing the Honourable Horst A. Schmid, Minister of Culture, Youth and Recreation in Peter Lougheed's first government.

In his maiden speech in the Legislature, Schmid noted the then-current belief that modern technology was on the verge of producing a splendid new leisure society (don't you wish), complete with a three-day workweek. It was important, he argued, that people have something to fill all that extra time. "Art," he said, his emotion rising, "is the very root and fibre of our existence. ... I believe," he said prophetically, "that, in this province, we are going to have a blooming of talent such as our pioneer fathers may never have dreamed of." Culture, he said, is "a thing beyond value. It's a backbone, the measure of how advanced a society is." One of the first things he did in his new portfolio was to order a review of department spending in relation to other provincial budgets. In this position, with escalating budgets over the next eight years, he became the person that many called Mr. Alberta Culture. His definition of culture clearly included

Lieutenant-Governor, the Honourable Ralph Steinhauer, swears in the Honourable Horst A. Schmid as Minister of Culture, Youth and Recreation. *Photo: Government of Alberta*

multiculturalism, and Alberta was one of the first provinces to make a formal commitment to cultural diversity.

After being sworn in, Schmid went quickly to Edmonton's CN Tower building, where the staff of his department had its offices. The first person he met when he got off the elevator was Les Graff, the department's supervisor of Arts and Crafts. Graff wished him well in his new job, but told the new minister that he had nothing to say to him. When Schmid asked him what he meant, Graff, a successful visual artist, told him he was quitting. He listed a long list of complaints, about bureaucracy, about the lack of real support for the arts. "Give me six months," Schmid pleaded, "and then decide." Graff stayed the six months and continued with the department through Schmid's tenure and beyond.

The next person Schmid met was Les Usher, the department's quiet, soft-spoken deputy minister. If Horst Schmid was the engine, if Jeanne Lougheed brought the inspiration and if Peter provided the fuel that made culture run in Alberta, Les Usher was the oil that kept the engine from seizing up under the breakneck speed at which it operated. He is one of the unsung heroes of Alberta's cultural development. Usher was and is financially independent. He did not have to work to earn a living, especially not in the pressure cooker that the Department of Culture, Youth and Recreation (later the Department of Culture) became in the 1970s. His family owns a substantial cattle ranch, large enough to be measured in townships, in central Alberta. His curriculum vitae still lists him as president of Usher Ranching Ltd.

A modest, self-effacing man, Les Usher is not the kind of person who takes over a room when he enters. But if there is work to do, he's the one who stays until all the loose ends are tied up. He came into government in 1949 with a fresh University of Alberta Bachelor of Science degree in agriculture, first to work as assistant supervisor of 4-H programs, then, in 1955, as supervisor. The next year, Premier Ernest Manning made him the first deputy minister of the new Department of Youth. Early in 1971, Harry Strom converted it into the Department of Culture, Youth and Recreation. Usher recruited the outstanding team that stayed to back up Horst Schmid's extraordinary commitment to making the arts matter in Alberta.

When the Lougheed government decided to leave the department intact, one of Schmid's most astute decisions, I would argue, was to keep Usher on as deputy minister. He was a skilled administrator, a true public servant, in the best sense of the term: dedicated to his work, not for money or power, but out of a strong sense of making a contribution to his community. He remained throughout Schmid's tenure in the Culture portfolio, a quiet but efficient counterpart to his minister's blustery ebullience.

Both were workaholics. Usher says he put in as many as 80 hours a week to make sure that the department could deliver what their peripatetic minister promised. In the era before computers, Usher's staff included two secretaries whose job was to keep up with the correspondence he spoke into a Dictaphone after he went home at night. He told me he didn't mind the late night calls from Schmid (admitting to taking calls as late as 11:00 p.m., but Schmid says it was often later than that) with some news, or some directive. Usher helped to make Alberta Culture a leading presence at the national level, pressing strongly for inter-provincial cooperation in culture, youth and recreation programming. He was the first chair of the Council of Provincial Deputy Ministers of Recreation and later chaired the first Council of Provincial Deputy Ministers of Culture. He produced major reports on the financing of both historical resources and of the arts. Alberta's approach to legislation, programming and financing of the arts, overseen by Usher, became models in their field and were echoed in other provinces across Canada.

Usher and Schmid were as unlike as chalk and cheese, but Usher greatly admired his Minister. In an unsolicited letter to Peter Lougheed dated February 1, 1974, Usher praised his boss as one of the most dedicated ministers he had ever worked for.

> It has occurred to me that too often we fail to express appreciation of the talents and labours of those to whom we are responsible—or worse, we take them for granted. Objectively at this point, I doubt if I have ever known anyone whose efforts are more unsparing, or who keeps himself so personally involved, concerning the needs of Albertans generally...I feel obliged to convey to you the pleasure and inspiration it has been for me to work with him these past two and a half years.

It was Horst's first term. There was no election in sight. The letter was marked confidential and not copied to Schmid. He never saw it.

Under Schmid and Usher, the Department of Culture, Youth and Recreation re-invented itself with a barrage of new cultural support programs that came with accelerating rapidity.

It was, without doubt, the network of grants programs established by the Lougheed administration, flush with oil and gas revenues, that turbocharged the arts environment, allowing creators in all disciplines to mature and flourish. Schmid, with the active encouragement of Jeanne Lougheed, began making grants to any artistic organization that seemed to have a shot at success. Those grants were soon organized into a constellation of programs that offered structured support to arts organizations, libraries and cultural heritage groups across the province.

For the Lougheed government, the links between art and cultural heritage were clear from the beginning. Art flows from culture. Both give us a sense of who we are and where we came from, of what it is to be fully human. In June of 1972, less than a year after assuming office, the new government assembled the Alberta Cultural Heritage Conference. Its principal purpose was "to focus attention on the provincial government's deep concern for and serious commitment to the preservation and promotion of Alberta's cultural background." Among the items on the agenda were the following:

- arts development and cultural development
- Canadianism
- education and language
- human rights and values.

It is important to note the connection between arts, culture, heritage and human rights and, as we shall see later, a demonstrated concern for less fortunate people throughout the world. These are, in my view, chief among the factors that define a truly advanced society.

In the spring of 1974, Schmid and Assistant Deputy Minister Walter Kaasa organized the Arts and You Conference in Red Deer.[68] Communities from across the province were invited to send representatives to meet with Alberta artists in the disciplines of dance, drama, the visual arts and crafts, creative writing, film and photography. Some 1000 people attended a three-day conference "to enrich understanding between artists and the people of Alberta." They were treated to a bountiful smorgasbord of performances and displays.

That spring I received a phone call from Horst Schmid which would have a significant impact on my life. He wanted to know if I could help with the organization of the Arts and You Conference.

"Who is taking care of the film festival?" I asked.

"What film festival?"

And that's how Alberta's first film festival came to be—but more about that in Chapter 8.

The Arts and You was followed in November 1974 by the Alberta Music Conference, with a parallel agenda, also held in Red Deer. Following these and other conferences, Alberta's maturing support of the arts delivered advice, training and education, scholarships, expert consultation and, most importantly, money. The Cultural Development Branch offered programs covering the visual arts and crafts, the performing arts in all their variety, film and literary arts. The Cultural Heritage Division established guidelines for grants to support a broad variety of heritage projects.

Alberta Summer Residential Drama Schools, run by George and Enid Botchett in Drumheller, offered three-week courses for high school students in all phases of theatre. In the mid-1970s my son Randall, still in high school, came to me one day. "There's a summer drama workshop in Drumheller, Dad," he said. "I've saved up half the tuition fee. Will you give me the rest?" It was my first inkling that he was seriously interested in theatre. Now in his 40s, he is an established member of Edmonton's theatrical community. Millions of people around the world saw the beautiful figures, carried by stilt-walking actors, that he created for the opening and closing ceremonies of the 2000 World Athletic Games held in Edmonton. In 2002 he won a Sterling Award for best costumes for his creations for a 2001 production of *The Hobbit*. (No proud father here!) He is one of hundreds of actors, directors, designers and other theatre crafts people who got their start at the summer residential programs, many of them going on to enter the Bachelor of Fine Arts program at the University of Alberta.

The Search for a New Alberta Novelist competition, part of the Film and Literary Arts Program managed by the brilliant short story writer turned cultural bureaucrat John Patrick Gillese, provided the springboard for a number of award-winning writers, beginning in 1974 with Fred Stenson and followed by Pauline Gedge, Aritha van Herk, Jan Truss and others. Gillese's own homespun, grab-you-by-the-heart stories had been published in such prestigious American magazines as *The Saturday Evening Post* and *Colliers,* as well as in

Horst with John Patrick Gillese, receiving an award from the Alberta Writers' Federation, 1976. *Photo: unknown*

such early Canadian mainstays as *The Star Weekly.* He inspired a generation of writers, novelists, screenwriters and poets.

In drama, between 1968 and 1985, the Citadel on Wheels and Wings was given the resources to make it possible for communities and schools, as many as 325 of them, in all parts of Alberta and northward into the Arctic, to experience first-class theatre. The Performing Arts on Tour program took individual artists and groups, ranging from the Stettler Gilbert and Sullivan Chorus to the Alberta Ballet Company, to more than 150 communities in the province. Artists-in-residence programs allowed artists, from the late blues singer Big Miller and opera star Bernard Turgeon to the classical ensemble One Third Ninth, to work with communities and schools to help broaden Albertans' understanding and appreciation of the arts.

In addition to programs managed within the Culture, Youth and Recreation Department, a number of arms-length institutions with specific mandates were established. They included the Alberta Art Foundation, established in 1972, which purchased works from Alberta artists for display in government-owned buildings and as the basis for touring visual arts exhibits; the Alberta Foundation for the Literary Arts; and, later, the Alberta Foundation for the Performing Arts, on whose initial board of directors I sat.[69] On the heritage side, there were the Alberta Historical Resources Foundation and the Ukrainian Cultural Heritage Village Advisory Board.

But, without doubt, the most important cultural assistance program launched during the 1970s was the Alberta Matching Grants Program. Schmid's department matched private donations to arts organizations, dollar for dollar, up to 25 percent of their budget. If an organization could raise 25 percent of the money it needed from non-government sources, it immediately found itself with half its budget in hand. The rest could reasonably be expected to come from box-office receipts and other fund-raising activities. It was a lot easier and much more satisfying to make donations to the arts when you knew that, in addition to your tax receipt, your contribution would be matched dollar-for-dollar by the government. The program opened wide a door that saw substantially increased private-sector support for theatre, ballet, opera, dance and the symphony.

The program was available to both professional and amateur performing and visual arts organizations. In 1975–76, the first year of the program, the renamed Department of Culture (Youth and Recreation had been transferred to other departments) paid $903,539 in matching grants to 16 professional organizations and $58,356 to 16 amateur organizations.[70] Most of the money was spent on employing artists.

The late Dave Billington,[71] the lovable professional maverick who wrote the *Edmonton Sun*'s entertainment column during the 1970s, lauded the province, which "through its ministry of culture, helped create and maintain the environment in which the arts were encouraged to grow. Its matching grant policy, brought in under the irrepressible Horst Schmid, is the most enlightened such policy in the country."[72]

In 1971, the year Horst Schmid became minister, the Department of Culture, Youth and Recreation had dispensed $282,797 on arts scholarships and grants to organizations, virtually doubling the amount spent by the Social Credit government. "By and large," wrote Deputy Minister Les Usher in the 1971 annual report, "the demand stems from increasing leisure (the result of shortened work weeks in some areas of business life, a more affluent society and the better health and longevity of retired citizens), rapidly growing interest in the arts themselves and concern for the worth of our cultural heritage." By 1979, Schmid's last year in the portfolio, the amount had exploded to $7,511,647. Some demand. Some response. The idea of the once-anticipated "leisure society" has disappeared into the never-never land of the Jetsons. But since the 1970s, the arts have claimed their place in Alberta, both as an essential ingredient in the daily life of a great many citizens and as an important part of the economy. "It is no longer necessary to think of support in the arts as welfare," Schmid's department reported.

The only Canadian province that supported the arts as enthusiastically was my native Québec. When I left Montréal in 1958, Maurice Duplessis was still in power, a virtual dictator who, with the help of the Catholic Church, ran a corrupt government that shamed Quebeckers and left English Canada with ample justification for its poor treatment of *la belle province*. I was almost sorry I had left when I learned that Jean Lesage had swept into power in 1960 and launched the Quiet Revolution.

Lesage opened Québec to an exciting rush of political, economic, cultural and artistic development. The Quiet Revolution changed the relationship between Québec and the rest of Canada forever. "The party which I lead," Lesage said, "wishes to give priority to cultural and educational questions." One of his first legislative acts was to establish the Ministry of Cultural Affairs, followed closely by the *Office de la langue française*. The *Ministère des affaires culturelles*,

Lesage said, was "a department of French Canadian civilization...to act as the most effective instrument of the French fact in North America, of the soul of our people." In 1965, one of his ministers, Pierre Laporte, later to be executed by the Front de Libération du Québec (Québec Liberation Front), or FLQ, put the case eloquently: "The role of culture itself in the heart of a nation should be emphasized. It creates liberty, it innovates, it constructs an internal order...the status, the vital forces, the very essence of a nation, all meet and find their greatest fulfilment in culture."[73] The explosion of culture triggered by Jean Lesage in the 1960s continues to this day. No other province had supported the arts so wholeheartedly as Québec.

Until Alberta.

Perhaps the greatest single exposition of the arts in Alberta was the program developed for the province's 75th anniversary in 1980. The province devoted $75 million to the celebration, and a good part of it went to culture and the arts. The celebration included a province-wide Festival of the Arts, the funding of Mel Hurtig's landmark *Canadian Encyclopedia*, a Discover Alberta Art Program and, to top it all off, *Alberta!*, an original musical production created by Jack McCreath, head of the drama division in the Department of Culture.

John Reid,[74] in the *Festival of the Arts Final Report* produced for the 75th Anniversary Commission, described the $3-million arts extravaganza as a fitting celebration in "an arts conscious province." The program included 13 major performing arts attractions, three arts exhibits and a number of special events that toured the province. It was, he said, "designed to encourage maximum participation in the anniversary celebrations."

Major attractions included an Alberta Festival for Young People; the Alberta Pops Orchestra, a 63-piece ensemble directed by Tommy Banks; W.O. Mitchell's play *The Black Bonspiel of Wullie MacCrimmon; Dance, Dance, Dance,* a "dance gala featuring world-class dancers (including Evelyn Hart and Frank Augustyn) in classical *pas de deux* and jazz performances; and a travelling *Folk Festival and Goodtime Medicine Show,* featuring well-known stars such as Sylvia Tyson, Stan Rogers, John Allan Cameron and Connie Kaldor.

There was a Festival of the Arts for the Disabled and an Alberta Art Foundation Caravan. The first attraction opened in Grande Prairie on May 14 and the last in Okotoks on September 7, 1980. Through the summer, festival attractions appeared in communities large and small, from Acadia Valley to Whitla in the County of Forty Mile, from Vegreville to Pincher Creek, from Lac La Biche to Vauxhall.

The 75th anniversary celebrations gave many hundreds of artists a boost and a foundation that would carry them through the end of the century, long after those golden years had passed. *Alberta Views* magazine, in May 2000, reported, "Estimates from the province assert upwards of 2.3 million people attended arts festivals last year. There are 48 established arts festivals across the province, with more cropping up every year. And that doesn't include the rodeos, the busy pow-wow circuit or commercial 'fests' also thriving here." The arts are part of our lives, our culture and our economy. Through it all, Horst Schmid had been part "Energizer Bunny," part Daddy Warbucks,[75] expanding and redesigning a wide variety of support programs.

Schmid's long-standing love of native culture led him to what he considers one of his proudest accomplishments. Schmid ordered the return of a medicine bundle that had been housed in the Provincial Museum to the Blood Reserve for use in their sacred Sun Dance ceremony. The chief of the reserve, discussing the spiritual importance of the sacred bundle, had asked Schmid if a Mass could be held without a chalice, or an evangelical service without a Bible. When museum staff said they could not give away what had become official provincial property, Horst found a regulation that allowed artefacts to be sent out on "permanent loan." The province may still, on paper, "own" the artefacts, but they are in the hands of the people to whom they really belong.

In 1997, the Samson Cree Band at Hobbema bestowed on Schmid the honorary title of Chief Flying Eagle. It was an ironic choice of name given his fear of flying. But, now a private-sector entrepreneur, Schmid has proudly named his company Flying Eagle Resources. And, as it happens, in German, *horst* means "eagle's nest."

One significant sidebar to Alberta Culture's programs was the international aid program. While you might not think of international aid as culture, there was a developing sense in the Department of Culture, and in the Lougheed Cabinet, that a "civil society"[76] should also be concerned about those in the world who were less fortunate. The program, created in late 1973, was designed to provide financial assistance to non-governmental organizations (NGOs) that wished to support projects and programs of assistance and/or emergency relief in less developed countries. In a move unequalled in Canada, Alberta matched private contributions dollar for dollar. An extraordinarily broad cross-section of community organizations, ranging from the Aga Khan Foundation to the Zonta Club of Edmonton, rose to meet the challenge. They included the Alberta Teachers Association, the YMCA, the St. Joseph's Save the Children Club, the Baptist Union of Western Canada, the Sir Edmund Hillary Foundation and Operation Eyesight Universal. Both religious communities and secular organizations stepped forward to meet the challenge.

The response was massive.[77] International disasters seemed to dominate the daily news. Idi Amin's inhuman Uganda massacres, the Guatemala earthquake, and what seemed like an endless parade of world crises generated urgent calls for agricultural development, food relief, potable water, health, education, vocational training, refugee rehabilitation and social services. One of the more poignant disasters was the plight of the Vietnamese "boat people." Between 1978 and 1981, several hundred thousand Vietnamese escaped from their homeland by boat, any kind of boat, in a desperate search for safety and freedom. Alberta's—and Canada's—response was tremendous, with community groups banding together to create a chain of support for the boat people. Under refugee sponsorship provisions of the new Immigration Act, thousands of refugees were brought to Canada.

> News Item– *The Calgary Herald:*
> Calgary, Dec. 21, 1978: Extra contributions by Albertans to international aid have prompted the government to increase its matching support by $600,000, Premier Lougheed said Wednesday. The province started matching donations from individuals in 1974. He said Alberta is one of three provinces

> with international aid programs, "I am pleased to say that we lead Canada by far in contributions," he said. "Albertans have given $4.3 million in the past year, through church and secular agencies," he said. "The money is for food, shelter, clothing, medical and schooling in less developed countries," said Lougheed. "By adding $600,000 to its share the government brings its international budget to a matching $4.3 million…That's up from the $3.7 million in matching grants that the government contributed last year for 201 projects in 62 countries," he said.

The international aid program was an extraordinary extension of the province's commitment to enriching the life of its own citizens.

The transformation from the old, inward-looking, defensive Social Credit Alberta, to Lougheed's let-the-sunshine-in revolution saw a general loosening of what were generally known as the "blue laws." Liquor laws were relaxed (you could actually buy a glass of wine during intermission at the Jubilee Auditorium). Schmid refused to ban *Penthouse* magazine. In its first legislative session, the new government allowed cameras into the Legislature. The Censor Board stopped cutting scenes out of films. "The day of government censorship is over," the board proclaimed. "This board will neither cut nor reject any film."[78] Albertans were allowed to see, uncensored, Bertolucci's *Last Tango in Paris*.

Lougheed's office received a minor flood of letters of protest from organizations such as the Women of Unifarm about the changes in censorship. Some of his advisors worried that the government would lose votes in rural Alberta, but Lougheed's reply was firm. "I really don't know how deep-seated fundamentalist thinking may be in the southern rural areas…however, I don't agree that this is a valid reason for imposing censorship on Albertans over the years ahead."[79] It was characteristic of the way Lougheed faced down the more fundamentalist elements in his caucus and in the province throughout his career. The sheer force of his personality, bolstered by the fact that he was chiefly responsible for the rebirth of the

Progressive Conservative Party and its electoral success, made Lougheed almost impossible to challenge.

Schmid's eagerness to support the arts had made him, Peter Lougheed aside, one of the most popular and most visible members of the Conservative Cabinet. Everyone knew that, in his enthusiasm, he cut corners and red tape. There is a story, which has no doubt been exaggerated along the way, about a rural Alberta community seeking provincial funding for a swimming pool.[80] It was well known that the best route to success was to get to Horst personally, but Schmid usually travelled with an aide who helped insulate him from being cornered. As a delegation from the town was trying to petition the minister, the aide stressed the necessity of submitting the request through the normal channels. Horst eventually excused himself to go to the bathroom. And that's where they got him. A member of the team had been stationed, astutely, in the men's room, ready to present a quick, intense pitch. The community got its swimming pool.

One of Schmid's challenges was to win over A.F. "Chip" Collins, Lougheed's no-nonsense, dot the i's, cross the t's, deputy provincial treasurer, who signed off on all government expenditures. His rapport with Collins was greatly improved after a serendipitous meeting in Paris when an Alberta government team, which included Collins, was attending a conference in the French capital. Sunday was a free day and Horst took the opportunity to visit the Louvre, one of his favourite haunts. He was surprised to come around a corner in the great museum and literally run into his budgetary adversary. The discovery of their shared interest warmed the relationship. "I never had a problem with him again," Schmid said. Collins supported the proposal for the Alberta Foundation for the Arts, which bought works from Alberta artists for display in government offices and other venues around the province.

Most people in the arts and cultural communities knew that Schmid had a tendency to make promises easily, relying on Les Usher and the department to back him up. But there was never any suggestion that his actions led to personal gain. He was, as publisher Grant Kennedy has pointed out, a diamond-in-the-rough. People who knew him trusted the integrity he brought to his work.

But Len Grant, then a newsman at Edmonton radio station CHQT, was looking for a good story. He submitted a grant application for a phoney cultural organization, the "St. George's Gaelic Language School," headed by a fictitious C.A. "Angus" McTaggart. The name sounded like that of Sandy McTaggart, an Edmonton entrepreneur and a well-known patron of the arts. "Margaret Thatcher" was listed, mockingly, as one of the 19 students. The request slipped through the department, and the "school" received a grant for $185 plus $2000 for "equipment and facilities."

Grant went public with the story on Monday, May 5, 1975. Horst was hurt and bitter. "I despise a person who would cast that kind of reflection on ethno-cultural groups in Alberta," he said.[81] It was also a reflection on him and his department. The Lougheeds, the Cabinet, and the arts community rallied in his support, and the incident blew over fairly quickly. Lougheed's office received scores of letters about the incident, the great majority of them supporting the embattled minister. But following an investigation by the auditor-general (which reported mismanagement and irregularities in the office of the Special Programs Division, which reported directly to Schmid), the department's procedures were quickly tightened up. So tight that later that year, when a student asked the Minister for a grant to take a Banff drama class, Schmid told the *Calgary Herald*'s Kathryn Warden,[82] "Before I would have said yes. I would have told my staff to provide the gentleman with the funds he needs. Now I have to have the application approved through the appropriate channels and then come back to me for approval."

But if Len Grant's challenge was worrying, it was nothing compared to the personal tragedy Schmid had faced earlier in his career. The new government was barely in place when, on November 12, 1971, Lougheed received a letter formally soliciting his government's support for the City of Edmonton's bid to host the 1978 Commonwealth Games. Lougheed's response was quick and to the point. The government *would* support the bid, and Horst Schmid would quarterback the province's participation. Schmid became part of a team led by Edmonton Mayor Ivor Dent and including Dr. Maury Van Vliet, dean of the University of Alberta's Faculty of

Physical Education, later to become chair of the Commonwealth Games Foundation of Edmonton.

Early in 1972, the Edmonton team, with substantial community support, won out over Toronto to become the official Canadian city bidding for the games. That summer, a fired-up Alberta delegation was in Horst Schmid's home town, Munich, where Commonwealth officials were meeting to award the games to one of the two leading contenders, the City of Leeds in Britain—or Edmonton. Throughout the day and evening before the formal presentations were to take place, the Alberta team went from delegation to delegation, mounting their last, best efforts at lobbying delegates from throughout the Commonwealth. At the end of a long day, Schmid and Mayor Dent were ready to go back to their hotels. Horst insisted on walking, politely refusing Dent's offer to walk with him.

The Edmonton mayor arrived at his hotel to find an urgent message from Energy Minister Don Getty, one of Horst's close friends in the Alberta Cabinet. He told Dent that there had been a terrible accident. Horst's son was in hospital fighting for his life. Getty wanted Dent to find Horst, and to make sure he was all right. Dent sat in the lobby of Schmid's hotel late into the night before the minister appeared, obviously having gone for a very long walk. The following is based on Ivor Dent's account, taken from his book *Getting the Games*.[83]

"What's up, Ivor?" he said, wondering why the mayor was there.

"Nothing," said Dent. "Just dropped over to see how you are."

"So you've heard," Horst said.

Dent was forthright in telling Schmid that his Cabinet colleagues and the premier were concerned about how he was dealing with the crisis.

"Look, Ivor," he said, "I've been speaking to Arleen, my wife, and our son is fighting for his life. She says we can do nothing but wait and pray—and that I might as well be doing that here as at home. I'm concerned that I'm not there with her during these trying hours. But she's a wonderful person and I know she's thinking of me. Arleen knows that in times of crisis I'm best if I'm busy. So she says to keep busy at getting the Games."

The next day, the mayor introduced Schmid, who was scheduled to make a major presentation, to the Games committee. With intense passion he told the story of how he had come to Alberta from Munich with no language and no money, and how, in a very few years, had become the first postwar immigrant to become a government minister. He gave his audience an eloquent testimonial to the fact that he was living proof that racial discrimination was not a factor in western Canada. African members of the Commonwealth committee were visibly impressed.

In Ivor Dent's words, "When Horst had finished, so sincere was his emotion that a hush fell over the room. …Very shortly after the verdict was announced he disappeared from sight and I never saw him in Munich again. I was informed that he'd caught a flight home to be with his family."

News Item: *The Edmonton Journal:*
Bike Fall Kills Son of Culture Minister

Edmonton: Aug. 4, 1972: The nine-year-old son of Culture, Youth and Recreation Minister Horst Schmid died Monday from injuries suffered Thursday when he fell off a bicycle.

Mr. Schmid was on an emergency flight back from Munich where he had been with Edmonton's Commonwealth Games delegation when he was informed his son, Bernard Charles Claudius Schmid, had died.

Bernard, of 7215–83 Ave., fell on his head and went into a coma after he and Laurence Brokop, 10, fell off a bicycle on a steep path leading to the Mill Creek Swimming Pool. Lawrence was also injured, but was released from the University Hospital the day after the accident. Mr. Schmid said today that his son had told his mother he was going swimming at the Bonnie Doon pool, but apparently got a ride

on Lawrence's bicycle to Mill Creek when they discovered the Bonnie Doon pool was closed. Police
say Lawrence lost control of the bicycle on the steep
grade and both boys were thrown from the bicycle.

Walter Kaasa, who was an unofficial godfather to the child, has
poignant memories of the tragedy. "Just a few days before, he was
sitting on my knee," he told me, "It had a terrible impact on me.
He was just a sweet, sweet little boy."

The funeral delivered another blow: the priest apparently delivered
a pro forma address that left the mourners cold. "He was terrible,"
Peter Lougheed told me. "It was the worst funeral I ever attended."
Horst's greatest comfort, he said, came from his remaining children,
Carla and Vernon.

There is a plaque in a forest in Israel that reads: *The members of
the Alberta trade mission have decided to contribute a unit in the development of Galil Canada in memory of Bernard Charles Claudius Schmid.*
And, on a rock beside Mill Creek Bridge in Edmonton, another
plaque placed there by staff of the Department of Culture, Youth
and Recreation honours Charlie's memory.

The tragedy probably hastened the end of Horst's marriage to
Arleen. Not comfortable as a political wife, she had been left largely
on her own by Horst's workaholic lifestyle. Intelligent and energetic, she took up aviation, first as a hobby, then as a vocation,
earning her pilot's licence as well as papers as a certified aircraft
mechanic. One day Arleen invited me out for coffee, suggesting we
meet at Edmonton's Municipal Airport, where, as pilots, we were
both members of the Edmonton Flying Club. We had crossed
paths a number of times at the club and swapped stories about our
flying escapades. But this was not to be an ordinary cup of coffee.
Arleen had restored an old blue and white Cessna 172 she had
bought as a wreck. The plane had just received its certificate of air-
worthiness, and she wanted to show it off. We climbed aboard, got
clearance for an unusual flight plan—she piloted the aircraft from
the Municipal Airport located close to the city centre, to the
Edmonton International Airport 25 miles (40 kilometres) south of
the city. We had coffee in the pilots' lounge and then flew back to

the city centre airport. As I write this, I've learned that Arleen is in hospital, battling cancer.

Schmid continued in the portfolio until the 1979 election. In fact, he was the only minister who retained his post following the March 1975 election. In 1979, he was named Minister of State for Economic Development and International Trade and threw as much energy into his new post as he had into his culture portfolio. The records show that he brought many millions of dollars worth of trade to the province. But he never lost his connection to, or stopped boosting, Alberta culture.

Horst was both a good friend—and a tough boss—to his staff. He expected everyone to work as hard as he did, and he had a well-known reputation for dressing down staff members who didn't live up to his expectations. He could be impatient, his already-loud voice getting even louder when he was annoyed. He was known to burst into a room and, in a rapid fire, sometimes hard-to-under-stand delivery, give what he must have thought were very explicit instructions about some project or other. "What was that about?" someone would ask after he'd left the room. Heads would shake. No one dared ask him to repeat himself. "I guess we'll just have to fake it." And they would piece together, and deliver, whatever they thought was needed.

Some staff members had bruised feelings but learned soon enough that Horst never held a grudge and, in fact, he usually forgot about such incidents by the next day. His former employees and associates are full of stories about this "Daddy Warbucks" of culture with his boundless energy and enormous dedication. One of them told a reporter, "If they took a photograph of his aura it would be all red and yellow and sparkles."[84]

Dick Wong, who later, as chair of the Wild Rose Foundation, would play an important role in the development of the Edmonton Heritage Festival,[85] had gone to work for Horst shortly after the latter's appointment. Young, bright, energetic and single, Wong worked hard, day and night, for Schmid and still considers him to be one of his mentors. On his first day on the job, Horst drove him home in the new government minister's car. Dick's mother was astounded. "Is that really a *minister* of the *government* driving *YOU* home?" Part of

A government photographer thought this picture of the Alberta Legislature Building was ruined because the lights had been left on in one of the offices. The office is Room 324, where Horst Schmid often worked late into the night. *Photo: Government of Alberta*

the job was accompanying the minister to social functions organized by various cultural communities, sometimes as many as six or seven in a single evening. Horst would always eat (out of politeness, of course) at every event, which no doubt contributed to his description as a "fireplug of a man."[86] Wong, also out of politeness, also ate— everything from Tandoori chicken to cabbage rolls to chow mein.

Some 225 of Horst's friends held a roast for him on June 6, 1979, with Tommy Banks as MC. Describing him as the "Medici of Prairie Culture," and the "Stomach That Ingested Alberta," we poked fun at him for close to five hours. The late CBC television personality Jo Green described Horst's "pretty basic" wardrobe, and wondered if he was getting kickbacks from Edmonton haberdashers Henry Singer and Pat Henning for announcing that he did *not* shop at their stores. I weighed in with the suggestion that, even though he really hated it, Horst actually took airplane trips to keep his weight down—he could sweat off three pounds just going from Edmonton to Calgary. Mary LeMessurier, who succeeded him as Minister of Culture, ribbed him for his habit of always having a handful of Alberta lapel pins in his jacket pocket, giving one to everyone he met, and suggested he had probably given five or six to everyone in the room. Former Citadel Theatre artistic director John Neville flew in from Halifax to note that when Horst first came to Edmonton he said, "Well, it's a funny looking place," but when he saw the Legislature Building he said, "but thank God it's got an opera house." Playwright Warren Graves confessed, "Being asked to roast Horst Schmid is like being asked to cover your navel and reject your mother." The knives were indeed made of rubber. Horst ended

Horst Schmid and Les Usher at a farewell party for Horst. *Photo: unknown*

the evening with a characteristic ringing declaration: "We have only just begun!"

Schmid's Department of Culture staff also threw a farewell party for him when he was moved to the Economic Development and International Trade portfolio. In a wild skit involving a large cadre of department employees, a receptionist named Miss Uneeda Grant said, "You wonder how I got this position. It was easy. I have all the qualifications. I don't need sleep, I love *lederhosen*, I understand the minister's every tiny little word on the phone and I am an instant supplier of plaques and pins." Miss Grant directed a line-up of applicants into the minister's office—including a kick-line of dancing "culture cuties," a filmmaker (not me), a woman who wants to take over the Ukrainian Village and the auditor general. A chorus sang, "He's just a guy who can't say no." The skit poked serious fun at Schmid. Far from being intimidated by their boss, the staff knew he could take a joke and, with a considerable amount of affection, let him have it.

Someone at the party told the story of accompanying Schmid on a trip to Germany when he appeared the morning after their arrival in a brand new suit. When asked where he had found a tailor who could work so fast, Horst replied he had bought it off the rack. "Munich is probably the only place in the world," the wag reported, "where a man built like Horst could buy a suit off the rack."

In an uncharacteristically flattering editorial, no doubt written by the flamboyant publisher J. Patrick O'Callaghan, the *Edmonton Journal* said,

> Thank you, Horst
> Culture Minister Horst Schmid deserves love and kisses for his decision to classify the Ritchie Mill and Alberta Hotel as historic sites. But propriety restrains us to congratulations.
>
> It is terribly important that people feel affection for their human and physical environment. Mr. Schmid knows this and has moved to save two elements of our shared past that are widely loved and would be sorely missed. His action makes a visible, lasting contribution to Edmonton.

> We nominate Horst Schmid for Minister of Culture a
> third time around. And (what the hell), love and
> kisses Horst.

There was no third time. But even though he changed portfolios, he has never wavered in his support of the arts. There is, of course, much more to the story of this remarkable man, but that telling will be interwoven with the stories of the events and successes he helped to make possible. What is clear is that you can not understand Alberta's cultural explosion without understanding Horst Schmid.

A city has to have a soul, a city has to have a heart, and the heart and soul of a city is its culture, and at the heart of that culture is the theatre.

—Joe Shoctor

Chapter 5

Joe Shoctor:
A Theatrical Colossus

J oe Shoctor was a one-in-a-million "somebody" who combined sophisticated business smarts with a passionate love of the theatre. Smart, stubborn, driven by an insurmountable ego and a fierce dedication to public service, he stood for more than three and a half decades like a colossus over Alberta's theatrical scene. His great legacy is the Citadel Theatre, which since its creation in 1965 has grown to house five stages and an indoor tropical park with a nine-metre-high waterfall. It is acclaimed as the finest and largest theatre complex in Canada. The $40-million complex has offered as many as 500 performances a year, with an annual subscriber base that at one time reached 22,000. It provides more jobs for actors and stages more world premieres than any other theatre in Canada.

A nattily dressed Joe Shoctor (right) and footballer Annis Stukas celebrate the Edmonton Eskimos' first victory in September 1949. *Photo: Citadel Theatre/City of Edmonton Archives*

Joseph Harvey Shoctor, O.C., Q.C., LL.D., was born in Edmonton on August 18, 1922, and grew up in the Boyle Street community on the city's poor east side, part of a small Jewish community. His father, Morris Shoctor, managed to succeed in a tough social and business environment and through the equally tough Great Depression. He operated a junk dealership on the present site of the Edmonton Art Gallery, just up the street from where the Citadel Theatre complex is today. "My parents taught me, by example, to be a survivor, to conquer adversity and to do it with spirit and zest," Joe said.

Much like the Ukrainian, German and other communities of European origin, Edmonton's Jewish community played an important role in the city's cultural life. The Hebrew Musical and Dramatic Society mounted annual revues in which locals such as Joe Shoctor, Arthur Hiller, Mary Samuels, Shelley Superstein, Ted Cohen,

Hazel Cristall, Dasha Goody, Mimi Newhouse and Phillip Silver (who was later the art director at the Citadel, the Stratford Festival and of my movie *Marie Anne*, where I came to know him well, and who is now Dean of Arts at York University) developed their skills. It was typical of the strong values brought by those who came to the Edmonton area from countries in Eastern Europe. The British presence was never as dominant here as it had been in Calgary and in other parts of Canada. Thoughtful people credit the city's early cultural diversity as the foundation for the flowering of the arts that, in the face of economic downturns and political indifference, continues to flourish to this day.

Exceptional teachers and mentors influenced Shoctor early in life. The first was Eva Howard, a teacher at Victoria High School, who directed him in plays, variety shows and a very funny film, *It Happened at Vic*.[87] Eva Osyth Howard came to Edmonton during World War I, having graduated from Montréal's McGill University in 1913. She taught in various city schools before joining the staff of Victoria High School in 1927 to teach literature and composition. It was there that her interest in drama took root and matured. The school offered no drama courses, so Miss Howard began directing her students in plays on her own time. Her charges included Joe Shoctor, Arthur Hiller (who became a celebrated Hollywood director), Erik Nielsen (who went to Parliament) and his brother Leslie (who went to Hollywood), Olga Larushka (who changed her name to Dianne Foster when she became a Hollywood actress) and Jack McCreath (later the provincial drama supervisor in Horst Schmid's Department of Culture).

Howard mounted a three-act play at the school every year and was an active participant in the growing Edmonton little theatre movement where a young Shoctor tested his talents as an actor and director. In addition to teaching at Vic, Howard lectured on drama in the University of Alberta Department of Education summer school. In 1940 she received the Dominion Drama Festival's (DDF) Canadian Drama Award, for her outstanding contribution to the work of the DDF. And, in 1986, the theatre at Victoria Composite High School, later designated as Edmonton's performing arts high school, was named the Eva O. Howard Theatre. When Tom Peacocke, who later won the best actor Genie for his performance as Father Athol Murray in my film *The Hounds of Notre Dame*, joined the Victoria staff as a drama teacher in 1956 (replacing Walter Kaasa), Howard was still teaching English. Oddly, she had never actually taught drama as a high school subject.

I have a video copy of *It Happened at Vic*, a 1941 school production described as a "plotless playlet" directed by Eva Howard. The lead in the show is a "flashy newcomer" named Carl, played with near manic energy by Joe Shoctor. He makes his entrance driving a fancy coupé (as two-door cars with rumble seats were called) and strides into the picture wearing a snazzy suit, a natty fedora and a cocky attitude. He is clearly the star, a whiz at track and field, and, at the end of the film sort of gets the girl. His abundant confidence is already obvious.

But the broadest shoulders on which Joe Shoctor stood belonged to the legendary Elizabeth Sterling Haynes. She recognized that Shoctor had "it" from the beginning—a tenacity and sense of showmanship that would make him a star at whatever he tried to do. "Elizabeth wanted me to be in theatre," said Joe. "Theatre became as important to me as breathing."[88] Haynes contributed encouragement, knowledge and training, and directed him in several plays, which gave him the foundation that allowed him to become synonymous with theatre in Alberta.

Haynes was, unquestionably, a major driving force behind the early development of community theatre in Edmonton, inspiring scores of students who went on to become major players in theatre. She was a striking figure, six feet tall,[89] red haired, with an imposing, some would say intimidating, demeanour. Her voice could stop you in your tracks. Tom Peacocke was sitting atop a high stepladder, setting stage lights above the stage in the Quonset hut that housed the university's Studio Theatre, when he first heard her speak. He deliberately dropped a wrench so that he could come down and see who was behind that astonishing voice. He was then a student, working on an education degree in history and English and taking a course in drama. "It was at that moment," he told David Leighton,[90] "that I subconsciously began to reconsider the direction my life would take." With Haynes's urging and inspiration,

Peacocke made his commitment to a life in theatre. Haynes is remembered today in Edmonton's annual Sterling Awards for theatre. But her greatest contribution to Alberta was in the founding and initial development of the theatre program at the Banff School of Fine Arts, a story I include in the chapter on Banff.

Another Haynes protégé was Isadore (Izzie) Gliener, a younger contemporary of Shoctor's and a promising young actor in his high school and university days. He offered some interesting insights into Joe and his era. While he greatly admired his friend and celebrated his success, he was also sharply aware of Shoctor's ego. Gliener was cast for a small part in *The Man Who Came to Dinner*, directed by Laurier Picard, who taught drama at Archbishop MacDonald High School and who was a leader in the development of drama in the Catholic school system. Shoctor was the assistant director. According to Gliener, Shoctor never got around to rehearsing him for his part in the play. As opening night approached, with his few lines solidly memorized, Izzie asked Joe, older and more authoritative than he, when he was going to rehearse. Shoctor delayed and delayed and finally replied that there wasn't enough time, it was too late. He would have to play the part himself. And, a still-offended Gliener told me, he did.

Shoctor later made up for the slight by casting and directing Gliener in several other plays. It was Joe who first sent Izzie to see his mentor, Elizabeth Sterling Haynes, then at the University of Alberta, where she was the acknowledged heart of the drama program. "She was," Izzie told me, "a very wise woman, warm and empathetic." When he knocked on her door saying, "Joe Shoctor sent me," she swept him in. Gliener was mesmerized. He had lost his mother when he was 16, and Haynes came close to being a replacement. "She was the greatest influence in my life," he said. "I really did love her. She could get more out of a word than anyone." She showed her students unexpected depth and meaning in the plays she directed. Gliener was active in Edmonton's little theatre scene for years, working with Ron Wigmore (later manager of the Edmonton Jubilee Auditorium), Jack McCreath and Frank and Mary Glenfield to help establish the (amateur) Walterdale Theatre. When I asked him why he had abandoned what might have been a promising career as an actor, Gliener explained that after university he wanted to go to London to study at the Old Vic, "but by then I had a wife and a child." Today Gliener is a successful businessman and a strong supporter of the arts community, but he hasn't been on a stage in years.

Nothing was going to stop Joe Shoctor, even as a student at Victoria High School. With powerful mentors Eva Howard and Elizabeth Haynes, he had a solid foundation upon which to build his dream. A fellow Vic student, Edmonton businessman Jim Hole, remembered that the word about the abundantly confident Shoctor in high school was that "Joe is almost as good as he thinks he is."

Arthur Hiller, who lived in the same neighbourhood as Shoctor, says that when they were six or seven years old, Joe taught him everything he needed to know about street hockey in the winter and baseball in the summer. Later at high school, Joe directed Arthur as a performer in a Victoria High School variety show. Hiller had a terrible headache, but Shoctor, crying, "The show must go on!" tried to solve the problem by feeding him aspirins. The headache, however, persisted, and by the time the evening was over, Joe had fed the increasingly light-headed Hiller 10 aspirins. Somehow, Hiller got through the show. Years later he reminisced, "I'm glad Joe didn't become a doctor."

While still in high school, Shoctor independently produced shows such as *Guys and Dolls,* with then football player (and later Member of Parliament) the late Steve Paproski in the role of Nicely Nicely. Anyone who knew Paproski, whose sense of humour was as wide as his girth, can easily imagine him in the role. "Steverino" Paproski was a good friend who appeared frequently on my radio programs, at one time phoning me with regular reports from Parliament Hill. I wish I had seen him in *Guys and Dolls.*

In 1946, after graduating from Victoria High School, Shoctor went audaciously to Hollywood to try his chances as an actor. Reports say he was told, we don't know how gently, that he wasn't handsome enough and, furthermore, that he was too short. Short, they could deal with. For years, the diminutive Alan Ladd starred as a leading man. When, as was often enough the case, the ladies were taller, the directors would stand him on a box. If the scene called for walking, *she* walked in a trench beside him. I think that Joe was handsome enough, but no way was he going to stand on a box. Later he said, "After I was admitted to the bar I was offered a chance to go into movies in California, but decided to stick with the law because the pay seemed more secure."[91]

His friend Arthur Hiller did succeed in Hollywood, developing an impressive filmography that includes *Love Story* and *Man of La Mancha*. At the 2002 Academy Awards show he was given the Jean Hersholt Humanitarian Award for, among other things, his service as past president of Hollywood's Academy of Motion Picture Arts and Sciences. "It feels humbling," he said in his acceptance speech at the show that night, "to receive a humanitarian award for doing what my parents brought me up to do." Part of what they brought him up to do was to remember where he came from. Hiller has maintained his connection with his home town and, as I write this in the spring of 2003, is the honorary chair of the Victoria High School Foundation for the Arts. In the fall of 2002, the University of Alberta awarded him an honorary degree. He comes back every year to work with students at the performing arts school and with Joe Shoctor, who, until his death in May 2001, was an honorary director.

While studying law at the University of Alberta, Shoctor was busy. He took his first cracks at being an impresario, organizing shows for American servicemen passing through to the Alaska Highway on what was known as the Northwest Staging Route. "When I was going through law school," he said, not shyly, "I brought the Happy Gang, (the) Ink Spots, Alan Jones, Freddie Martin and his orchestra, *Music Man, Guys and Dolls.* ..." He launched the U of A Varsity Show, served on Student Council and was president of the Literary Association. Shoctor also won a Literary A ring, the Inter-Collegiate Debating Trophy (the McGowan Cup) and a football letter A and Bar with the U of A Golden Bears.

Shoctor's high-spirited approach to life showed up in his courtship of his wife, Kayla. They first met, she told me, when she was on a visit to Edmonton from her home in Saskatoon. She was 16. He was 22. "Who's that cute little fat girl?" he asked a friend. Kayla was not impressed when he told her, "Here's a nickel, kid, call me when you grow up!" But she couldn't help noticing him. She was in Saskatoon when they met again two or three years later, and she noticed him again.

On a later visit to Edmonton, Joe and Kayla spent part of an afternoon together at the Purple Lantern restaurant on what is now Edmonton's Rice Howard Way. "Why don't you stay and marry me?" asked subtle Joe. "He even came to Saskatoon and worked on my mother," says Kayla, but Kayla had other plans. The plans included a degree in social work from McGill University. "You'll marry me one day," Joe kept on. Instead, she moved west to take a social work job in Vancouver. But Joseph Shoctor never gave up at anything he set out to do. He borrowed money from his father, bought a ring and went to Vancouver. They met for lunch at the Hotel Vancouver.

"I brought you a present," he said, producing the ring. Before she could say anything, he had it on her finger. "Now we're engaged."

"What do you mean?"

"Well, you're wearing my ring. That means we're engaged."

Kayla thought for a long minute. "OK."

"He was kind of neat." A year after his death, her eyes still danced when she told me the story. For years after they were married, he would tell her, "Look at the good life you've had with me." Kayla doesn't disagree. "We had so many 'best' times…he was a man who could do anything." It was a lifelong romance.

Shoctor's love of the theatre did not stand in the way of his becoming a successful lawyer. In 1960, he became the youngest lawyer in Canada to achieve the status of Queen's Counsel (Q.C.). His talent for business and for raising money already apparent, he decided that if it couldn't be Hollywood, maybe it could be Broadway. Kayla remembers a trip to New York during which they saw the Broadway version of *A Raisin in the Sun*. The play, written by Lorraine Hansberry,[92] the first Black woman to have a play produced on Broadway, was about to fold. At the end of the performance, Hansberry's husband, Robert Nemiroff, one of the show's producers, came on stage to plead with the audience. Could anyone help raise money to keep the show open?

Joe jumped up.

They met the producers after the show and Joe was enthusiastic, but, after some nudging from Kayla, he had second thoughts and backed away. The couple learned more about the ways of Broadway after attending the opening night of a show called *Love That World,* joining the crowd of insiders awaiting the reviews at New York's famous Sardi's Restaurant. The mood was upbeat as the first reviews came in. But when the *New York Times* review came in panning the show, the air went out of the room. It was an experience Shoctor would come to know firsthand. The Internet Broadway Data Base lists four productions with Shoctor's name attached to them. First there was a musical called *Billy,* which opened in the Billy Rose Theatre on March 22, 1969. Shoctor is listed as the producer, in association with Bruce W. Stark. The show closed on March 22, 1969. I don't know if they got the news at Sardi's.

But Broadway Joe, as his Edmonton friends called him, was no quitter. He is listed, along with Albert I. Fill, Marcel Akselrod and Norman Twain, as a producer of *Hamlet,* starring Nicol Williamson. The production was a modest success in Broadway terms, with 52 performances between May 1 and June 14, 1969. Shoctor had better success a decade later. *A Life,* directed by Peter Coe and first presented on the Citadel stage, had a moderately successful Broadway run with 64 performances between November 1980 and January 1981. *A Life* won four Tony nominations. It was more successful than *Mister Lincoln,* also directed by Coe and produced by the Citadel in association with David Susskind and Isobel Robins. The show ran for only 16 performances in the spring of 1980. The Citadel's musical *Duddy,* about which I write later in this chapter, never made it to Broadway.

Back in Edmonton, Shoctor was building a reputation as Alberta's greatest producer and promoter. He was one of the original founders (with haberdasher Henry Singer and fellow lawyer Moe Lieberman) of the Edmonton Eskimo Football Club and served as its first secretary manager. He was instrumental in making the team part of the Canadian Football League. In the early days, he was also the sidelines announcer, describing the plays to the crowd, and running the half-time show, which featured everything from dancing girls to mud-wrestling contests. He held season tickets to Eskimo games all his life. But Shoctor also took care of business, becoming, in addition to a respected lawyer, a successful real estate developer and hotel owner.

The Manitoba Theatre Centre takes pride of place as Canada's first regional theatre, established in Winnipeg in 1958 by John Hirsch and Tom Hendry. In December 1960, Circle Eight, one of Edmonton's community theatres for which Shoctor had directed a production of Tennessee Williams's *A Streetcar Named Desire*, organized a meeting in which John Hirsch talked about locating a theatre centre in Edmonton, to "save the north." It's not clear whether Joe Shoctor attended that meeting, but he was present in June 1962 when the Allied Arts Council called a meeting to mount a campaign for a theatre in the Edmonton civic centre. Shoctor joined a committee that included Jack McCreath, Dick Morton and Hugh Currie.[93]

Soon after that meeting, the old Salvation Army Citadel on Edmonton's 102 Street went on the market. The brick building had been built in 1926 for $39,300 and had a solid, timeless look to it. "I took one look at it and I knew at once this could be the site for a theatre," Shoctor declared. "Edmonton is big enough for it."[94] He needed to raise $100,000 to buy the building and another $150,000 to convert the Citadel into a first-class theatre.

In 1963, Tommy Banks and his partner Phil Shragge were operating a downtown establishment that offered both good food and good entertainment. Shoctor and his friends were frequent and valued customers. "One day," Banks told me, "Joe asked me to come to his office, in the old Petroleum Building on 102 Street, south of Jasper. He said he was thinking of buying the old Salvation Army Citadel, which was directly across the street, and turning it into a theatre. I replied that I thought that might be a good idea…the Strand was just around the corner, and you could run either art films or second-run features and probably do okay. He said 'No, no! I mean a THEATRE! Not a movie house…a THEATRE. With actors. Live. So how much would you like to invest?'

"Joe had somehow got the impression that I had some money." Banks said. "It is to laugh. So then he asked if Phil and I would like to establish a good restaurant in the lower level of the building, which we did, and that was that. While I was sitting in his office, he received callbacks from Jim Martin and from Ralph MacMillan, from both of whom he extracted on-the-spot commitments for substantial amounts of money to start his theatre."

It was the beginning of a series of unmatched fund-raising campaigns. Joe told investor Sandy McTaggart that the building was such a good real estate investment that they couldn't lose money on it. Later when Shoctor built the new Citadel and sold the old building, McTaggart was not entirely surprised to find himself being persuaded to put the profits into the new building. When Shoctor called on Jim Hole, he was told, "Come back when you have a little bit more to show." "I'm not leaving until you give me something," Joe retorted, settling into a chair. He was not empty-handed when he left.

Ron Wigmore and a group that included Frank Glenfield had also been looking at the Salvation Army building on behalf of Theatre Associates. But, with Joe already in motion, Wigmore and his group stepped back. Theatre Associates generously contributed their subscriber lists to Shoctor, who reciprocated, saying, "Without the ground work by Theatre Associates and [the University of Alberta Drama Department's] Studio Theatre, we wouldn't be able to confidently launch this project."

The Citadel Theatre opened on November 9, 1965, with a production of Edward Albee's *Who's Afraid of Virginia Woolf*, starring the husband and wife team of Bernard Engel and Bette Oliver. Through the run, it played to 76 percent full houses. The theatre had 285 seats, with the restaurant operated by Tommy Banks and Phil Shragge in the basement. Everything in the Green Room was green. John ("We'll still be putting down carpets on opening night") Hulbert, who had been head of drama at Allegheny College in Pennsylvania, was the first artistic director.

The board of directors was composed of the first investors—Jim Martin, Sandy McTaggart, Ralph MacMillan—and David Bentley, Mary Mooney, Ken Higham, Hazel Cristall, Eve Willox, Rose Bogoch and, of course, Joe. The dedicated staff, many of whom stayed with the theatre for years, included Olive Finland, Marjorie Knowler,

Don Boyes, Wilf Rowe, Monty Montgomery and Margaret Mooney, a former governor of the Dominion Drama Festival. They sold 1350 season tickets. It was a huge success. "We've been able to lay the foundation for professional theatre here without one dime in grants or subsidies," Joe boasted.

That didn't mean that they would not aggressively pursue grants from every available source. In 1966 the Canada Council approved a grant of $15,000.[95] In 1967 Mayor Vince Dantzer announced that the City of Edmonton would come through with a grant of $7500, beginning a trend that has seen the city develop, over the years, as a major supporter of the arts. The Citadel sold 1800 season tickets. "We're reaching people who have never gone to live theatre before, and these are the ones that count," Shoctor told reporter Ron (later alderman, and still later councillor) Hayter. In 1968 Alberta's Social Credit government finally joined the parade with a modest grant of $5000.

Shoctor ran the operation hands-on. After the heady success of *Who's Afraid of Virginia Woolf,* the theatre experienced a downturn. Hulbert's next shows, *Under the Yum Yum Tree* and *Bell, Book and Candle,* were acknowledged flops, playing to half-full houses. Although the next offering, *Come Back Little Sheba,* did better, Hulbert's time was up. "We had to let him go because his primary interest was in administration, rather than staging, and frankly," said Shoctor, "that is a luxury we cannot afford."

He brought in Robert Glenn from New York's American National Theatre to direct three plays to finish the inaugural season. Attendance boomed, and Joe persuaded Glenn to return for a second successful season. The late Barry Westgate, then writing the entertainment column for the *Edmonton Journal,* said the theatre was "the most significant jolt in years to Edmonton's cultural scene." Sean Mulcahy, a flamboyant Irishman, took charge of the Citadel's third season in 1968, driving from Toronto to Edmonton in his MG sports car. He had trained at the Abbey Theatre in Dublin before coming to Canada, where he worked at the CBC and later helped found the Shaw Festival. Mulcahy was as tireless a promoter as Shoctor. He once had the audacity to try to sell season tickets to Shoctor himself. Now, that's chutzpah. Together, they raised the profile of the theatre, achieving new audience records every season. They launched the Citadel on Wheels and Wings, which toured thousands of miles to schools and communities as far north as the Arctic Circle. Professional instructors offered drama classes at the Citadel to more than 500 students.

In 1969, the Citadel Theatre turned a profit. Joe could have stopped right there and received due recognition as a giant of Edmonton theatre. But he was not satisfied. By the turn of the decade, the Citadel was playing to virtually full houses. Mulcahy had declared that if Shoctor didn't build him a bigger house, he would leave. (Joe didn't need to be persuaded, but when he built that bigger house, Mulcahy was not part of it.)

When Peter Lougheed and his government swept to power in the fall of 1971, the way was opened for a new Citadel. The dramatic change in attitude toward the arts, the province's rising economy and Horst Schmid's "How can we do this?" boosterism opened the province to winds of change unprecedented since Social Credit swept into power in 1935 riding a very different kind of storm. Shoctor, better than anyone, caught the new wind in his sails.

He launched the greatest fund-raising campaign to that date in the history of Edmonton, probably of Alberta. Shoctor, who didn't hesitate to put his own money on the line, was relentless. I got one of my best insights into how aggressive he could be from a friend, the late William (Bill) Lutsky, a very rich Edmontonian who was on the top 10 list of people you went to if you wanted to raise money for any civic project. Lutsky is commemorated in the William Lutsky YMCA in south Edmonton, even though for most of his life he was a regular at the city's downtown Y, where members of the "men's club" would sit around in the afternoon, and, after a good steam, play cards and talk about their investments. Lutsky told me how Shoctor had approached one of his friends, a financially substantial member of the community, seeking support for his new Citadel. The friend agreed and, in the fullness of time, sent what he thought was an appropriate, even a generous, amount. Shoctor, Lutsky told me, thought the cheque should have been for more, much more. Personally insulted, Shoctor stormed into the man's office and dramatically tore up the cheque in front of him. He left

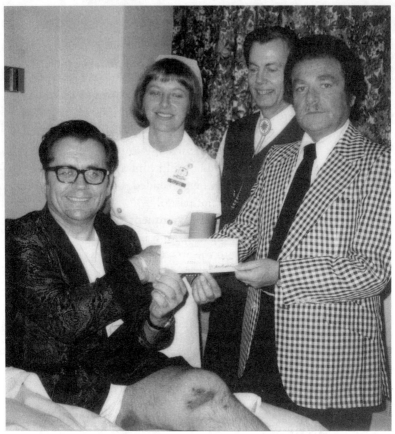

Horst Schmid in hospital for a few bruises received in an accident. It did not prevent Joe Shoctor from visiting the hospital to collect a cheque from Horst. A nurse and Deputy Minister Les Usher look on. *Photo: Horst Schmid*

with a significantly larger donation. Variations on the story have become part of the lore surrounding the man, a true marvel of his times.

Members of his board of directors were expected to put their shoulders to the wheel. Stories abound of Shoctor motivating, cajoling, wheedling, sweet-talking, berating, whatever worked, urging his board members to do more. His boardroom performances, some told me, equalled anything you might see on the stage. Businessman

Bill Weir, whose construction company was doing some work on the new building, at prices close to cost, complained to Joe that his payments were late—everyone else was being paid on time. "Well," said Joe, "you haven't done any fund-raising."

Shoctor was, if it is possible, even more aggressive with the Lougheed government, who were pretty well on his side to start with. He was so persistent in his need to get the money into the bank that, on more than one occasion he collected cheques from the minister in his sick bed. During the pre-construction phase of the theatre, four Government of Alberta cheques were due. Horst Schmid always liked to deliver the big cheques personally, but on two occasions he was in the hospital when Shoctor's cheques were ready. Once he had kidney stones; the next time he was in briefly for repair after an accident. Joe was not going to wait. He visited Horst (who had arranged to have the cheques ready) in the hospital and came away with the money.

The campaign was immensely successful. Few could say no to Joe. Practically everyone who had the means, including all levels of government, kicked in. By 1974, the ground was broken, and on November 13, 1976, the sparkling new Citadel Theatre building, in the heart of Edmonton, opened with a production of *Romeo and Juliet.* "The heart and soul of a city is its culture, and at the heart of that culture is the theatre," Shoctor said. Edmonton had its heart. Part of the Citadel's success is its accessible location in the city centre on Edmonton's Sir Winston Churchill Square. The square is used as a setting for many concerts, festivals and gatherings and is surrounded by the Edmonton Art Gallery; the newly renovated Edmonton Public Library; Edmonton City Hall, one of the most accessible city hall buildings in the country and regularly used for celebrations and commemorations of all kinds; the superb new Francis Winspear Concert Hall, with the finest acoustics and the largest pipe organ in Canada; the Provincial Court House; major hotel and shopping facilities; and, of course, the Citadel Theatre.

"He was," said John Neville,[96] "the greatest fund-raiser I ever met." Neville, who came to Canada in 1972 after enjoying a solid career on the British stage, was the first artistic director of the new Citadel. In addition to being a great director, he is, to my mind, the

The Citadel at night showing Shoctor Alley on the right. *Photo: Citadel Theatre*

finest Canadian Shakespearean actor now living. He *speaks* the lines, giving them nuance and shape, shades of meaning you never knew were there. Since seeing Neville, I am always infuriated by actors who "declaim" Shakespeare, shouting at the top of their voices, and by the directors who either urge or allow them to do so. Neville was and is a legitimate star of both stage and screen. But he brought more than acting skills to the Citadel. He put the Citadel on the national and international map. I remember stunning performances by Dame Peggy Ashcroft, Martha Henry, Brent Carver, Kenneth Haig and many others during his tenure at the Citadel.

Neville was succeeded by the equally distinguished directors Peter Coe and Robin Phillips, who each added their contributions to the Citadel's growing national and international reputation. In addition to big shows on the main stage, there were also wonderful performances offered in the Rice Theatre, the "black box" theatre

space in the complex. I particularly remember Sharon Pollock's *The Komagata Maru Incident*, starring Angela Gann and Jean Pierre Fournier and directed by Jim DeFelice.

The Citadel was the first major theatrical company in the country to hire a Canadian, Duncan MacIntosh, as artistic director. Today's artistic director, Bob Baker, is an Edmontonian, a graduate of the University of Alberta drama program, and the former artistic director of Edmonton's Phoenix Theatre and Toronto's Canadian Stage. In the spring of 2002, he renewed his contract for another six years. Way back in the days of the old Citadel on 102 Street, Joe was challenged for not hiring more Canadians. "This is professional theatre," he said, "and it has to be professional." It is no small part of his legacy that Edmonton has been able to grow professionals that animate stages across Canada and beyond.

Through it all, Shoctor kept a strong hand on the tiller of his ship. He fought with the directors and argued with critics, once banning the acerbic *Edmonton Journal* writer Keith Ashwell from the premises. (I applauded, having tangled with the haughty Englishman myself.[97]) When Liz Nicholls, who replaced Ashwell as theatre critic, showed up for her first opening night, Shoctor told her, "It's your opening night, too. Don't blow it."

Joe's heart may have belonged to the Citadel, but he had other interests. In addition to his impressive contributions to theatre, he was a tireless booster for development of the downtown, raging at the disrepair into which so many buildings on Jasper Avenue, Edmonton's main street, had fallen. He developed a master plan for the renovation and development of the area, chairing a number of committees to promote the initiative.

In 1981, the Canadian Radio-television and Telecommunications Commission (CRTC) opened the door for applications for the first of the Canadian broadcasting system's specialty channels—which would only be available on cable and for which subscribers would pay a fee. Seeing an opportunity to promote the arts, Joe led a group that included Tommy Banks, Wendell Wilkes, Doug Hutton and me in an application for a licence for an arts channel. We worked hard at developing what we believed was a credible application, but the eastern decks were stacked against us. Doug Hutton recalls that when one of the CRTC commissioners asked Joe what was so Canadian about the channel (Canadian content had to be an important ingredient of the plan), Joe exploded, slamming his fist on the table, "I'm Canadian, and that should be good enough!" The commissioner quickly abandoned that line of questioning. Happily, in retrospect, the licence went to the late-lamented C Channel, which proved that Canada was not yet ready to support a television service dedicated to music, drama, dance and literature. We thought that the rest of the country had the same appetite for the arts as we did.

Joe and I had worked together on another project a year or so earlier. APEGGA, the Association of Professional Engineers, Geologists and Geophysicists of Alberta, had commissioned me to produce a documentary celebrating a major anniversary. The documentary, which I titled *The Unseen Hand*, showed how the work of engineers provides essential support for the success of structures for which architects usually received the major credit. The documentary looked at some of Edmonton's most interesting structures: Douglas Cardinal's dramatic Space and Science Centre,[98] Peter Hemmingway's Coronation Park swimming pool and the pyramids of Muttart Conservatory, the five-acre domed water park at West Edmonton Mall and the Citadel Theatre. I hired writer Peter C. Newman to host the program, but I put Joe on centre stage of the Shoctor Theatre to describe his building. It happened that the show on the main stage had a set that included a larger-than-life golden throne, which moved across the stage on invisible tracks. Joe sat on the throne, and, as it moved from background into close up, he told the story of the engineering that went into the theatre.

Shoctor had a tendency to react to anyone who said "It can't be done" with a ferocious assault on whatever barrier was placed before him. I was in the full flood of my movie-making years, having produced the successful *Why Shoot the Teacher* and the pure, but flawed, *Marie Anne*, and was hell-bent to prove to the world that made-in-Canada Canadian movies could work. My Fraser Film Associates Ltd. had acquired rights to a number of works by Canadian icons, including W.O. Mitchell's *Back to Beulah*, Patrick Watson's *Alter Ego*, Pierre Berton's *The Secret World of Og*, Ken Mitchell's *The Meadowlark Connection*, Maria Campbell's *Half Breed*, and Peter C. Newman's *Bronfman Dynasty*. The story of my adventures in the screen trade (with a bow to William Goldman[99]) is touched on in Chapter 8, but my adventure with Joe Shoctor in trying to produce a movie called *Mr. Sam*, based on Newman's book about the Bronfmans, belongs here.

Peter Newman is one of Canada's greatest political writers. A former editor of *Maclean's*, he has carved an unmatched career with his ability to understand and explain the personalities and motivations of our country's political and business leaders. I still go back to his slim early volume, *Home Country*, to re-read some of the most insightful writing about Canada I know. The book is the source of my earlier quotes about the Social Credit Leader Robert Thompson. Newman introduced his chapter on Thompson with the sentence

"This is a requiem for a lightweight." His book about Sam Bronfman, the powerful founder of one of Canada's great fortunes, is a daring classic.

I was convinced that a movie about Bronfman, one of our most fascinating national characters, could be an international hit. I paid Newman a substantial fee for the rights to the book, commissioned a writer to produce a screenplay, and set about raising the money. And then peculiar things began to happen. When I approached financiers, I got, without fail, an enthusiastic reaction. Everyone agreed that it was a great story, that Newman had told it well, and that it would make a great film. But, without fail, within weeks everyone cooled and backed off.

So I went to see Joe. He was convinced that he could raise the money. We had a long and, shall we say, strenuous negotiation about which of us would control the project and who would get what credit. Finally we agreed on a deal that essentially gave each of us a veto over what the other might do. And Joe set out to climb the financial mountain. Three weeks later he was back. "It can't be done," he stated flatly, refusing to elaborate.

Years later, I was a speaker on a panel at a Canadian Conference on the Arts event in Ottawa. One of Sam Bronfman's sons was on the panel with me. During a break I told him about our experience. "Oh, we knew all about you," he said. The family simply did not want any film about Sam Bronfman to be made while his widow, Sadye, was still alive. I learned, from a variety of sources, that whenever a major financier showed an interest in the project, they would get a call subtly suggesting it would not be wise to invest in the film. (I eventually sold the rights to another producer, who has yet to make what I still think would be a great film.)

One of Joe Shoctor's greatest desires was to have a Citadel play become a bona fide hit on Broadway. The Tony nominations he had received for *A Life* had whetted an appetite that never really left him. And the greatest chance, he thought, was to base a musical on Mordecai Richler's famous novel *The Apprenticeship of Duddy Kravitz*. Director Ted Kotcheff (whom I had invited to Edmonton to chair the jury for the first Alberta Film Festival) had turned the book into the first real Canadian movie hit. Many thousands of people in

Canada and beyond knew and loved Richard Dreyfuss's portrayal of the street-smart Jewish kid who set out to make it big in the movies, starting with films of bar mitzvahs and weddings. The story had become part of Canadian culture, and the things that made Duddy run were not foreign to Joe Shoctor.

And so *Duddy, the Musical.* I still have the blue and gold lapel pin, with musical notes at the top of a stairway spelling out "duddy." Opening night was a dazzling affair. Edmonton's glitterati, and all of Joe's supporters, turned out in gowns and tuxedos. Ted Kotcheff was there. Shoctor's investors were hungrily there, expecting a blockbuster. So was Mordecai Richler, looking nervous. The first act ended with a rousing song and dance number with the book's Boy Wonder, played by Henry Ramer, leading the entire cast. The audience erupted into applause and spilled out into the foyer. "Mazeltov!" I said to Richler, but he wasn't smiling. He had been at the rehearsals. When the second and final act closed, the response was subdued, and the Citadel's second floor foyer, where opening night audiences usually lingered for up to an hour enjoying drinks and hors d'oeuvres, emptied within minutes. We were all embarrassed for Joe and didn't want to show him our disappointment. Duddy went through a number of re-writes, played the National Arts Centre in Ottawa, but never made it to Broadway.

Joseph Shoctor received many honours in his lifetime. He was an Officer of the Order of Canada. He received the Governor General's Performing Arts Award, an honorary doctorate from the University of Alberta, the Sterling Award for his "outstanding contribution to the performing arts," the State of Israel's Prime Minister's Medal and membership in Edmonton's Cultural Hall of Fame. He was also inducted into the Alberta Order of Excellence.

In a video tribute to Shoctor assembled by his friends, there is a voice recording of Joe as he reminisced about going into the empty Citadel Theatre, dark except for the illumination from one stage light. "I remember," he says, "when I was going to have open heart surgery, I was told I had a bad heart. It was Sunday morning, and I went over to the theatre and I sat down—there was nobody in there—and I sat there, and I sat there, and it was quiet and beautiful and sort of eerie—and I literally felt that I was in a synagogue or in a cathedral, and I said, you know, if I never live another day—if I never live another day—and I have experienced this, I'm thankful."[100]

Joe Shoctor died in Edmonton on April 19, 2001. He was 78. He enriched his city with the finest theatre complex and the strongest theatre organization in Canada. His contributions to the Edmonton, national and international Jewish communities, perhaps not as well known, were also significant. He was the major fund-raiser for the new Beth Israel Synagogue, where his funeral was later held. He had overseen much of the construction of the building and had seen to it that all of its systems were state of the art, which may have led to a heart-wrenching disagreement with the rabbi about the sound system. As a consequence, Joe never attended a service there. Joe's funeral was the first service in which he was a participant at the synagogue.

His friends mounted a warm, affectionate tribute to him in the theatre that he built. There were poignant remembrances of stories going back to his high school days, emotional thanks and farewells. But perhaps the most touching tribute came from Dino Polti, who managed the Citadel's physical plant for 20 years. He said that Joe had always told him that when people give you a hard time to remember "there's a boss behind you." "When I retired," Dino recalled, his eyes filling, "I remember that he said, 'This is my key, Dino. I give it to you. It's the master key.' "

For me, Joe Shoctor's most important legacy is the belief, no, the conviction, that he instilled in generations of Canadians, that our actors, our directors, our producers and all of the other creative people who work in theatre can be as good or better than any in the world. He was the inspiration who showed the way for many others who, following his lead, have developed a vibrant, truly Canadian theatre. I doubt that my movies would have received the support of Edmonton's financial community had Joe Shoctor not paved the way by creating an environment where support for the arts was seen as a socially acceptable thing to do. I was inspired by his can-do, damn-the-torpedoes approach. It is substantially to his credit that Edmonton remains one of the most lively theatrical communities in the country.

If you want to make money, you're better off putting your savings into Canada Savings Bonds than going into publishing.

—Mel Hurtig to Allan Shute

Chapter 6

Mel Hurtig's Magnificent Gift

Mel Hurtig is one of this country's great citizens. Like Joe Shoctor in theatre, Hurtig was the larger-than-life figure who stood tallest in Alberta's publishing industry through the 1970s and 1980s. He is one of a very small circle who has mounted successful careers in all phases of the world of books. Jack McClelland may have discovered and brought to prominence some of Canada's greatest novelists—Atwood, Laurence, Richler, to name a few—but Hurtig created one of the country's most successful bookstores, published some of our most important and challenging political books and continues as a best-selling author. His success is self-authored. He worked and fought for everything he accomplished. There was no silver spoon, no family fortune.[101]

Mel Hurtig, a master book seller, during his publishing days. *Photo: Mel Hurtig*

Mel Hurtig was born in Edmonton on June 24, 1932. He grew up in an era when, if you were Jewish, a strong entrepreneurial sense was almost a necessity for survival and success. Better, in that generation, to make your own job than to hope that someone would give you one. His uncles and father were in the fur business, but young

Hurtig discovered early that helping women try on fur coats was not for him. Any possibility of a career in furs was ruined when, while working in his father's store, a very large woman asked him if a muskrat coat, the biggest one he could find in the store, made her look heavy. Mel turned his back, trying to keep a straight face, but unable to contain himself, doubled over with laughter. No sale. The event was a catalyst that set him on his own entrepreneurial journey. It was the last time in his life that he worked for someone else.

It was 1956 when, with $3500 borrowed from the bank on the strength of his reluctant father's signature, he opened Edmonton's first bookstore. It was all of 425 square feet. In spite of his father's skepticism ("If it's such a good idea, how is it that no one has done it already?") and his banker's open cynicism, the store was successful from the beginning. Hurtig demonstrated that he knew how to run a business, how to attract and satisfy his customers. By the summer of 1962, Hurtig Books had moved into its third location on the busiest part of Jasper Avenue. With some 7000 square feet, it was Canada's largest bookstore. It soon became one of its best. A British publisher, André Deutsch said, "Mel Hurtig's bookstore is certainly the finest in Canada and one of the best I've seen anywhere." Toronto critic Nathan Cohen added, "Who would expect Edmonton to have the best classified and most up-to-date bookstore in Canada?"[102]

By the time I moved from Regina to Edmonton in 1965, Hurtig Books was the literary centre and one of the intellectual centres of the city. Those were the days when Jasper Avenue was still the liveliest part of town. Henry Singer's Men's Wear store was on the north side, offering stiff competition to the Johnstone Walker department store down the street, not far from Hurtig Furs. Henry Birks & Sons still had a classy store in its own building at the corner of 104 Street. Diagonally across the street was Sol Reichert's Carousel Restaurant, a few doors from Hurtig's bookstore. CKUA was broadcasting groundbreaking radio from the then-in-good-repair Alberta Government Telephones Building, a block and a half west. I worked out of an office on 103 Street, a short walk away from the action on Jasper and soon became part of the downtown scene. When we were not at the Carousel, the nearby Seven Seas (a pretend Polynesian restaurant that included a comfortable bar) was a gathering place for some of the city's more interesting characters.

Mel Hurtig's store was a large and welcoming oasis with an open invitation to sit in one of the comfortable chairs scattered about the store, enjoy free coffee and doughnuts, and read enough of a book or a magazine to decide whether you wanted to buy it. If a few people read books from cover to cover (sometimes over several days) without buying them, it was, for Mel, no big deal. The store was a meeting place; you would often find local intelligentsia browsing the latest best sellers, checking the bulletin board for messages, or playing chess or the Japanese game GO at the back of the store. Canada's better- and lesser-known authors gave readings, signed books and revelled in the accommodating environment. I was often there on a Saturday morning with my son Randall enjoying one of the best children's book sections I had ever encountered.[103]

But if Mel ran a great bookstore, he was, in my view, an even better publisher. From the beginning, he produced works that meant something to Canada, starting, in partnership with the American publisher Charles Tuttle, with the Canadiana Reprint Series. The series offered facsimile reproductions of significant but out-of-print books that had lapsed into the public domain. Tuttle would publish them in the US, Hurtig in Canada. The first title, released in 1967, was an Alberta-based rhapsody, *Johnny Chinook: Tall Tales and True from the Canadian West* by Robert Gard and illustrated by none other than Walter Phillips. Hurtig published the book with a new introduction by Grant MacEwan, later to become lieutenant-governor of Alberta. Hurtig Publishers sold out the print run within a year. The second Hurtig book, *An Idiot Joy* by Eli Mandel, won the 1968 Governor General's Award for Poetry. But, for me, the most significant of his early titles was Harold Cardinal's *The Unjust Society*, a closely reasoned attack on then-Indian Affairs Minister Jean Chrétien's plan to dismantle the Indian Act. Chrétien's department had published a white paper that would have dramatically changed the relationship between "status Indians" and the federal government. Cardinal, 24, was then president of the Indian Association of Alberta. He responded with his own "Red Paper" and went on, at Hurtig's urging, to write *The Unjust Society*. Published in 1969, it made a mockery of the Trudeau government's championing of the "Just Society." The book was not only a flat-out best seller; it changed the government's course. Chrétien withdrew the white paper, and the Department of Indian Affairs continued, more or less, with business as usual. It was, for Canada's First Nations, at least the devil they knew.

In 1972, Hurtig decided to concentrate on publishing and sold the bookstores that had by then expanded to three locations in the city. From humble offices under a since-dismantled overpass on 105 Street, Hurtig Publishers produced a string of best sellers and award winners, books that frequently had an impact on the political life of the country. Out of curiosity, I did a scan of my own library and was not surprised to find more than a dozen titles with the stylized "H" imprint on the spine (not counting others I would likely find in the boxes of books I don't have shelf space for). And an eclectic lot they are. There is a 1981 book on Canadian separatism; Peter Gzowski's book about *This Country in the Morning*; Hugh Dempsey's *The Best of Bob Edwards*; *Edmonton, A History* by J.G. McGregor; *Great Golf Stories*; *Colombo's Canadian Quotations*; the story of *Tatanga Mani*, the legendary Indian leader Walking Buffalo, by Grant MacEwan; and, of course, *The Canadian Encyclopedia*. I bought copies of the encyclopedia for each of my children.

Hurtig and I often crossed paths. We were both members of the Mayfield Tennis Centre when it opened in the early 1980s and played together on a number of occasions until his obsession with golf took over his recreational life. Hurtig has an odd sense of humour. He loves to set people up. He gives a hint of it in his autobiography. "When I take friends from Toronto to the [Mayfair Golf] course for the first time I prepare them for an hour-long drive. But much to their astonishment, four minutes later we're in the locker room putting on our spikes."

Here is another example. In the days when *This Hour Has Seven Days* was practically required viewing on television, Mel and I were at the Carousel having coffee with a local accountant. Mel related how, on the previous evening, the CBC personality Larry Zolf had, in characteristic fashion, made a number of outrageous statements to stir up arguments all over the country. Without mentioning Zolf by

A tireless promoter, Mel Hurtig wears *The Canadian Encyclopedia.* The project remains the greatest accomplishment in the history of Canadian publishing. *Photo: Mel Hurtig*

name, Hurtig proceeded to repeat, in a bit of a caricature, the statements he had made. "What do you think of that?" he asked the accountant, his eyes glinting. The accountant exploded with words to the effect that he had never heard such rubbish in his life. Hurtig, closing in for the kill, calmly told Michael Zolf that the author of the "rubbish" was his brother, Larry.

Hurtig experienced a kind of epiphany one day in 1971 or 1972 (he can't remember the exact date) while waiting to give a speech in Swift Current, Saskatchewan. He was in a school library when he noticed that almost all of the reference books were American. There were few Canadian texts. It was typical of Hurtig, as we shall see, that when he encountered a "somebody oughta do something about this" situation, he elected himself. I do not say this in a derogatory sense. When National Film Commissioner Sidney Newman said that we couldn't make movies in Alberta, I elected myself to prove him wrong. But that story is for a later chapter. Suffice it to say here that I understand the motivation. For Hurtig, the challenge to publish a real Canadian encyclopedia was too great to resist.

There had been an *Encyclopedia Canadiana*, a 10-volume set published in 1956 by the American publisher Grolier. By the 1970s, the books were sadly out of date, but Grolier was not interested in producing an updated edition. In 1975, Hurtig had been gathering support for a one-volume, 1744-page encyclopedia. Schmid's Department of Culture offered to contribute $50,000 a year for five years toward a $2.5 million budget. There was support, interestingly, from the University of Toronto, which considered providing free office and library space. Hurtig asked the Canada Council for $150,000 a year for five years, a total of $750,000. The council, after several delays, unrealistically insisted that the encyclopedia had to be published simultaneously in English and French. It then announced that the project was too big for it to handle; it could not come up with the needed funds. The project was left twisting in the western wind.

But Hurtig was not about to give up, and Horst Schmid remained committed to the idea. The wind changed when Alberta decided to mark the 75th anniversary of the province in 1980 with a multi-million dollar extravaganza celebrating the province's history, its many cultures and the arts. Money flowed to arts organizations, to libraries and to publishers. Lone Pine Publishing's first book, *The Albertans,* which profiled 75 of the province's leading citizens, was one of the smaller projects. With Schmid working behind the scenes, Hurtig wrote Peter Lougheed with the suggestion that the anniversary presented a great opportunity for Alberta to celebrate with *The Canadian Encyclopedia,* which the province could present as a birthday gift to Canada. It was 1979. Schmid had been moved from Culture into the Economic Development and International Trade portfolio. But it was he who, working with Mary LeMessurier, his successor in the Culture portfolio, organized the pitch to Cabinet.

Hurtig asked the government to put up $2 million (the project would eventually cost $12 million), part of which would be used to purchase copies to present to every school, every college and every university in Canada. He hoped that Ottawa would match the Alberta contribution. Bob Dowling, a former Lougheed Cabinet minister, then out of government and serving as head of the 75th anniversary celebrations, called Hurtig with Alberta's response. The government would not give him $2 million, Dowling said. Then, after a beat, during which Hurtig's hopes crashed, Dowling announced that Alberta would give him not $2 million, but $4 million, provided Hurtig keep the federal government out of it. The provincial government, Dowling said, wanted the encyclopedia to be an all-Alberta project. The encyclopedia became one of the projects of the 75th anniversary celebrations, during which the province spent $75 million on a broad variety of community, infrastructure, arts and cultural projects. The province would underwrite the costs of research and development, about $3.4 million, and for $600,000 would buy 25,000 of the three-volume sets for distribution across the country (the idea of a single-volume encyclopedia was shelved when it became clear that the book would be too heavy for some people to lift). Harry Gunning, then president of the University of Alberta, offered office space and the use of the university's computer system in return for a modest fee and a share of the profits. The French-language rights would be made available free to any Québec publisher willing to take up the challenge. Hurtig's account of the twists, turns and near-death experiences that he and a large team of editors, writers, designers and many others went through is fascinating reading. You will find it in his memoirs, *At Twilight in the Country: Memoirs of a Canadian Nationalist,* published in 1996 by Stoddart.

On June 28, 1985, in a ceremony in the rotunda of the Alberta Legislature Building, publisher Hurtig proudly presented a copy of a specially bound edition of *The Canadian Encyclopedia* to Premier Peter Lougheed. Astonishing! Has any other province in Confederation celebrated its birthday, or any anniversary or event, with a gift to all of Canada? Lougheed himself presented the numbered, specially bound, first copy to Prime Minister Brian Mulroney and the second to Governor General Jeanne Sauvé. On September 6, about 1100 people attended a party at the Citadel Theatre to launch the encyclopedia.

Four days after its publication date, the first edition of the encyclopedia had sold out its entire print run of 154,500 sets, the greatest accomplishment in Canadian publishing history. Hurtig was out of debt and had $2 million in the bank. A second edition, published in 1988, sold 113,300 sets of an expanded work. Part of the promotional package for the second edition allowed owners of the first to trade in their volumes for the updated version. I wish I had kept that first set. As it is there are still two sets of the second edition in my library.[104]

The Canadian Encyclopedia took Mel Hurtig to the highest pinnacle of publishing in Canada. *The Junior Encyclopedia of Canada* led to his downfall as a publisher. With the wind in his sails, Hurtig planned "the most extensively and beautifully illustrated reference books in Canadian history." He insisted that *Junior* would not be a scaled-down version of the senior edition. It would be written in language that young people could understand and identify with, it would be tested in schools, and it would pay careful attention to school curricula at elementary and secondary levels. It would turn out to be significantly more expensive to produce than the adult versions.

Mel Hurtig could have rested on his laurels, the bankers off of his back, money in the bank and a respected member of the Canadian establishment. He could have waited for someone else to raise the money and approach him to produce a junior version of the encyclopedia. He was, after all, the only Canadian with the experience, knowledge and organization to do it. He might have sought the support of schools and educational organizations across

Canada, including provincial and national teachers, principals and other educational organizations. But, he told me, he wanted to keep the talented team that had produced the encyclopedia together. At the peak of its production, some 40 people had worked full time on the project (all told, some 3000 people from across Canada were directly involved in the encyclopedia) under the direction of Editor-in-Chief James Marsh. Perhaps Hurtig thought that, having dodged so many financial bullets in his career,[105] his lucky star had settled in for the long haul. Maybe he thought he couldn't lose, that no matter how tough things would get, he could always find a way to succeed. I think he just didn't know how to quit.

So, once again, he "bet the farm," and set out to find money and support for a project unprecedented in Canadian publishing history. He almost pulled it off. The federal government, which had made no contribution to Alberta's gift to Canada, agreed to put up $950,000 if Hurtig could match the amount, either from private sources or from other governments. As he had done with the earlier editions, Hurtig went deeply into debt to publish the junior version. He had learned some hard lessons about merchandising with the second edition of the encyclopedia, when major booksellers heavily discounted the books, cutting deeply into his profits. For *Junior* he decided to bypass the distributors and retail stores and sell the encyclopedia through his own organization with a massive direct sales campaign. But as the publication date approached, advance orders were seriously below expectations. *Junior* was launched at a massive party at Toronto's Roy Thomson Hall on September 10, 1990, with a multi-million dollar advertising and promotion campaign. But this time the sales weren't there. By the end of the year, with mounting bank charges and a disappearing cash flow, it was clear that Hurtig Publishers could not survive.

Mel literally went begging for help. He asked the Alberta government, now headed by Don Getty, for a six-month loan guarantee of $750,000. The answer was clear and abrupt. The chickens of his politics, in which he had fiercely attacked governments at all levels, now came home to roost. He reports in his memoirs[106] that Doug Main, then Alberta Minister of Culture, told him, "Hurtig, now you're going to pay for your politics."

A corroborating view of Hurtig's difficulties was reported in an essay by Alberta writer Fred Stenson in the March–April 2001 edition of *Alberta Views* magazine. It's worth quoting the article at some length.

> Immediately before our conference [the annual conference of the Writers' Guild of Alberta], the Hurtig publishing company of Edmonton was denied a bailout by the Alberta government and ceased to be. As a general rule, culture ministers were invited to address our AGMs and they usually declined, but in 1991, Doug Main said yes. It was like a volunteer appearance before the lions at the Roman coliseum.

> The inimitable Jon Whyte introduced the minister. He said the minister came from a family so well known in Alberta that principal streets in a great many towns were named after it. Then, probing the sore point at its very centre, he brought up Hurtig's *Canadian Encyclopedia*, the junior version said to be responsible for the company's financial difficulty. Whyte had been in Mr. Main's office recently and was pleased to see a set of the *Junior Encyclopedia* on a bookcase. Whyte added that it might do the minister more good were he to remove the shrink-wrap.

> Perhaps riled by this, perhaps delivering the speech he came to give, Main gave a stunningly abrupt address. After a few preliminary rudenesses, he leapt voluntarily into the Hurtig subject. Hurtig had made a point of having no friends in the Alberta government, he said. Why the surprise that he would get no dough? I'm not sure if buns were thrown, but verbiage certainly was. There were calls of "What about your buddy, Pocklington?" Several writers, Myrna Kostash and Helen Rosta being two, rose to say how much good Mel Hurtig had done for Albertan and Canadian writers.

> I tell that story in such detail because it seems to have
> been a watershed. Not that anything happened
> because of the things said that night, necessarily, but
> it does seem to mark a time beyond which the rela-
> tionship between Guild and government became for-
> mal and distant.

Stenson's report is, for me, a chilling account of the change in
attitude toward the arts that ended the once-in-a-lifetime era that is
the focus of this book. What a stunning difference from the days
when the standard response from Horst Schmid and the government he represented was not "No," but "How can we do this?"

I had a poignant meeting with Mel Hurtig early in 1991. Hurtig
was close to defeat when he called, inviting me to his office for a
"visit." He was more than cordial as he welcomed me, offering me a
copy of a beautiful coffee table book *Alberta, A Celebration*, by Tom
Radford and Harry Savage. I still have the book, duplicated by a
copy given me by Horst Schmid, who, when he was Minister of
Culture, helped Hurtig mightily by buying copies of his books to be
used as gifts for visiting dignitaries and others.

I knew quite a bit about Hurtig's political woes. I was at the time
chief commissioner of the Alberta Human Rights Commission.
And, because of my work on the Federal Broadcasting Task Force
and later as a member of the Spicer Commission, I had access to
many people in government at both federal and provincial levels. I
also knew that Mel had already exhausted every possible avenue of
assistance. I could only offer the faintest, most desperate hope. The
financial establishments and the government of Alberta had turned
Hurtig down cold. His last hope was with the federal government
of Brian Mulroney, a government he had trashed mercilessly for its
"betrayal of Canada."[107] He asked if I would talk to people I knew
in the federal Cabinet to try to enlist their help to save, not Hurtig
himself, but one of Canada's most important publishing enterprises.

As a journalist I had come to know Don Mazankowski,
Mulroney's deputy prime minister.[108] In an effort to help, I contacted him, saying that regardless of what Hurtig had said about
him and his party his publishing enterprise was important to

Canada and needed to be saved in spite of the political views of its owner. "This is bigger than Mel," I told him as I urged him to put politics aside, to hold his nose, if he must, and keep western Canada's greatest publishing house afloat. I will not quote Mazankowski's red-in-the-face response, spit out with uncharacteristic venom. There were no circumstances under which the federal government would lift a finger to save Hurtig's enterprise. Mel was not surprised by the news.

Avie Bennett is another Canadian hero. The former developer and businessman had rescued McClelland and Stewart after Jack McClelland had run out of money and options. And, in the spring of 1991, he did the same for Mel Hurtig, buying out his publishing enterprise. *The Canadian Encyclopedia*, both senior and junior edition, now have a new life, and as I write this, have been updated and are available free to Canadians on the Internet, funded by Avie Bennett, private foundations and the Government of Canada.

No one needs to take up a collection for Mel Hurtig. Bennett was very fair in the purchasing arrangements. The *Edmonton Journal* editorial on May 30, 1991, said,

> "Nobody, for a second, should feel sorry for Mel Hurtig," the man himself said on Tuesday as he announced the sale of Edmonton's best-known publishing firm to McClelland and Stewart of Toronto.
>
> Fine Mel, we won't express sympathy. Pity wouldn't sit well on your shoulders. But permit us to feel sorry for a country, a province and a city that have benefited enormously from the contributions of Hurtig Publishers Ltd. And will miss its independent, creative spirit.
>
> The country is losing one of the few unabashed voices for Canadians nationalism in its corporate sector.

Mel later told the *Edmonton Journal,* "If I had the choice of walking away with a million dollars cash and not publishing *Junior,*

I would still choose to publish it. I am extremely proud of what we did." Ah yes, Canadian nationalism and the Hurtig hubris.

If Mel Hurtig was vulnerable to the notion that somebody ought to do something in the world of publishing, he was mesmerized by the call of politics. Early in his career he had become concerned about the growing ownership of Canadian business and industry by American firms. He joined the Liberals and ran for an Edmonton seat in the midst of the western Trudeauphobia of the 1972 federal election. By election day he had become disillusioned with Trudeau's policies, particularly with respect to foreign ownership. He lost the election and went on to be a co-founder of the Committee for an Independent Canada, sharply critical of what he perceived as the government's weak policies. By 1985 he was the founding chair of the Council of Canadians, with many of the same concerns, and in 1992, was the principal founder of the National Party of Canada, leading it unsuccessfully into the 1993 federal election.

I have already stated that this is not a political book. Mel Hurtig's battles as an economic nationalist have been widely reported and commented on. But it is important to appreciate the catastrophe of how his political idealism consistently overruled his well-honed business sense. Hurtig is an excellent researcher; his attacks on government stung because they had the fact-checked validity to score serious points. But many politicians saw him as an irresponsible alarmist; "Chicken Little," some called him, accusing him of going around shouting, "The sky is falling, the sky is falling." I prefer to see him as a political Don Quixote, searching for honourable solutions in a political arena overwhelmed by cynical cronyism and corruption. It will always be interesting to speculate on the fate of Hurtig Publishers had its owner stuck to publishing. What is clear is that his attacks on the financial establishment, on the banks and on governments, did his business and his dreams as a publisher no good at all.

Hurtig is nothing if not an idealist. He told me that, after the collapse of the National Party of Canada he wrote, "Even if we had only one chance in a hundred of success, it would be irresponsible not to take that chance." That idealism propelled him into his third

Mel Hurtig's campaign against US corporate takeovers of Canadian companies takes him on a treadmill of a speaking schedule. Some call him "Mr. Canada."
Photo: Mel Hurtig

career in the world of books as a highly successful author. He brought all of his passion to his first book, *The Betrayal of Canada*, which topped the bestseller lists in 1991. Other books, the poignant *Pay the Rent or Feed the Kids: The Tragedy and Disgrace of Poverty in Canada,* his autobiography *At Twilight in the Country: Memoirs of a Canadian Nationalist,* and his latest work, *The Vanishing Country,* have carved a place for Mel Hurtig in Canadian letters that almost equals his role as an extraordinary bookseller and a ground-breaking publisher. Today, he maintains an active speaking schedule; his deep-voiced, articulate delivery, his meticulous research and his passion attract audiences all over the country.

When I visited him in his comfortable heritage log home overlooking Edmonton's river valley to talk about this book, I found a man at peace. He had accepted his reversals, was satisfied with his accomplishments, and was busy at work on his latest book. His passion for Canadian nationalism still burns bright. His essays often appear as guest editorials in newspapers across Canada. Mel Hurtig has been well recognized by his country. He is an Officer of the Order of Canada. He has been the recipient of several publishing industry awards and six honorary doctor of law degrees from Canadian universities. The Humanist Association of Canada lists him, along with Margaret Atwood, June Callwood, Henry Morgentaler and Farley Mowat, among notable modern humanists.

The lesser-known part of Hurtig's story is the influence he had on other Alberta publishers. Allan Shute and his wife, Katherine founded Tree Frog Press on October 9, 1971, within six weeks of the day Lougheed's Progressive Conservatives swept into power. Shute describes Hurtig as both a mentor and a friend, always ready with advice about everything from marketing and accounting to how to determine the size of a print run. He told the Shutes which booksellers paid promptly and which had to be kept on a short leash. Tree Frog Press was located in a garage on 106 Street, a block or so away from Hurtig's 105 Street location. Shute laughingly described the area as the "publishing district" of the early 1970s.

Hurtig Publishers, along with Tree Frog Press, the University of Alberta Press, Red Deer College Press, and J.M. Lebel Enterprises, were the founding members of the Book Publishers Association of

Alberta, launched in March 1975. And through its early days, Hurtig went out of his way to support the organization.

If Alberta's small publishing community could look to Hurtig for practical advice, John Patrick Gillese provided both inspiration and government money. I still smile at the infectious enthusiasm of this man who came to Canada from County Tyrone in Northern Ireland at the age of six, homesteading with his family near Rochfort Bridge, Alberta. By the time he became director of Literary Arts in Walter Kaasa's Cultural Development Department, Gillese had developed a highly successful career as a freelance writer. As a boy he had written letters that were published in the children's pages in the *Free Press Prairie Farmer* and *Western Producer*. During his career, he published some 5000 articles, short stories and columns in Canada, the United States, Britain and elsewhere. He loved to tell the story of how, when he was 19, he won a short story competition, "not in Canada, but in the United States of America," with a $1000 prize. It was an astonishing sum in 1939, with North America just coming out of the Great Depression. Gillese's 1957 short story, "Kirby's Gander," became the basis for the movie *Wings of Chance*.

There is no doubt, according to Allan Shute, that the early success of Alberta's publishing industry is in no small measure due to Gillese. He tells a great story about the launch of his company's first book with a party at The Hovel, which was a 1960s-style hangout next to a hole-in-the-wall pizza take-out establishment on 109 Street in Edmonton. The book, *39 Below,* showcased the work of 39 Edmonton poets and had been produced on an antique press at Tree Frog Press. As he tells it,[109]

> The poets were moaning on, reading their poetry at great length, when this older fellow came in—the average age in the room was probably 19.6—in a trench coat with a fedora on. He stood out like a sore thumb. He sits in the corner at the back of the room, and the word went out that there was a NARC attending. Some of the kids came up to me and said, "Hey Shute, this is your party, you go check him

out." So it was my job to go over and shake this NARC down, and this fellow stands up and shakes my hand and says, "Hello, I'd like to introduce myself, I'm Johnny Gillese, and I'm from the Alberta government and I'm here to help Alberta publishing."

Gillese asked Shute to figure out how much *39 Below* had cost to publish and insisted Shute see him on Monday morning. Shute thought the book cost about $250 for paper and plates "and, I go in there and he gives me a cheque." In the years ahead, Tree Frog Press received ever-increasing annual grants from the Culture department. The grants helped them to develop a sizeable book list that included titles ranging from the once-popular *Edmonton Access Catalogue* to

Mel Hurtig promoting his most recent book, *The Vanishing Country. Photo: Mel Hurtig*

writer Jan Hudson's award-winning *Sweetgrass* to *Especially Babe*, the best seller by the esteemed Alberta writer R. Ross Annett. "It was *exciting*," Shute told me, "that the Government of Alberta was allowing this kind of thing to happen, and sponsoring it too." Subsequent grants helped to establish the Book Publishers Association of Alberta.

If John Patrick Gillese was a friend to publishing, he was a virtual godsend to a generation of Alberta writers. According to Fred Stenson, he "ran the department's literary arts branch in a populist, grassroots way. He favoured contests and workshops as a means of helping writers. The novel competition, in particular, was of great help to many, including me. Its purpose was to discover Alberta novelists; among others, it found Jan Truss and the perennial bestseller Pauline Gedge."

The Writers Guild of Alberta was founded on June 21, 1980, when 35 writers gathered at the University of Alberta and each attendee anted up $10 to help launch the organization. The guild set up headquarters in Edmonton, but it was essentially broke until the Department of Culture granted the organization $10,000 in operating funds. The guild is now a province-wide organization with more than 700 members.

John Gillese passed away in 1999. A new scholarship has been established by the Alberta Writers Fund to honour him, "whose encouragement of writers young and old has left a lasting legacy in Alberta."

And as for Mel Hurtig, the undisputed giant of Alberta publishing is still writing his story. And dreaming big dreams.

The Fringe is very important to me; it's definitely part of my growth and development as a playwright, as an artist. You can afford to take chances at the Fringe, you can try things you've never tried before.

—David Belke, playwright

Chapter 7

Road to the Fringe

The Edmonton Fringe Theatre Festival is the most successful theatrical event of its kind in North America and one of the great legacies of the Lougheed years. It gives the city and the province a leading role in the world of alternative theatre. Edmonton's Fringe has spawned similar festivals across Canada and in the United States. Its development could not have happened without the decade of explosive growth in Edmonton's theatrical community that preceded it.

By the time Brian Paisley came to Edmonton in 1980, the foundation for the creation of Canada's most successful theatrical movement was solidly in place. Joe Shoctor had created the Citadel, Alberta's first and most successful professional theatre. Alberta Culture's innovative support programs, with substantial additional

Posters vying for attention at the 1989 Fringe Festival. *Photo: Alberta Government Archives*

funding from the City of Edmonton, had put the city on the road to developing a vibrant theatrical community. "At the present time there are five (and sometimes six) professional theatres in Edmonton, and the statistics regarding audience attendance and the frequency of openings support local claims that Edmonton is, in per capita terms, the liveliest theatre centre in Canada," wrote Alan Filewood in the winter 1978 edition of the *Canadian Theatre Review.* "Both the Citadel Theatre and Theatre 3 have completed their opening seasons in impressive new playhouses and public boosterism is fashionable."

Edmonton, according to *Alberta Trivia*,[110] had more live theatre per capita than any other city in North America. There were more theatrical companies, more theatre spaces and seats and more bums in those seats. Alberta, with 30 publishers, had the second-largest publishing industry in English Canada, and the second-largest indigenous film and video industry in Canada. Albertans were the largest consumers of cultural products in English Canada.

A quick scan of Edmonton's theatrical community gives a good overview of how dynamic the Edmonton scene, following Shoctor's lead, had become.

Mark Schoenberg and Anne Green[111] founded Theatre 3 in 1970. Schoenberg was a drama professor recruited by the University of Alberta at the same time as Jim DeFelice. DeFelice tells how Schoenberg, originally a New Yorker, crashed the line ahead of him when the U of A Drama Department was interviewing prospects at a 1968 convention in Chicago. Schoenberg, as brash in his way as Joe Shoctor was in his, believed that the city needed another company as an alternative to the Citadel. Theatre 3[112] started out in the Theatre Beside, a 90-seat venue at Victoria Composite High School, next to the Eva O. Howard Theatre. From time to time, the company also mounted plays in the 175-seat Centennial Library Theatre. In 1976, with growing support, Theatre 3 acquired its own space in a former autobody and welding shop in the warehouse district on Edmonton's 95 Street. Keith Digby took over artistic directorship of the company in 1978, when Mark Schoenberg left with high hopes to direct *Parallels*, a movie produced by my friend and sometime partner Dr. Jack Wynters.

Then, in 1981, disaster struck. A local lawyer, who had talked himself into the position of president of Theatre 3's board of directors, was found to be playing fast and loose, not only with their funds, but with those of a number of other city organizations. Theatre 3 collapsed under a debt load of $800,000.[113] The lawyer went to jail. The creditors took over and found the cupboard to be, for all practical purposes, bare.

It is a testament to the strong following Theatre 3 had developed for its highly professional work that, within a year, Keith Digby was able to revive the company as the Phoenix Theatre. The Phoenix offered plays in the Students' Union Building of the University of Alberta. In 1982, Bob Baker took over artistic directorship, and the Phoenix grew steadily until it closed its doors in 1997, Baker having gone east in the early 1990s to run the Canadian Stage Theatre in Toronto.

Northern Light Theatre was an adventurous lunch-hour theatre company founded in 1975 by four young thespians who moved to

Edmonton from Vancouver. By then it was a fact of theatrical life that, with a welcoming cultural environment and the Department of Culture's generous funding programs, there was more work for actors in Edmonton than in the much larger city of Vancouver. Scott Swan, Alan Lysell and two sisters, Merrilyn and Angela Gann, were talented actors who quickly developed a following for their lunch-hour performances in a small theatre in the then relatively new Edmonton Art Gallery. At first the only lighting the company had came from turning the lights away from the paintings and onto the actors. By the end of their second season, now working in the gallery's basement lecture hall with a few more lights, the company had mounted 25 productions, playing to some 30,000 people.[114] Scott Swan, the artistic director, was a persuasive recruiter. Jeanne Lougheed, Jim DeFelice and I were, at various times, on his board of directors. By 1977, in addition to the one-act lunch-hour performances, Northern Light was producing full-length plays in the evening and the following year began offering Shakespeare in the Summer. One of my son Randall's first acting jobs was appearing in *A Midsummer Night's Dream* and *As You Like It.* Another member of the cast was a young Paul Gross.

From 1982 to 1988, under Jace Van Der Veen's artistic direction, Northern Light joined the growing number of companies that mounted productions in the theatre named for Walter Kaasa at Edmonton's Jubilee Auditorium. Northern Light Theatre celebrated its 25th anniversary in 1999–2000 having established a reputation as an alternative theatre dedicated to development and innovation. On its silver anniversary, Northern Light Theatre won public acclaim for its productions *Wreck Beach* and *Alphonse,* nominated for two Sterling Awards. Theatre Network, formed during the same year as Northern Light by Mark Manson, produced works on Alberta themes and toured them across the province and the country. One of their early success, *Hard Hats and Stolen Hearts,* was based on stories from Alberta's northern oil treasure trove, Fort McMurray. I still remember enjoying it. By 1981, Stephen Heatley had taken over as artistic director with a mandate to produce plays written by western Canadian playwrights. Among them were Frank Moher, Robert Clinton, Connie Massing, Ken Mitchell, Paul Gross,

Ken Brown, Ray Storey and Kelly Rebar. All of the actors were Canadian. The company is still performing successfully at the Roxy Theatre, a renovated movie house on 124 Street.

Workshop West Theatre, founded in 1978 by Gerry Potter, was also devoted to the development and production of Canadian plays. As it grew, Workshop West became another significant source of new plays by western Canadian playwrights. David Fennario launched *On the Job,* and Brad Fraser's widely produced *Unidentified Human Remains and the True Nature of Love* originated as a commission for Workshop West (under the title *Friends*).

Other companies included Catalyst Theatre, which produced socially relevant plays for both adult and young audiences, and Nexus Theatre, which offered lunch-hour plays in an underground shopping centre in the heart of downtown Edmonton. John Juliani's[115] Savage God company, launched in the summer of 1978 by the former director of York University's Graduate Theatre Program, offered a variety of avant-garde readings and performances at various venues around Edmonton, including an art gallery named Latitude 53, which is Edmonton's actual latitude.

The highly competent amateur sector continued its development, led by the venerable Walterdale Playhouse, founded in 1959. Amateur theatre played, and continues to play, an important role in the creation of western Canadian dramaturgy. Walterdale is one of the country's most exciting amateur theatres, part of the training ground for many actors, writers and other artists who have gone on to professional theatre. The theatre is located in Strathcona Fire Hall No. 1, the city's oldest fire hall, in the heart of the district where hundreds of thousands of people gather every summer for the Edmonton Fringe Theatre Festival.

Calgary companies also formed part of the rich resource base that allowed the Fringe to succeed with such flourish. Theatre Calgary, the city's oldest professional company (founded in 1968), produced high-quality classic and contemporary plays and musicals. Christopher Newton, of Shaw Festival fame, was one of its first artistic directors. Harold Baldridge, later director of the Neighborhood Playhouse School of the Theatre, a famous acting school in New York City, headed Theatre Calgary from 1972 to

Bob Westbury (left) with Sheila and Jim Edwards at the 2001 Fringe Festival. Westbury led a fund-raising drive that resulted in the renovation of the Old Strathcona bus barns in time for the 2003 festival. Edwards, the head of Economic Development Edmonton at the time, was a major player. *Photo: Fringe Festival photo by Karen Smith*

1978. It was he who premiered W.O. Mitchell's *Back to Beulah* and followed that with *The Black Bonspiel of Wullie MacCrimmon* and *The Kite*, by the same author.

Lucille Wagner (later a producer in London's West End), Douglas Riske and Paddy Campbell founded Calgary's Alberta Theatre Projects in 1972. ATP began as an offshoot of a children's theatre organization, and at the beginning it presented works aimed at young audiences. Later it moved into the Canmore Opera House, an old building in Calgary's Heritage Park. Playwrights Sharon Pollock and John Murrell presented some of their early works at ATP.

The avant-garde One Yellow Rabbit is one of Canada's most well-known and leading producers of original work, often, according to Tom Peacocke, ahead of its time. The company, founded by Michael Green and Blake Brooker in 1982, produces, among other things, the High Performance Rodeo, an annual festival of new and experimental performance theatre. One Yellow Rabbit is a cult favourite on the international Fringe theatre circuit.

Calgary's Loose Moose Theatre, formed in 1977 by Keith Johnstone, created a distinctive theatre based on improvisation. Johnstone, who had come to Calgary with credentials that included a stint at the Royal Court Theatre in London, helped to create one of the more popular forms of contemporary theatre, Theatre Sports. In the early 1980s, Theatre Sports, in which two teams of improvising actors compete against each other for points awarded by a panel of judges, appeared as a demonstration event in the 1984 Alberta Winter Games. During the 1984 Fringe, the performances of Theatre Sports were among the best attended, attracting two-hour-long line-ups. Theatre Sports is now a popular feature in television comedy, and there are Theatre Sports teams on five continents.

There is one other important theatrical enterprise in Alberta, unmentioned, I regret, in the annals of the "legitimate theatre." Howard Pechet, an English major and a Blake scholar, is the scion of an Edmonton family that owned, among other things, the well-appointed Mayfield Inn. Howard created the Mayfield Dinner Theatre, which brought in Hollywood movie and television stars during the winding down years of their careers to perform in popular light entertainment theatre fare. He occasionally departed from that path to stage more serious works, which usually lost money, but salved his artistic soul. The Mayfield Theatre still attracts full houses, and attracting whole families to its performances is of crucial importance in building future audiences for theatre. And it pays its actors well. The Mayfield gave birth to the Stage West Dinner Theatres, which continue to operate in Toronto and Calgary and, in spite of some down-your-nose disdain from some quarters, to provide professional work for many Canadian actors, designers and stage managers.

Important, I would say critical, support for this growth came from the University of Alberta's Bachelor of Fine Arts (BFA) drama program. The university, whose commitment to drama was sparked in the early 1930s by Elizabeth Sterling Haynes, has graduated generations of well-trained actors, designers, directors, stage managers and playwrights. Today, they animate stages across the country. If you were to gather the playbills of every professional theatre in Canada on a given fall night, I would venture that a large percentage of the professionals working there, if not a majority, would have received their training in the BFA program at the U of A. You could see stars such as Tom Wood and Paul Gross literally being born at the university's well-attended Studio Theatre student productions.

None of this growth would have been possible without the constellation of government programs, including matching funds for professional and amateur companies, and support for summer schools, for writers and for facilities such as the Citadel and the Calgary Centre for the Performing Arts (renamed the EPCOR Centre for the Performing Arts in the 1990s). So when Brian Paisley came to Edmonton, he found himself quickly immersed in a very rich theatrical environment.

Like many who were part of Alberta's artistic explosion during the Lougheed years, Paisley had a colourful past. He was born of solid Protestant stock in Belfast. His parents, looking for a better life, immigrated to Canada when he was still a boy. Before moving to Edmonton, he operated Chinook Theatre from a base in Fort St. John, British Columbia, successfully touring plays for young people throughout the Peace River Country, on both sides of the British Columbia–Alberta border. The life of the theatre had grabbed him when he was in high school in Burnaby, British Columbia. It started with a drama course he admits he took to get an easy mark. At the end of the year the school put on a big musical, *The Wizard of Oz*. The actor who was playing the lion got sick just before the play opened. Brian, who still does not think of himself as an actor, was recruited as a last-minute replacement. Muhammad Ali was then much in the news, and Brian decided that his lion would adopt Ali's "float like a butterfly and sting like a bee" attitude. The cowardly lion with the boxer's bravado—and Brian—were a great success. The heady rush that comes with feeling an audience responding to his every word, gasping, laughing, guffawing, was overwhelming. He was hooked.

After high school, it was on to the drama program at UBC, where he learned that his strength was in directing, not acting. After graduation he took a couple of years to see the world, including an

Children always have a place at the Fringe Festival. *Photo: Alberta Government Archives*

overland trip across Africa from Morocco to Tanzania. Then it was back to his childhood home in Northern Ireland and teaching jobs there and later in England. The experience taught him that Canada was his true home, and he returned to work at the New Play Centre and the Playhouse Theatre in Vancouver.

He then took a job as a theatre consultant for the British Columbia government and travelled the province offering advice and assistance to local theatre groups. While visiting Fort St. John, he was offered a job as head of the newly formed Northern Lights College, which included Stage North, a vehicle for the community's drama students. It was there that he created what he describes as "a professional wing," the Chinook Touring Theatre. The theatre soon became Paisley's main preoccupation, successfully playing to school audiences throughout northern British Columbia, and stretching into the Alberta communities of Peace River, Grande Prairie and Fairview.

It was almost inevitable that, with government support for the arts at its peak, Paisley would check out the prospects of creating a new base for his children's theatre touring program in Edmonton. He knew that Joe Shoctor's Citadel on Wheels and Wings was already performing for thousands of students. But he believed he had something different to offer. Paisley was stunned when Jim Robertshaw, an official in Alberta Culture's Performing Arts division, told him, "You get the audience. We'll give you the money." There was no such support in British Columbia, or, for that matter, anywhere else in Canada. Moving to Edmonton, he was amazed at the warm reception he found in the city's theatre community. Rather than seeing him as competition, they welcomed him into the fold. By the fall of 1980, he had developed a respectable tour for the new Chinook Theatre, which included the schools he had already served in the Peace River Country and a substantial number of new schools in central Alberta.

Paisley's creation of the Edmonton Fringe Festival came about almost accidentally. In fact, you can indirectly credit Scott Swan, the artistic director of the Northern Light Theatre, with starting it all when he objected to a 50 percent cut in the Northern Light's grant, causing the theatre to close and the money to be freed for a new project. By the late 1970s, the City of Edmonton's Summerfest umbrella organization provided funding for the city's growing number of festivals. Northern Light Theatre received an annual grant of $100,000 for its Shakespeare in the Summer program, held in a tent on a bank overlooking the North Saskatchewan River. But in 1982, the economy faltered and the city announced that grants would be cut in half. Swan, idealistic and somewhat headstrong, thought that the Shakespeare in the Summer's success was too important for the city to cut his grant. He flatly refused to work for half the money, possibly believing that Summerfest officials would cave in at the last minute and give him the full amount. But the financial crunch was real, and Swan was "hoist with his own petard."

Sheldon Wilner, in charge of the Summerfest organization from 1981 to 1985, had to come up with something to replace Northern Light's offerings. With $52,000 in hand, he called Brian Paisley, who had by then developed a local reputation as a well-organized professional. Could he come up with something? It was February 1982. Chinook Theatre, now playing to thousands of school children across Alberta, had moved its offices to the basement of the Princess Theatre on Whyte Avenue in the heart of Edmonton's Old Strathcona district.

Paisley knew the run-down, somewhat funky area well. Whyte Avenue, actually 82 Avenue in Edmonton's numbered grid system, was lined with small, owner-operated shops, restaurants and bars. The Princess Theatre, now a beautifully restored facility, was boarded up; the Strathcona Hotel, across the road from the old Strathcona railway station, was a low-rent beer parlour in serious need of renovation. The old Army and Navy Store, on the corner of 104 Street, was selling discount whatever and war surplus items. The area was interesting, but hardly a destination for anyone who didn't live nearby.

Paisley had visited the famous Edinburgh Fringe Theatre Festival. He told Wilner he would try to come up with an Edmonton version and immediately got on the phone to everyone he knew in the theatre community, pleading for help. One of the people he called was Jim DeFelice, a drama professor at the University of Alberta. DeFelice was and is a mainstay of Edmonton theatre, writing and directing plays, acting in dozens of productions and helping to launch some of the city's theatre companies. Playwright Stewart Lemoine calls him "the king of reference letters," partly because of his reputation for maintaining contact with, and supporting, his acting students long after they have graduated. He has given direction and sometimes life-altering inspiration to hundreds of students in the university drama program. DeFelice had been a member of the founding boards of many of the city's theatre companies, including Northern Light Theatre, Workshop West, Nexus Theatre, Shadow Theatre and, early on, Theatre 3. Many of his plays are produced in theatres across the country.

DeFelice promised Paisley he would recruit drama students, actors, directors and writers for the festival, and over the years both he and his students have been ubiquitous presences in Fringe Festival productions. So were many university-owned props and costumes. In the run-up to the second Fringe Festival, Paisley called to say that he still had 18 open slots. DeFelice and his students filled

Brian Paisley being interviewed at the 1989 Fringe Festival. *Photo: Alberta Government Archives*

eight of them. He has been involved, in some way, in virtually every Fringe Festival event since the beginning.

On February 19, 1982, in a tight page and a half, Paisley sent Sheldon Wilner a basic outline that, more than 20 years later, still describes the Fringe Festival. Some excerpts follow:

> The purpose of the Fringe is to involve as many theatre "components" as possible in a community and tourist-oriented event which would complement other main stage performing and visual arts activities being offered during the festival.

> The Fringe would take place in five venues, within walking distance of each other, in Edmonton's Old Strathcona district.

> The theatre productions themselves would be solicited from the Edmonton theatre community—professional, semi-professional and amateur—and invitations would be sent as well to interested groups or individuals [outside the province]....
>
> The Summerfest Fringe would provide a performing space with resident technician, a coordinated schedule of events and "general" publicity for all Fringe productions. In return, each participating company would keep the gate receipts from their performances.

And that, basically, was it.

From the beginning, Paisley's drive for the Fringe was obvious. "Welcome...to the first annual...*Fringe Theatre Event*," Paisley wrote in the inaugural program, "—nine days of theatrical colour and chaos in the heart of Edmonton's Old Strathcona district...What is a *Fringe*? Well, at best it's an exciting, often irreverent, sometimes outrageous, always entertaining collection of theatre pieces which may never find their way into 'regular' performing arts seasons."

During the first year, plays were staged in the renovated Princess Theatre, an art store, a vacant space in the Tower Mortgage Building, the Strathcona Hotel and the Orange Hall (a tiny building that might have once been a one-room prairie school). The only real theatre space was the Walterdale Playhouse. The first Fringe offered 225 live performances and drew an attendance of some 7500. Performing artists took in $30,000 from admission prices ranging from two to five dollars.

By 1987 Gone with the Fringe[116] had a budget of $400,000, offered 160 shows on 14 stages and attracted an audience of 172,000 to 750 performances. It was undisputedly the largest event of its kind in North America.

Paisley produced an 80-page "Guide for Production," which has become the bible for new festivals. In all of his years at the helm (1982–90), he stuck determinedly to a handful of basic principles. Prices would be kept low. There would be no advance sales. Seats would go on sale an hour or so before each performance. There would be at least four shows a day, starting at lunch time, in each of five venues, breaking wide open in Canada the tradition that theatre was something that happened in the evening and that you dressed up for. The Fringe provided the venues; participating theatre groups, who got access to the stages on a first-come-first-served basis, covered their own production and other costs.

That first Fringe attracted some very talented performers, many of whom have gone on to great success. Calgary's Loose Moose Theatre brought an early version of the now popular Theatre Sports. The fabulous puppeteer Ronnie Burkett brought *The Plight of Polly Pureheart*. Calgary's One Yellow Rabbit Theatre presented *Leonardo's Last Supper*. Edmonton's Theatre Network weighed in with a Henry Van Rijk monologue called *Nocturnal Admissions*. Maria Formolo and Keith Urban, pioneers in Canadian modern dance, teamed up on stage for the first time. A few groups set up on streets and alleyways and performed for spare change.

Even in its infancy the Fringe proved to be an economic boon to Old Strathcona and to the city at large. Whyte Avenue became trendy, increasingly upscale, one of the most interesting parts of the city because of the Fringe. With festival audiences growing to be measured in the hundreds of thousands, merchants got Christmas twice a year. The shops became more interesting, the restaurants more varied.

The Fringe also generated a huge volunteer community. Many built their summer holidays around the event. An economic study of the third Fringe by the University of Alberta's Dr. Clive Padfield[117] noted that in 1984 the festival sold in excess of 30,000 tickets to 500 performances. The study determined that the local economic impact of the festival in that year was close to half a million dollars.

Over the years, thousands of performers, designers and stagecraft creators got their start, honed their skills and developed their reputations at the Fringe. In addition to plays performed in specific venues, the Fringe attracted a growing number of street performers, or buskers. These performers included the Green Fools from Calgary, David Aiken and his Checkerboard Guy and Bob Palmer's Flying

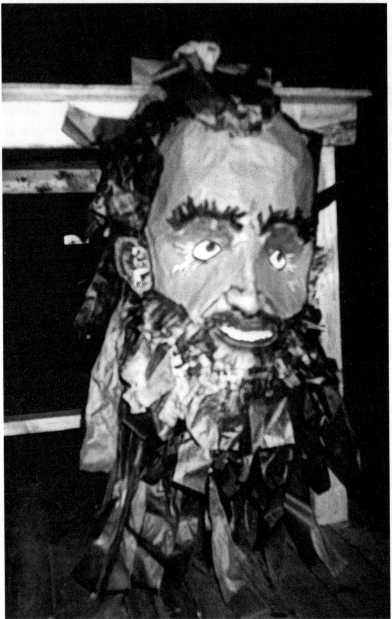

Piñata of Brian Paisley's head created by Randall Fraser. *Photo: Randall Fraser*

Debris. A group from Texas that called itself the Flaming Idiots was shocked one year to be faced with an inch of snow—in the middle of August. As Edmontonians know, it can snow in any month of the year. Only slightly daunted, the Flaming Idiots performed anyway, managed to attract a small audience, made lunch money and have been telling the story ever since.

According to my son Randall, who has worked as a "techie" ("It's like a summer holiday, Dad!") on every Fringe since 1990, many performers at first brought little more than raw talent. But year after year he watched them grow, in some cases, to international stature. Randall, sometimes to my dismay, also performed from time to time as a busker. During one Fringe, my daughter Tanice called to tell me he had burned his nose off. Randall had been doing a fire-eating act in which, lit torch in hand, he took in a mouthful of something flammable and blew it out in a spray of flame. By then an adult living on his own, he managed to avoid seeing me for three weeks. When I did catch up with him, the burn had healed. And he still had his nose.

The Edmonton Fringe, providing what some performers describe as "the best audiences in the world," is an important stop on the international professional buskers' circuit. A sampling of theatre companies that grew up with the Fringe includes Leave it to Jane Theatre, Trevor Schmidt's Unconscious Collective, John Hudson's Shadow Theatre, Calgary's One Yellow Rabbit, Three Dead Trolls in a Baggie, Mump and Smoot, Ken Brown of *My Life in Hockey* fame, and a spelling bee of writers, including David Belke,[118] Brad (no relation) Fraser, Marty Chan, Wes Borg, Chris Craddock, Tololwa Mollel and Trevor Schmidt.

But no one has had a longer and closer connection with the Fringe than writer/director Stewart Lemoine. His Teatro La Quindicina, "a group of five corybantic performers augmented for this production by a Hungarian concert pianist, a platinum-blonde French maid, a portly cubist writer and her long-time companion," produced *All These Heels* for the first Fringe. With the exception of 1995, there has been a Lemoine play at every Fringe up to and including 2002, when he announced that he was retiring from the event to get some summers off and to write for the regular theatrical season. His first play, which offered 50 percent off the regular four-dollar admission to anyone born in 1932, needed a piano. Lemoine moved his mother's upright piano to the theatre (actually an art store) and persuaded Paisley to split the $70 cost. The play was a hit, partly because of a review by the *Edmonton Journal*'s Keith Ashwell panning the play. It was part of the conventional wisdom of Edmonton theatregoers at the time that any play Ashwell panned must be worth seeing.

Lemoine was working on a BA at the University of Alberta when the Fringe was born. A self-taught playwright, he literally grew his talent at the event, along the way winning three Sterling Awards and a Dora Mavor Moore Award. He has written 50 plays. He has a quirky sense of humour and an excellent ear for dialogue, and he works with a company of actors whose talent extracts every nuance of (usually hilarious) comedic sense from his offbeat, occasionally socially relevant plays. "The Fringe," he says, "was a self-made school of theatre."

Anyone with the determination and ability to create and run an operation as successful as the Fringe is necessarily strong willed. Brian Paisley, according to those who knew him, could be "irascible"; he knew what he wanted and he wanted what he wanted. He was also very well organized. Paisley had determined early in the festival's development to plan for his replacement—to have someone on the ground who could take over. So by the time he decided that he wanted to pass the torch, Judy Lawrence was ready to step up from her role as assistant artistic director.

Lawrence was a talented stage manager who, when Paisley found her, was in Kamloops, British Columbia, working with a touring children's theatre company. Paisley and his wife, Julia, were driving from Edmonton to Vancouver in the spring of 1988. It was early in the morning, but they decided to stop and interview the candidate. Lawrence was staying with friends and had attended a theatre opening, and its ensuing party, the night before. She had stayed up "until 5:30 or 6:00 a.m. discussing folk music, Samuel Beckett and I don't know what else. I crawled into bed extremely tired," she told me. She still has no idea how Paisley got her address. It was before 8:30 on Saturday morning when he knocked on her door. Paisley says she came to the door in her bathrobe, but according to Lawrence, "I've never owned a bathrobe in my life. It was worse, a long shirt, *avec* underwear." But realizing that her next job was standing on the doorstep, she invited the couple in and, with great aplomb, Paisley says, managed coffee, aced the interview and got the job.

A blithe spirit with a workaholic ethic, Lawrence also knew how to have fun. At the opening of her first festival, the 1988 Fringe Daze, there was a plan to send Paisley up for a hot-air balloon ride over the city, but by the time they were ready to launch, it was snow-ing,[119] and a nasty wind had blown up. Lawrence sent the balloon up anyway, but on a 100-foot tether. Paisley was relieved when they finally pulled the thing down. When he decided to retire in 1990, Judy Lawrence planned a huge party at the Varscona Theatre, by then a major Fringe venue. Most of Edmonton's theatrical commu-nity and many Fringe volunteers turned out. My son Randall was commissioned to build a huge piñata in the shape of Paisley's head. Trouble was, Randall tells me, "I overbuilt the piñata, and it wouldn't break." Participants had a great time whacking away, with consider-able relish, at Brian's "head" before finally breaking it open to get at the goodies inside. Brian's own recollection of the party was, he says, without explaining, "a tad foggy." He now lives in Victoria, British Columbia, where he teaches screen writing and successfully writes screenplays for film, television and new media.

The Fringe could be frantic. The first-come-first-served policy for performing venues led, in the early years, to line-ups that stretched into several days. Actors, playwrights and directors, as many as 50 or 60 of them, would show up with sleeping bags on Thursday to line up for the Sunday opening of the doors. It hap-pened in December. Lawrence worried about people spending nights out in −20°C weather, and opened the doors to the old bus barns, where the Fringe had its offices, so that they could keep rea-sonably warm. Still, she thought, the system was unfair. Among other things, it penalized working actors performing on stages throughout the province and beyond who couldn't line up, and it favoured the young and the unemployed. A mini-industry grew up in which applicants would hire people to hold their places in line. Lawrence thought about moving the date, but that presented other problems. It could not be earlier because applicants for Fringe venues had to have finished shows; it could not be later because of the huge amount of planning that had to take place based on the number and kind of shows that would be offered. Lawrence finally devised a lottery system, which guaranteed 50 percent of the venues for local performers, 30 percent for regional companies and 20 percent for out-of-country shows.

But the Fringe is, above else, fun. It reinvents itself every year, with fanciful themes that delight performers and audiences alike. A Fringe Theatre Event of 1982 became The Fringe Strikes Again two years later. It was Home on the Fringe in 1985, Frankenfringe in1998, The Bride of Frankenfringe in 1999 and, of course, A Fringe Odyssey in 2001. In 2003 it was Attack of the Killer Fringe. Shows picked up the mood with wild titles such as *Barbies on the Tundra, Still Life with Dinosaur* and *The time is now $2.70*. Those titles are from the first Fringe; they got a lot stranger over the years.

When I asked Judy Lawrence about the greatest challenges of her decade at the Fringe (1988–98), the first words out of her mouth were "*The Happy Cunt.*" The Fringe, by definition, pushed, stretched and frequently tore the envelope of what was acceptable in theatre. *The Happy Cunt*, which appeared at the (Come in if You Dare) Frankenfringe in 1998, was produced by three women from Vancouver and explored that "unmentionable" part of the anatomy from a feminist perspective. People who never saw, or intended to see, the play were outraged long before it opened. Funding agencies made threatening noises about "community standards." Others refused to allow the poster advertising the show to be displayed. But the play had already been presented at Fringe festivals in other parts of Canada and, with the exception of the resignation of a board member in Saskatoon, there had been no other incidents.

Lawrence consulted lawyers who told her that *The Happy Cunt* broke no obscenity laws. She facilitated a discussion between the artists and community organizations including the Old Strathcona Foundation, which had offered to pay the cost of producing a new poster without the offending word, or, worse still, the illustration of a hermaphrodite character with a "third eye" on his or her forehead that looked dangerously like a vagina. Lawrence, noting there had been no great outcry when previous Fringes had offered plays like *The Fuck Machine* and *Penis De Milo,* stood her ground. The *Happy Cunt* went on, of course, to sold-out audiences. "And how was the play?" I asked her. "Not that good," came the reply.

As the years passed, avant-garde productions at the Fringe became more acceptable. Lawrence remembers a less heated, but amusing, controversy that developed over *Condomania,* mounted on one of the Fringe's outdoor stages. A businessperson, thinking it was about condominiums, brought his young son to see the show. He was outraged, demanding that Lawrence censor the show. She told him that because the play was an outdoor venue, there was no admission charge—it was free. Performers earned their money by passing the hat. If he didn't like it, she told him, trying to keep a straight face, it was his prerogative to leave. In 2002, the play *Nymphomania* hardly raised an eyebrow and got good reviews.

As the Fringe grew to the point of filling every available space, Lawrence inaugurated the "bring your own venue" category. It allowed artists who didn't make the cut for the established spaces to perform in any space they could find in the area. Stages sprung up in restaurants, bars, auto body shops and anywhere else you could string a few lights and accommodate an audience. A Winnipeg company run by Ron Jenkins put on a production "written and performed in a garage." The play started with a car screeching in the door. A feature was the discovery of a body in the trunk.

The Edmonton organization spawned a Fringe movement across Canada and beyond. There is a circuit of Canadian Fringes that include Ottawa, Montréal, Toronto, Winnipeg, Saskatoon, London, Vancouver, Calgary, Victoria, Thunder Bay, Saskatoon, Abbotsford, Prince George, Athabasca and Dartmouth. There are also United States versions in Orlando, Minneapolis, San Francisco and Seattle, and the numbers are growing. But none is as big or successful as Edmonton's annual Fringe Theatre Festival.

The Fringe continues to offer everything from street corner poetry readings at midnight to cutting-edge explorations of topics that set the so-called conventional wisdom on edge. In 2002 more than 450,000 people attended See Spot Fringe. Some 70,000 people attended indoor events. The Fringe hosted 27 venues, 12 indoor,

12 Bring Your Own Venues and 3 outdoor stages. There were busking circles throughout the area. Coming from nine countries and six provinces, 989 artists representing 140 different theatre companies produced shows. More than 1300 people volunteered close to 29,000 hours. Ticket sales exceeded half a million dollars.[120] And the executive vice-president in charge of casting for the Fox network came to the Fringe to scout for talent. The cast of *Die Nasty*, an irreverent, loosely structured comic soap opera and a perennial Edmonton favourite, was invited to Los Angeles for consultations.

Judy Lawrence describes the Fringe as "democracy at work." Artists are free to take risks. Their only limits are what their audiences will put up with. It was and is permeated by a delightful anarchy. While it needs strong leadership and clearly established rules, any interference with its artistic elements is, almost by definition, unacceptable. For 10 days the Fringe is its own "little city," with a population of up to 500,000. As other Fringe theatre festivals developed across North America, Lawrence brought them together under the umbrella of the National Association of Fringe Festivals.

By 1998, Judy Lawrence felt that her time at the Fringe was done. The Fringe needs to constantly re-invent itself, she said. So, like founder Brian Paisley, she too planned her own succession, bringing in David Cherios as assistant director, leaving it in good hands when she moved on to a position with Alberta Theatre Projects in Calgary.

But the Fringe goes on, and on.

What is an Alberta filmmaker? Whether a quixotic fool or a hardy survivor, an Alberta filmmaker may simply entertain the notion that a Canadian should be able to ply his or her trade in any part of the country, or may have a burning desire to tell Alberta stories onscreen.

—Linda Kupecek, writing in *Alberta Views*[121]

Chapter 8

Making Movies in Alberta

Sidney Newman said it couldn't be done. Here the story gets personal. In the fall of 1975, for the first time in its history, the Canadian Film and Television Association (CFTA) held its annual meeting away from central Canada, in, of all places, Edmonton. The meeting, held in tandem with the 2nd Alberta Film Awards (now known as the AMPIA Awards), was a rare recognition by Toronto of Alberta's developing film industry. In 1973, a group of producers, led by Nick Zubko, Bill Marsden, Ron Brown, Gerry Wilson and Dale Phillips, had formed the Alberta Motion Picture Industries Association (AMPIA), with a membership made up of incorporated film production companies. Len Stahl was the executive secretary of AMPIA at the very beginning and through the early years. Filmmakers in Alberta produced documentaries, educational films, corporate promotional pieces and whatever else would bring in a buck. Within a year, the association counted a dozen companies, including my Fraser Communications Ltd., which focused on educational films for Alberta School Broadcasts and for ACCESS, the provincial educational television network.

Sidney Newman, the National Film Commissioner and head of the National Film Board (NFB), was a near-legend in film and television. He had become famous at the BBC where he created television hits such as *The Forsyte Saga* and *The Avengers*. He had come home to run the NFB. In a speech to the convention, he advanced the persuasive argument that if Canada were to produce successful feature films, we had to develop a critical mass of writers, actors, directors and producers, and, he said, the only logical place to do that was in Toronto. He romanced us with tales of London, England, where artists could work in the theatre one day, in television the next, and then go on to do a movie; great synergies produced great work.

I jumped out of my seat to tell Newman that he was wrong, that we could and would make movies in western Canada, telling our own stories with our own creative people. I took his declaration as provocation, which triggered a deeply rooted flaw in my character. Don't tell me I can't do something. My life has been filled with adventures, great and small, climbing supposedly unassailable mountains, sometimes, admittedly, with all of the success of Sisyphus.

We (and particularly a younger, more naïve I) were not persuaded by Newman. By the 1970s, feelings of alienation by people who lived in "the regions" were gathering strength and potency in many parts of the country, but nowhere more than in Alberta. The energy wars that pitted Peter Lougheed against the eastern establishment grew out of a sense that we were being short-changed in Confederation. In 1973 we watched the CBC gut production capacity in Alberta, cancelling the *Tommy Banks Show*, which had brought classy big band jazz to national television. It was the same mentality that killed successful East Coast musical shows such as the *Don Messer Show*, and later, Rita MacNeil's much-loved program. The largest proportion of federal cultural budgets, delivered through such vehicles as the Canada Council, the CBC, the NFB and the recently established Canadian Film Development Corporation (CFDC), were disproportionately spent in central Canada. We felt marginalized, left out. I was convinced that if we were going to succeed at making movies in Alberta we would have to build the infrastructure to support the enterprise.

Move to Toronto to make movies? I would sooner move to Siberia to write Russian novels.

I admit that at the time of Newman's admonition, I had already started down the path to movie making in Alberta. A close friend, Maria Campbell, had written *Half Breed*, a stunningly evocative book about growing up Métis in western Canada. A number of American producers offered to buy the rights, but they sounded like they wanted to exploit the seamier side of Métis (and Maria's early) life. I told her the movie should be made in Canada and promised to make it. It was a special promise because, in addition to being a close friend, Maria had adopted me as her brother. The Plains Cree have a tradition, honoured by Métis Cree, that allows you to replace a lost relative. If someone in your family dies, you can, within a certain period of time, ask someone close to replace that individual. When Maria's brother died in a drowning accident at Batoche, Saskatchewan, she asked me to take his place. A year after his drowning, we returned to the banks of the North Saskatchewan River, and in a quiet, dignified ceremony, I became a member of her family and part of her culture.

With a travel grant arranged by Horst Schmid, I went to Hollywood, the heart of movie land, in search of advice on how to make films. Luck was with me. Arthur Hiller, whose long and distinguished list of credits includes *The Americanization of Emily* and *The In-laws*, grew up in Edmonton. He is related to the well-known Edmonton Pechet family. Howard Pechet arranged for me to visit his uncle. Hiller turned out to be a gracious mentor, inviting me to his Beverly Hills home as I sought advice on how to produce a feature film.

I was, at the time, making part of my living as a radio and television personality, running radio station CJCA's *Talk Back* open-line show in the morning, and then moving over in the afternoon to

CJCA publicity photo. At the time I was hosting *Talk Back* as well as the daily *Fil Fraser Show* on Edmonton's ITV. *Photo: Parker and Garneau Studios*

ITV, Dr. Charles Allard's new television station,[122] to host *The Fil Fraser Show*. Many of the people I interviewed on those programs and on the CBC television supper-hour show, which I co-anchored through the 1971–72 and 1972–73 seasons, were authors. Most of them were sent across the country by publishing icon Jack McClelland, inventor of what I described as the Great Canadian

Book Tour. McClelland sent almost every author he published on a national media tour, and most of them ended up on my program. Max Braithwaite and his wife, Eileen, were in Edmonton in 1974 promoting *Lusty Winter*. It was their 37th wedding anniversary, and my then-wife Ruth and I had invited them to our house for dinner and drinks. Max was the author of a series of books about growing up on the western prairies, and, in what I thought was the best of them, about becoming a schoolteacher in a one-room school in a lonely farming community. After dinner, we were sitting in front of the fireplace, well into the brandy, when Max, glowing a bit, said, "Somebody should make a movie out of one of my books." "Which one?" I, glowing just as warmly, asked. That was the start of making a Canadian movie classic, *Why Shoot the Teacher*.

I took the books for both *Teacher* and *Half Breed* to Arthur Hiller and asked him which one he thought would make the better movie. To my astonishment and delight, he agreed to read them and give me his advice. When he got back to me a couple of weeks later, he told me that *Half Breed* would make a fine movie. When I asked him how to find a screenwriter, he suggested I find a film I admired, one that was close in feeling to what I was looking for, and then find that writer. I contacted Lon Elder III, credited with the screenplay for *Sounder*, a film about a poor family in the American South, whose marginalized existence was not unlike the "road allowance people" described in Campbell's *Half Breed*. Maria had tried hard to create a workable screenplay, but, as I was to discover a number of times during my film career, authors are almost always too close to their stories to make the necessary compromises that produce a good screenplay. So I tracked down Elder, and, at some considerable expense, brought him to Edmonton to work with Maria. It was heart breaking for Maria and me to learn that he was past his prime and unable to complete the task. It is one of the great regrets of my life that I have yet to fulfill my promise to make that film.

Max, like Maria, wanted to write the screenplay for his book. Each had written strongly evocative works that were poignant, deeply personal autobiographical accounts. But, like Maria, Max was too close to the story to succeed in one of the most difficult of writing challenges. Max finally agreed that he just couldn't manage it, and I, not wanting to repeat the Lon Elder experience, followed an intuitive hunch. Someone had told me about a professor in the drama department of the University of Alberta. He had written a book with a scene by-scene-analysis of the classic Carol Reed movie *Odd Man Out*, demonstrating that he knew a great deal about screenplays and their structure—what worked and what did not. He was also a successful playwright.

Jim DeFelice is one of the most unforgettable and surprising characters I've ever met. Balding, red-headed, of Italian heritage, Jim came to the University of Alberta from Boston where he had once been a sports writer for the *Boston Globe*. He was to become, as mentioned earlier, an important contributor to Edmonton's theatrical community, including the Fringe Theatre Festival. He had a mild conversational stammer, which, unlike his unmistakable Boston accent, has faded with the years. But any speech impediment miraculously disappears when he is on stage. He is a brilliant stage director, actor and writer, appearing in at least 16 of the annual Fringe Theatre Festivals in one role or another, sometimes both directing and acting. His stage direction is smooth and deliberate, allowing time and space for elements of the show—a gasp, a laugh, a tear—to sink in. His transitions from scene to scene are filmic in their smoothness—like watching a beautifully edited film. His trilogy of parable plays, *The Elixir, Fools and Masters* and *The Merchants of Dazu,* has been produced across Canada. He was awarded Edmonton's highly regarded Sterling Award for lifetime achievement in theatre.

Jim and Gail DeFelice met at Indiana University where she was studying English and he was majoring in drama. In those days, Canadian universities sent recruiting teams to well-known American schools in search of prospective faculty. In December 1969, Jim and his wife-to-be Gail were each interviewed by the University of Alberta, Gail in New York by the Department of English, Jim in Chicago by the Department of Drama's Frank Bueckert, and each made a good impression. There were other interviews, but Jim got a firm offer to come to Edmonton, where he joined the drama department, while Gail taught in the English department. Edmonton became their home, where they have raised two daughters (Amy DeFelice is now a theatre director), become important members of both the academic and theatrical communities, and Canadian citizens.

Jim and I met over a sandwich at the U of A Faculty Club, and, within minutes, I knew that he was the man for *Why Shoot the Teacher*. Happily, he also became a lifelong friend, and, from time to time, a wily tennis partner. It was one of the relatively rare times when my intuition was right on the mark. My brief involvement with Lon Elder was a costly disaster. But Jim DeFelice turned out a gem of a screenplay that won Alberta's first national feature film award, the Etrog.[123]

As I got more involved in producing the film, Horst Schmid's support of *Why Shoot the Teacher* never flagged, even though direct support of the film industry had passed to the Department of Business Development and Tourism. Partly because of his help, the film's world premiere was an unforgettable event for me as well as for the cast and crew and the citizens of Hanna. After the 1975 election, Schmid was not only the province's cultural tsar, but also the Minister of Government Services. The role included, among other things, responsibility for the government's small fleet of aircraft, hangared at Edmonton's Municipal Airport. He frequently made the aircraft available, both to Alberta and Hollywood producers, for aerial surveys of potential film locations.[124] I had decided to hold the world premiere of *Why Shoot the Teacher* where it had been filmed, in Hanna. Horst volunteered the government's vintage DC-3 to ferry the Edmonton actors and crew to the central Alberta town.

As a private pilot, I had been flying back and forth between Edmonton and Hanna throughout the filming and had promised the people of Hanna that we would open the movie in their town. But I wondered about the length of the runway at the Hanna airport, just 2500 feet long, long enough by far for the single engine, four-seat aircraft I usually flew. But could it handle the much larger DC-3, once the workhorse of Canada's national carrier, Trans-Canada Airlines? The government pilots told me that the runway was within the DC-3's limits, and the trip was on.

Schmid had an almost pathological fear of flying. For a man who spent a considerable amount of his time in the air, I found it

The crew and some of the cast of *Why Shoot the Teacher* before our flight to Hanna for the film's world premiere. *Photo: Government of Alberta*

remarkable that he managed to control his fear. On the few occasions when I flew with him, it was hard not to notice his white-knuckle trembling. The flight to Hanna almost put him over the edge. The pilot, wanting to make sure that he would not run out of runway, was determined to touch the tail dragger down within the first few feet. The run-up to the paved runway was gravel, and there was a bit of a bump where the pavement started. The wheels touched down in front of, not behind the bump, and the plane took a mighty bounce, coming down several yards farther down the runway. The pilot immediately applied full brakes, bringing the aircraft to a stop just before he ran out of runway. Horst was drenched in sweat as we left the aircraft—but didn't say a word.

The screening was a hoot. The Hanna theatre was filled to capacity. Members of the cast and crew were introduced. Horst and I each said a few words, and the show hit the screen. Few in the audience were able to take in the whole movie because of the constant din of coversation throughout the whole film. We had used many local residents, and some of their farms and houses in the film. The screening was interrupted throughout by hoots and shouts: "That's my cow!" "See, I told you they'd use my road!" "Hey look, I built that Bennett Buggy!" We all had a great good time, and after refreshments and conversation and promises to keep in touch, we climbed back into the DC-3 and flew back to Edmonton. Even Horst, exhausted and happy like the rest of us, enjoyed the trip home. The movie continued to play at the Hanna theatre for several weeks. Everyone in the district must have seen it several times.

It is too bad that, because of the weather, they missed one of the funniest scenes in Jim DeFelice's screenplay. The story was scripted to take place in a typical prairie winter, very cold, lots of snow. It was typical of the times that the way to get through winter was to get out and into it. DeFelice wrote a scene in which the rag-tag class of farmers' kids got together on a frozen pond for a game of lunchtime shinny hockey. The kids were having such a good time that they didn't want to go back to class. Max, the naïve protagonist-teacher of the film, took matters into his own hands and confiscated the puck, putting it in his back pocket, and herded the kids back into the one-room school. Halfway through the afternoon a terrible smell began to fill the classroom—and Max finally realized it was coming from him. The puck, as everyone but Max knew, was a frozen horse bun. In the original script, Max went downstairs to his basement room to change and finished the class in his bathrobe.

We had to lose the scene because, for the first time in years, Hanna experienced an early spring. We had planned the shoot for March on the basis of weather records that promised lots of snow and low temperatures. But in March of 1975 there was hardly any snow, and the ice had melted. DeFelice had to spend several days on the set rewriting the scenes that called for snow and ice. There is a sequence in the movie in which one of the characters gets lost in a blizzard. It was filmed using artificial snow in a Hollywood studio.

After the successful release of *Why Shoot the Teacher* in 1976, George Destounis, head of the American-owned Famous Players chain during the 1970s, gave me a sobering lesson in the realpolitik of feature film. "Fraser," he told me in the gruff manner that hid a warm heart, "that was a pretty good film, and we did well with it. And maybe two years from now you'll come along with another one under your arm, and want even more screen time. And I'd like to give it to you, but you have to realize that Fox and Universal and the other Hollywood majors each come in here with 20 or 30 films every year, any one of them might be a blockbuster like *Jaws*. They tell me which theatres they want and they tell me what dates they want them. I have no choice but to say, 'Yes, Sir,' and 'What else can I do for you, Sir.' Even if you did come in here with 20 films, Fraser, I still wouldn't like your chances. Hollywood has all the clout. They call all the shots."

Yes, you can make movies in Alberta, and, if you like, in Toronto. I produced three feature films for theatrical release and helped with a fourth. But, with the exception of Francophone Québec producers, any Canadian who thinks he or she can make money from the theatrical distribution of truly Canadian movies, using our own talent and stories, is sadly, sometimes devastatingly, wrong. It was and is impossible to succeed in making truly Canadian theatrical feature films in English, in Alberta, Toronto or anywhere else in Canada. The trouble is not in our ability to make interesting, compelling films. The hard, hard reality is the unassailable fact that Canada's screens are controlled by Hollywood.

No surprise, then, that Canadian films usually end up on the smallest screens in suburban shopping centre multiplexes, or in off-the-beaten-track alternative theatres. It is a rare thing to see them last more than a week. Even Paul Gross's highly touted *Men With Brooms*, with the largest promotion and advertising budget ever afforded a Canadian film, stayed in theatres for little more than a week or two—not long enough to make its money back, certainly not from the box office controlled by the United States.

I saw the effects of America's clout more than once during my producing days. Every time a Canadian minister responsible for culture made brave statements about getting more screen time for Canadian films, Jack Valenti, president of the Motion Picture Association of America, would make yet another trip to Ottawa, make a few calls, sometimes take the relevant minister out to dinner and within days the initiative would be shelved.

In an incident that had a profoundly negative effect on my second film, *Marie Anne*, then Secretary of State John Roberts, with great bravado, announced that he would impose a quota on theatres,

In the co-pilot's seat of the government's Queen Air turboprop aircraft. I loved to fly. *Photo: Fil Fraser*

requiring them to devote money or a percentage of screen time to Canadian films. That idea barely lasted a month, but had the effect of removing Famous Players as a financial partner in *Marie Anne,* an earnest but flawed film about the first white woman to live in western Canada, the grandmother of Louis Riel. Destounis needed some assurance that if the government scheme required exhibitors to spend money on Canadian films, his investment in *Marie Anne* would be credited. Pulling every political string I knew, I went to Ottawa and visited Roberts in his home. I left with the clear understanding that he would call Destounis and assure him that he would not be penalized for investing in my film. Roberts never made the call, and Destounis pulled the $250,000 that he had committed. With pre-production already under way, I spent most of the time the film was being made raising the rest of the budget, on a couple of occasions getting money into the bank just in time to meet the pay-roll. The time that I should have been spending fine-tuning the script and production was lost, and the film went ahead, so far as I, the producer, was concerned, virtually on autopilot. It is thanks to a fine cast and crew that it turned out as well as it did.

An even more dramatic example of Hollywood's power unfolded when Québec Premier Jean-Jacques Bertrand brought in legislation that would have required all US films to be distributed with a French soundtrack before the English version would be allowed to enter the province. Valenti ominously decreed that if the legislation were proclaimed, Hollywood would simply pull its films from the Québec market. The province's theatre operators, who knew the Americans weren't kidding, went ballistic. The government folded. This clout is the bone-shattering truth of our relationship with the US and it will never change.

America goes to extraordinary lengths to protect foreign markets for its movies, considering them among its most important exports. The movies create international markets for American products— Coca Cola, McDonald's (increasingly in the Third World), Marlboro cigarettes and American life-styles. But, they insist, it is not culture; it is the entertainment industry. The US, in the name of free trade and democracy, insists that its films have open access to the world's screens, and nowhere is that access more open than in Canada. At the same time, non-American films, from Canada or any other country, have about the same chance of getting anything more than token distribution on US screens as a Swiss Army knife has of getting through airport security.

There have been a few real Canadian movies. The earliest,[125] and certainly one of the strangest, *Back to God's Country,* is described in an *Alberta Views* magazine essay by Linda Kupecek.

> A silent film called *Back to God's Country* was made in
> 1919, becoming, for its time, a huge commercial and

artistic success, with a reported 300 percent return to its Canadian investors. More surprising was the fact that this film, starring the celebrated Nell Shipman, was shot on location in Lesser Slave Lake in northern Alberta, and the Canadian investors were Calgarians. Nell and her husband, Ernest Shipman (known as "Ten Percent Ernie"), had arrived in Calgary from Hollywood via Toronto amid much hoopla, then charmed the $65,000 budget out of the local community for their company, Canadian Photoplays Ltd.

The shoot, however, was marred by what Ernest described in a letter to a Canadian Photoplays stockholder as "obstacles unprecedented and trouble never dreamed of." What were presented in jolly press releases as minor inconveniences were in fact the mutiny and defection of the crew and carpenters once they experienced one day of –50° temperatures (they fled south *en masse* to the more civilized climate of California); the frostbite suffered by the production manager as he laboured, with one native helper, to build an entire set, including a ship, under these conditions, which left him with a lifelong limp; and the more than inconvenient death of the leading man from a "severe cold" which turned to pneumonia. But, in show-must-go-on tradition, after the actor's demise in an Edmonton hospital, he was quickly replaced, and the shoot staggered on under these horrific circumstances. Nell and Ernie were rewarded with international success, thanks to Ernie's marketing know-how, Nell's talent before the camera (including one of the first nude scenes onscreen) and—oh, yes—the Alberta scenery.[126]

But Americans have made most of the movies filmed in Alberta, beginning in 1907 with the Edison Company's tearjerker, *An Unselfish Love*. Alan Ladd came to Alberta in 1953 to star, ironically,

Receiving the 1978 Alberta Achievement Award for Excellence in Film Making from Premier Peter Lougheed. Broadcaster/MC Jo Green is in the background. *Photo: Government of Alberta*

in a film called *Saskatchewan.* Bing Crosby was in Jasper in 1948 for Billy Wilder's *The Emperor Waltz,* the first colour feature. Many others—Marilyn Monroe, Robert Mitchum, Jimmy Stewart, Paul Newman, Clint Eastwood, Richard Gere and Brad Pitt—came to use Alberta's magnificent scenery.

In 1961, an Albertan, Larry Matanski, made *The Wings of Chance.* It was the first really made-in-Alberta-by-Canadians movie. *Back to God's Country* was filmed here with Calgary money, but the cast and crew were Americans. Matanski followed it in 1963 with a racy little film called *The Naked Flame,* based on news reports and photos of Doukhabor women from the radical Sons of Freedom sect, who burned down schools and disrobed to protest against modern incursions into their world. With an eye on the box office,

Matanski hired a group of Las Vegas showgirls to play the women. Then Matanski disappeared from the Alberta scene.

That made *Why Shoot the Teacher*, released in 1979, the second made-in-Alberta-by-Albertans Canadian movie. But even though most of the cast and crew were Albertans, I had to go out of province or out of country, not only for the lead actors, but for the director, the first assistant director, the director of photography and, at the insistence of a US-based union, his assistant. It was clear that we needed programs to develop and train our own film professionals.[127]

And to prove that Sidney Newman was wrong.

I was not the only one making interesting films in Alberta. Among other groups was the Film West Studio, created in 1971 by Tom Radford, Dale Phillips, Harvey Spak, Allan Stein, Mark and Reevan Dolgoy and Bob Reece. Film West was an amalgamation of Film Frontiers and Barnyard Films, two pioneer documentary production companies in the province, and it grew to include Anne Wheeler and George Christoff. It launched the careers of notable filmmakers Tom Radford and Anne Wheeler. Filmmakers such as Nick Bakyta and Andy Thomson actually moved to Alberta from other parts of the country as we worked to build a supportive infrastructure for our enterprises. There were many in the Alberta film industry to acknowledge and celebrate.

The first Alberta Film Festival was launched in 1974 as part of Arts and You, a Conference on the Arts to be held in Red Deer, May 30 through June 2 with a grant of $10,000 from Horst Schmid's department and with the cooperation of our industry association, Alberta Motion Pictures Industry Association (AMPIA). As its organizer and chair, I invited any Alberta filmmaker to submit any film to Alberta's first provincial film festival. Len Stahl, who had helped start AMPIA, did the nuts and bolts work of pulling all of the elements together and making them work.[128] I wanted Arthur Hiller to chair the first Alberta Film Festival jury, and, had he not been committed to another event, I'm sure he would have agreed. So I called Canadian director Ted Kotcheff,[129] who had directed the first commercially viable Canadian film, *The Apprenticeship of Duddy Kravitz*, starring the young American actor Richard Dreyfuss. Kotcheff drove in from California with Dreyfuss's co-star,

The restored Princess Theatre was the principal venue for the first Commonwealth Games International Film Festival in 1978. *Government of Alberta Photo*

Micheline Lanctot, a budding Québec actor who has since become a respected writer and film director. With Kotcheff as chair, the jury was made up of Colin Low, a brilliant NFB filmmaker, originally from Cardston; Louise Bresky, the *Calgary Herald* film critic; the steadfast Ellen Watt from ACCESS Educational Television; and Jim Vincent, an advertising agency executive.

I then went looking for a trophy to present for the best film. My first stop was Horst Schmid's office. Room 324 of the Legislature Building looked like a strange combination of museum and tourist gift shop. Everywhere he went, on travels around Alberta and around the world, Horst acquired a wagonload of gifts—dolls, books, plates, plaques, paintings and sculptures as well as folk art crafts of all kinds. Don't even ask about T-shirts. From time to time, he would buy works from Alberta artists, often using them as gifts on special occasions. His Legislature office was filled, virtually from floor to ceiling, with an impressive array of art and other "stuff."

One of the works was a Roy Leadbeater sculpture called *The Celestial Visitor*. A heavy bronze about two feet high, it is a very free representation of an alien form. Leadbeater told me it was part of a series he created during an era when UFOs were much in the news, and his children suggested he should do some sculptures of what aliens might look like. Horst had visited a Leadbeater show, had personally purchased a pair of candleholders and, later, his office acquired the *Visitor*. Some might raise their eyebrows, but it has a powerful primitive charm that grows on you as you live with it.

"How about that?" Horst offered, pointing out *The Celestial Visitor*, unceremoniously sitting on the windowsill. Not wanting to look a gift Horst in the mouth, I accepted as graciously as I could. Jury chair Ted Kotcheff, at my behest, dubbed it the "Horst" as he presented it to Tom Radford, who won the prize for his film *Ernest Brown, Pioneer Photographer*. Several members of the cast of the docudrama are notable. William Thorsell, now the CEO of the Royal Ontario Museum and former chair of the editorial board of the *Globe and Mail*, was then a young man about town. Another member of the cast was the talented Anne Wheeler, who has gone on to a distinguished career as a film director, with movie credits including *Loyalties*, *War Story*, *Angel Square* and *Better Than Chocolate*. Well-known Alberta artists Harry Savage and Sylvain Voyer were also in the film, and the soundtrack was by Bruce Cockburn.

The "Horst" stayed with the festival, which AMPIA has continued as an annual gala event, until its displacement in 1981 by a more modern trophy. My movie, *The Hounds of Notre Dame*, was the last to win it. I was presented with a heavy bronze plaque, also created by Leadbeater, with *The Celestial Visitor* carved in relief. But the actual sculpture went missing for several years until I found it in a corner of the AMPIA offices early in 2002. The staff of the day were not sure what it was or whence it had come.

Many people and organizations worked hard during those early years of the 1970s to build an environment in which Alberta film-makers could develop and prosper. AMPIA organized an ongoing series of seminars on the various film crafts; lighting, sound, cinematography and others. The Department of Film and Literary Arts, headed by the enthusiastic, ever-optimistic author John Patrick Gillese, provided advice, guidance and material assistance to a growing number of screenwriters. At the Banff Centre for the Arts, I organized a series of courses, workshops and master classes on film to introduce Albertans to leading film professionals of the day such as cinematographer Richard Leiterman, writer Jim DeFelice, directors Silvio Narrizzano and Lethbridge-born Bill Fruet, among others.

In 1977, Schmid, as related in Chapter 4, had been part of the team that secured the 1978 Commonwealth Games for Edmonton. And, characteristically, he wanted to add a cultural element to what had always been a purely sports event. You won't be surprised, having read thus far, to learn that one of the components of the arts festival that would complement the sports spectacle was a film festival. Both the Commonwealth Games Arts Festival and Film Festival are now permanent features of the event that still rotates around the world's Commonwealth countries every four years. The Commonwealth Games Film Festival was a first—the forerunner to what is now the most important television festival in the world, the Banff International Television Festival. I tell that story in the next chapter.

Probably the most important factor in the development of Alberta's film industry came as the result of a task force stimulated by Horst Schmid but actually carried out under the auspices of the Department of Business Development and Tourism. There had been, for a number of years, an ongoing discussion as to whether film production was primarily a business or a cultural activity. Most members of AMPIA, producers of documentaries and industrial films, considered their activities to be part of an industry. After the first festival, launched with the financial support of Schmid's Department of Culture, support for subsequent festivals came from the Film Industry Sector office of the Department of Business Development and Tourism. I leaned toward a cultural approach to film development but saw and acknowledged that the reality of filmmaking, especially movie making, is a money game. I compensated by setting up the Fraser Films Award for best screenwriting,

Being congratulated by Prime Minister Jean Chrétien and Aline Chrétien after receiving the 1999 Harry Jerome Award for Excellence in the Professions. Looking on is BBPA member Jean Pierre. *Photo: Black Business and Professional Association of Canada*

a metal sculpture of a bird set on a piece of granite, which was, for a time, presented as part of the AMPIA awards.

In February 1977, with Horst Schmid's strong support, the Department of Business Development and Tourism created a film study committee with the following mandate:

- to suggest an overall government policy on film production
- to recommend an environment that is conducive to allow creative people to work and live in Alberta
- to suggest ways to encourage the private film producers and financial sectors of the province to become involved in the viable film industry. [130]

The task force was chaired by Bill Brese, an economist, and comprised Bill Marsden, a documentary film producer and then president of AMPIA; Brian McIntosh, a film exhibition executive; and me. Chuck Ross, director of Alberta Business' Film Industry Sector, organized a tour that took us to Arizona, California, Australia and Hong Kong. He was our wagon master, our purser and our mentor. And the trip was a genuine adventure.

We went to Old Tucson to visit a movie set that anyone who has ever seen a Hollywood western would recognize. Many of the old classics—*Arizona, The Last Round-up, Winchester, The Last Outpost, Gunfight at the OK Corral,* the TV series *Have Gun Will Travel* and many more—were made there. Part of our mandate was to explore the tourist potential of film sets. When movies are not being shot in Old Tucson, the area is a hot tourist destination, with people coming to see the daily simulated shoot-outs and other hi-jinks of the largely fictional American old west.

From the Tucson desert, we travelled over the mountains to the movie mecca, Hollywood. Our visit was a whirlwind of studio tours, meetings with senior executives from Samuel Goldwyn Studios, Twentieth Century Fox, Warner Brothers and Universal Studios. It was a crash course in the politics of film. If we didn't know it before, we now saw the raw truth of the film business: a relative handful of individuals exercise enormous power over what gets made, who makes it, how it gets distributed, who gets paid and in what order.

The airplane trip from Los Angeles to Sydney was the longest I had ever taken. We flew to Honolulu, changed planes and flew for some 14 hours across the Pacific to Sydney, Australia, watching three movies along the way and arriving severely jet-lagged. We discovered that the country, in some ways a smaller version of Canada, had a strongly emerging film industry. A new film, *Picnic at Hanging Rock*, had just made an international impact. Its director, Peter Weir, went on to crack the world market with *The Dead Poets Society* and achieved a place in Hollywood with films like *The Truman Show*. Bruce Beresford, a brilliant new director, had just made *Don's Party*, a breakthrough film that also moved him onto the world's stage. His Hollywood successes include *Tender Mercies* and *Driving Miss Daisy*.

What astonished us even then was that a country smaller, less populated and less affluent than our own could mount a viable film industry. Why, we wondered, could Australian films succeed in their smaller country, when Canadian producers had trouble getting paid, let alone making money on their films? It is the most frustrating question we face. And the answer tells us more about ourselves than about Australia. Australians are proud of, and delight in watching, Australian films. No such luck, Québec excepted, in Canada. A movie I saw in Adelaide, *Storm Boy*, was said to have recovered its entire budget from receipts from a single theatre in that city, which played the film for more than a year. It was the beautiful, simple story of a white boy and an Aborigine adult who meet on a beach where the boy has found a wounded bird. Together they nurse the creature back to health and set it free. Just the kind of story a Canadian producer might make.

We learned that Australia had a broadcasting and film infrastructure quite similar to our own. In fact, they borrowed it from us. ABC, the Australian Broadcasting Corporation, is modeled after our CBC. And the Australian Film Board thanks our National Film Board for helping set it up. But they don't live next door to the US, which in its corporate boardrooms considers Canada to be part of its domestic market. American films are seen in Australia and do well there. But Australians like their own films and celebrate their directors and their stars. Australia was a lesson and a challenge. I came home feeling envious of a country that celebrates, revels in and is proud of its own culture.

While we worked hard and learned a great deal in our meetings in Los Angeles and Australia, our visit to Hong Kong gave us insights into another kind of movie making. We wanted to get an inside look at one of the world's richest, most prolific film production companies, run by a man who was already a legend, Sir Run Run Shaw. He and his brother, Vee King Shaw, had practically invented the Kung Fu action movie genre and produced a constant stream of low-cost, high-action films that found audiences, in dozens of languages, all over the world.

A Mercedes picked us up at the airport and we set up shop at the Miramar Hotel on Hong Kong's "Kowloon Side." We toured the Shaw Brothers offices and studios, had long discussions with their executives, and visited the sets of several films in production. The shows, populated by scores of Jackie Chan-like characters, were all shot without sound, or MOS.[131] Hong Kong action movies show very few close ups of their actors, especially of their mouths. They spend most of their screen time engaged in increasingly complex fights. The sparse dialogue, with background sound and music, is dubbed in later in a variety of languages to serve various world markets. There was no question here of art. This movie making was all business—and a very profitable business. One of the highlights of the trip was seeing one of Sir Run Run Shaw's gold-plated Rolls Royces.

Back in Canada, the report of the study group was delivered in record time, eight months after our February appointment.[132] We had also visited Canadian centres: Montréal, Ottawa, Toronto and Vancouver. And what we learned made it clear to us that, with the right support, Alberta could develop an energetic film industry, a desirable goal. "Through the medium of film," we said, "international awareness of Alberta's progress, diversity and development potential can have important social, cultural and economic consequences for the province." We told the government that the development of a viable Alberta film industry made economic sense, that properly managed and with the right support, it could make money. We urged the establishment of a Film Development Corporation to be in operation by April 1, 1979.

The report and its recommendations were in the hands of the business development portfolio. There was a small tug of war between those who wanted the support program to be part of Culture and those who believed that an industrial strategy was required. I was *hors de combat*, out of the battle, trying to survive in the movie business. Horst Schmid moved from Culture to International Trade following the 1979 election and was replaced by the earnest, but less dynamic Mary LeMessurier. The momentum slowed.

It was not until 1982, five years after our report had been submitted, with the economy beginning to falter, that the Alberta Motion Picture Development Corporation (AMPDC) was established. Bill Marsden, who had given up independent production to take a job as director of Film Development, drafted the enabling legislation, Bill 24 (1981). The legislation called for the establishment of a $3-million revolving fund to be used to make repayable loans or to provide bank guarantees to film producers for up to 60 percent of the funds required for the pre-production stage of a motion picture. Pre-production costs include the screenplay, location scouting, recruitment of key personnel such as actors, directors and directors of photography, building sets and a compendium of other costs. It is the hardest money to raise.

AMPDC, as long as it was in operation, contributed greatly to the development of a successful Alberta film industry, producing a net revenue gain for the province. The Klein government killed it in March 1996. Tom Peacocke recalls an official of the Australian Film Development Corporation telling an AMPDC meeting, "You did the example. You gave us the idea and we ran with it. What happened to you?" Many of the province's dramatic producers, directors, writers and performers moved to British Columbia, leaving a handful of documentary producers to fend for themselves. At this writing, former Albertan filmmakers such as Anne Wheeler and Arvi Liimatainen are still on the West Coast.

But the larger malaise is national. It is not that Canada has not produced talented writers, directors and actors. It is just that they have to cross the border to "make it." Premier filmmakers get little respect in their own country. The list of expatriates is long. It begins at the earliest days of movie making with stars such as Mary Pickford, Mack Sennett, Louis B. Mayer (the M in MGM), Norma Shearer and Walter Huston—all former Canadians. And the modern list of Canadians in American film and television is staggering.

Dan Akroyd—*Saturday Night Live, Blues Brothers*
Pamela Anderson Lee—*Baywatch, Home
    Improvement*
Raymond Burr—*Perry Mason*
Neve Campbell—*Party of Five, Scream*
Jim Carrey—*Ace Ventura, Dumb and Dumber,
    The Truman Show*
Tommy Chong—*Cheech and Chong*
Hume Cronyn—*Cleopatra, Cocoon, The Pelican Brief*
Elisha Cuthbert—*24*
Colleen Dewhurst—*Anne of Green Gables*
Michael J. Fox—*Back to the Future, Spin City*

Brendan Fraser—*Encino Man, George of the Jungle, The Mummy*
Lorne Greene—*Bonanza*
Phil Hartman—*Saturday Night Live, News Radio*
Natasha Henstridge—*Species*
Michael Ironside—*Top Gun, Total Recall*
Margot Kidder—*Superman, The Amityville Horror*
Elias Koteas—*TMNT, The Thin Red Line*
Norm Macdonald—*Saturday Night Live*
Howie Mandel—*Little Monsters*
Rick Moranis—*Parenthood, Honey I Shrunk the Kids*
Mike Myers—*Wayne's World, Austin Powers*
Leslie Nielsen—*Naked Gun, Mr. Magoo*
Catherine O'Hara—*SCTV, Home Alone*
Anna Paquin—*The Piano, Amistad*
Matthew Perry—*Friends*
Jason Priestly—*Beverly Hills 90210, Calendar Girl*
Keanu Reeves—*Speed, Point Break, The Matrix*
Paul Schaffer—*Late Show with David Letterman*
William Shatner—*Star Trek*
Martin Short—*Three Amigos, Pure Luck*
Scott Speedman—*Felicity*
Donald Sutherland—*M*A*S*H, Ordinary People, Don't Look Now*
Kiefer Sutherland—*The Lost Boys, Stand by Me, 24*
Alan Thicke—*Growing Pains*
Dave Thomas—*Grace Under Fire*
Jennifer Tilly—*Bullets over Broadway, Bound*

And that's just a partial list of the actors and their films. Hollywood is full of Canadian writers, directors, cinematographers, editors and other film professionals.

I DO WANT TO LABOUR THE POINT.

Like a twist on the famous Groucho Marx saying, "I don't care to belong to any club that will have me as a member," we Canadians do not care to watch a movie that has our people as its stars, unless, of course, they have already made it you-know-where. Or, as Budge

Crawley has said to me many times, "There isn't the same pride taken by Canadians in achievements in a cultural field like this, as many other countries."

It is a reality that was brought home forcefully to me in 1987 when I was invited to take a small festival of Canadian films to the Soviet Union. The country has a distinguished film history, which includes such pioneers as Eisenstein, Kuleshov and Pudovkin. These filmmakers are virtually unknown to people in the outside world other than film buffs, but they are revered in their own country. I took three feature films, *Why Shoot the Teacher*, *Marie Anne* and Alan King's *Who Has Seen the Wind*, and a charming documentary by Bill Marsden, *Let Music Be the Message*. From the day we arrived, we were treated to screening after screening of films that had been banned by the pre-Gorbachev regime. Later, we attended a number of gala world premieres of films, some of them made up to a dozen years earlier, which had never had a public screening. The films were generally excellent, a few were outstanding, and we often wondered why they had been banned. A film about a farm wife who left an oppressive family for a new life in the city was suppressed, we were told, because it gave the appearance of challenging established (male) authority. Another film, in its time very daring, dealt with youth culture, showing teenagers break-dancing to bootlegged American music on Moscow's Arbat Street Mall.

There was a general air of celebration in the film community. They were among the first to embrace *glasnost* and *perestroika*. We drank significant quantities of fine brandy and champagne and ate caviar, and we toured Moscow's extensive studio facilities, treading in the footsteps of Eisenstein and other great Russian filmmakers. Many of the same studios, editing rooms and other facilities he had used were still in operation.

We saved *Why Shoot the Teacher* and *Let Music Be the Message* for Kiev, where the Ukrainian landscape was not unlike our prairies and where there were still close ties to Ukrainian heritage communities in western Canada. And the reception was even warmer than it had been in Moscow. At our film screenings, I found myself wishing they had been received as enthusiastically in Canada as they were in the Soviet Union. A large audience came to see *Who has Seen the Wind* and *Marie Anne* in Moscow.

Seven years earlier, when Tom Peacocke won the 1980 Best Actor Genie for his performance in *The Hounds of Notre Dame*, he stunned the audience at the awards ceremony by raging against the fact that he was being honoured for a film that few Canadians would see. "But you know what's really sad about it," he said, "I'm playing a hero, and no one's seen the movie. And that describes a great deal about our industry, and our country."

In addition to best actor nomination, *Hounds* was nominated for several other awards: Frances Hyland for best supporting actor, Zale Dalen for best director, Ken Mitchell for best original screenplay and Tony Lower for best editor, as well as a number of technical awards. (But the year belonged to a Québec film, *Les Bons Desbarets*, which swept the 1980 awards.)

The CBC paid $160,000 for the broadcast rights to *Hounds,* the highest licence fee it had ever awarded a Canadian movie. I made what I considered to be an honourable deal with a Canadian distributor, which allowed him to include the CBC sale as part of his deal, for which, in return, he agreed to spend a substantial amount promoting the film. By the time the film was ready for release, he went bankrupt. The distributor who succeeded him failed to honour his pledge. *Hounds* got token distribution in a few theatres. I lost control of the rights to the film. I never collected a producer's fee.

For a while I had really believed I could break the mould; that we could make truly Canadian films that Canadians would want to watch. That was, and sadly still is, a fantasy. I have spent more than a little time thinking that, had I done this or that differently, hired that writer, that actor, done a different deal, had different partners, found a better distributor, pushed government a little harder, that it might have come out differently. I might have, like some of those who started in the business when I did, made a lot of money by paying myself first—but (a possible flaw in my character) I thought my investors should get their money back first. The real flaw is that I have never managed money very well; it has never been a motivating factor in my life. Fatal for a movie producer. All that aside, with distance and time, I know now that there was no way to change Canadians' preference for American films, or to create a mainstream taste for what we can produce here. Too many of us think and act like Americans. Those few producers and directors who have enjoyed, if that's the term, some modest success by staying in Canada, have done so largely by making "American clone" movies: shot in Canada, but with American themes and with street names, licence plates, flags—anything that identified our country—carefully removed. And even if we could engage Canadians, create an appetite for real Canadian stories, as TV with the prodding of the CRTC is now beginning to do, we would still fail. We might have the occasional small success, but capturing the mainstream of Canadian movie viewing is just a fantasy. Hollywood's grip on the distribution system is crushingly strong.

It is our own fault. We are proud Albertans. And there are proud Nova Scotians and Newfoundlanders and Saskatchewanians and Québecers, and so on. We are more often in contention with each other as regions, attacking the federal government—and our country. Our writers capture international prizes, our armed forces are the most trusted peacekeepers, the United Nations rated us as among the best countries in the world in which to live. People, by the millions, including Americans, want to come here from other countries. But a startling number of us would just as soon be Americans. We have so little pride in things Canadian.

There are a few exceptional Canadians who make Canadian films. Atom Egoyan, especially, makes earnest, credible films that have a following. David Cronenberg has carved an international niche for his well-made thrillers. And now with new technology that has democratized the means of production, the way has been opened for a new generation of filmmakers to carve a better place for themselves. It is now possible, with a relatively few thousand dollars worth of digital equipment, to make technically credible movies that will play on the big screen. Shortly after my return to Edmonton, I was honoured to be asked to chair the jury for the 2001 AMPIA Awards. The winner was a clever, funny, technically innovative film that had been shot in a Calgary shopping centre using digital video cameras and effects. The movie, *waydowntown,* has had modest success and has probably made back its low budget cost. Perhaps television sales alone will cover its budget. You may have seen it on Air Canada flights, but not in very many theatres.

Following my success with *Why Shoot the Teacher,* an American distributor who once owned a string of car dealerships in the eastern US offered to distribute my films in the US, on condition that I make some films to which he had acquired the rights. He pressed hard to get me to make a movie called *Mrs. Bad Gun,* a violent story about a woman who hunts down and brutally murders a group of bizarre characters she believes killed her husband. The story line was strictly a device upon which to hang some of the most explicit, violent murder scenes I have ever read. The distributor wanted to produce these B-class movies in Canada as cheaply as possible using no name (read Canadian) actors, and to push them through his distribution system. It would have made me rich.

I was not the only one who wanted to prove that Sidney Newman was wrong. But we, including Newman, were all wrong. Movies made in Canada by Canadians for Canadians will always be a hard sell.

Horst Schmid's support never wavered. I was proud to be in the audience at the 2001 Alberta Film Festival when AMPIA recognized Horst with a special trophy, honouring him as the great friend of the industry that he was.

...a brilliant parade of artists, builders and dreamers who shared a vision and made it come true.

—David Leighton

Chapter 9

Cultural Treasures at Banff

Banff is a national treasure, the site of one of our most beautiful national parks, home to some of the best skiing on the continent, and a fabulous nature preserve where maintaining the balance between territories occupied by wild and human life is the subject of ongoing debate. But many Canadians are not aware that two of Canada's great cultural treasures also shine amid the Rocky Mountains—the Banff Centre and the Banff International Television Festival.

Of all the achievements in the development of culture and the arts in Canada, none is more impressive or more important than the Banff Centre. Since its creation in 1933 as a summer program of the Department of Extension of the University of Alberta, the centre has achieved international recognition for its dedication to

Tennis at the Banff Centre. With (left to right) Greg Kane, Adrianne Burns and Norm Green. *Photo: Fil Fraser*

lifelong creative and professional development. Artists from across Canada and around the world come to Banff year-round to hone their talents in disciplines ranging from opera to writing, from music to painting, from dance to sculpture, from drama to electronic media. For people attending its performances and exhibits, the centre offers Canada's richest banquet of creative artistry.

David and Peggy Leighton have told the story of the Banff Centre—"Campus in the Clouds"—admirably well in their aptly named book *Artists, Builders and Dreamers*.[133] One of these artists, builders and dreamers was Elizabeth Sterling Haynes. In a chapter titled "A Woman Ahead of Her Time," the Leightons write, "Her contribution to the Banff Theatre School was immeasurable. Had it not been for her talent and her ability to inspire others, the venture might easily have collapsed in those first years. As it was, she established high standards and provided the energetic leadership that captured the imagination of those who were to follow. It was Elizabeth Haynes who built the base upon which the future Banff School would grow."[134] It was not until I began the research for this book that I learned how essential Haynes had been to Banff.

Elizabeth Sterling Haynes was born in 1898 into a notable Canadian family. Her brother, Wallace Sterling, was a distinguished educator and president of California's prestigious Stanford University from 1949 to 1968. Elizabeth attended the University of Toronto where she established an enduring reputation as an actress, performing in the famous Hart House Theatre's first season. She moved to Edmonton in 1922 with her husband, Dr. Nelson Haynes, a dentist, who, according to some who remember him, was a self-effacing man who hated dentistry and would have preferred to be a farmer. Elizabeth Haynes launched herself into developing what theatre there was in the city—acting, directing, lifting it to new heights. In 1928 she was a founding member of the Alberta Drama League, which became a model for the Dominion Drama Festival (1932–39, 1947–78). When the Edmonton Little Theatre Company was formed in 1929, Dr. W.H. Alexander was its first president, but it was the dynamic Haynes who, as director and head of production, was its real inspiration and sparkplug. That same year, the stock market crashed and the Great Depression began. In a perverse way, the economic decline fostered the development of amateur theatre in many communities. The big travelling shows of more prosperous times stopped touring, and people had to make their own entertainment. Community theatre saw some of its best times during the years before World War II. In Alberta, Elizabeth Sterling Haynes stood at its centre. In her doctoral thesis, Moira Jean Day[135] noted, "the initial broad community and artistic base of the Edmonton Little Theatre truly made Elizabeth Haynes the most powerful and influential theatre person in Edmonton."

In 1932 Haynes took on the role through which she made one of her great contributions to Alberta's developing theatrical community. She became the first dramatics supervisor for the Department of Extension at the University of Alberta, becoming a pivotal figure in its development.

Gwen Pharis (later Ringwood),[136] who was a secretary in the department and later became a successful playwright, described Haynes as "a force; a creative energy unleashed at a time when creativity was suspect and in a place where creativity was often ignored in the hope that it would go away."[137] She had, and frequently

Elizabeth Sterling Haynes.
"When the house darkens and the lights go up
We remember Elizabeth, offering up beauty in an ancient cut."
From a poem, *For Elizabeth*, by playwright Gwen Pharis Ringwood, 1952.
Photo: Edmonton City Archives

expressed, a strong sense of social justice. Her support for the Council for Canadian-Soviet Friendship made her a controversial figure, both in political and academic circles. It may have been one of the factors that stood in the way of her advancement at the university. So, I think, was the rough reality that Haynes was a strong, assertive woman in an era when people of her gender were expected to take a much more passive role. In any event, even though she was the drama department's driving force, she was forever limited to the status of a sessional lecturer, never given a faculty appointment.

In 1933, with Dr. E.A. Corbett, head of the Department of Extension, she founded the Banff School of Fine Arts and was its first dean. In 1936, the Carnegie Foundation grant that had funded her work at Banff ran out. The Department of Extension was by then under the direction of Donald Cameron. Her contract was not renewed. From then until he retired in 1969, Cameron took control of the school and ran it with an iron hand—and claimed most of the credit for its success. Unfairly, Haynes's contributions to the development of the Banff School were later downplayed.

With no job in Alberta, Elizabeth Haynes was invited by the province of New Brunswick to help develop the literary and dramatic phases of its adult and child educational program, and, in 1937, she moved east, alone. She returned to her husband and children in Edmonton in 1939 and resumed work as a sessional lecturer in the U of A's Department of Drama. When, her health failing, she and her husband left Edmonton for Toronto in 1957, many of the family possessions were sold at auction. One of her protégés, Edmonton businessman Isadore Gliener, sadly recalls watching a beautiful dining-room suite being sold for $90.

If you'll permit me a small rant,[138] I find it unfortunate that while Eva Howard, Betty Mitchell and Walter Kaasa have all been appropriately recognized with theatres named for them, Elizabeth Sterling Haynes has been disregarded. At the Banff Centre there have been buildings or facilities named for Donald Cameron, for E.A. Corbett and for Eric Harvie, who gave the centre exceptional financial support. The artists H.G. Glyde and Walter Phillips are recognized, as are ballet's Betty Farrally and Gweneth Lloyd. But there is no facility, building or program commemorating the essential contribution of Elizabeth Sterling Haynes. It is not too late to redress this injustice.

The oversight may have been because of her unfashionable (to some) left-wing leanings.[139] And it was almost certainly because of her very forceful personality, not endearing to the men who called the shots in those days. Elizabeth Sterling Haynes died in Toronto in 1957 at the age of 59. She is honoured only in Edmonton with the excellent, but local, Sterling Awards, created in 1987 by the Performing Arts Publicists Association.

The Leightons' book also recognizes the "master builder" Donald Cameron as one of the major architects of the Banff Centre. Although he had no background in the arts, he was an effective and relentless fund-raiser. Cameron wrote and self-published his own history of the centre, a 1977 volume titled *The Impossible Dream*. His determined efforts were vital to the development of the centre's impressive campus on Tunnel Mountain, overlooking the Banff townsite. Cameron was one of the many inspired, strong-willed people who, over the years, brought the centre to its outstanding status.

Dr. David S.R. Leighton, one of Canada's most distinguished arts administrators, took over the presidency of the Banff School of Fine Arts in 1970, following the retirement of Donald Cameron. Born in Regina, Leighton followed a Queen's University undergraduate degree with an MBA (with High Distinction) and a rare Doctorate in Business Administration from Harvard, where he first met fellow student Peter Lougheed. Before coming to Banff, he had developed a distinguished academic career, holding teaching appointments at, among others, Harvard, the University of Western Ontario and the University of London, England. A talented amateur violinist, he had a great understanding of and appreciation for the arts. But he was also a brilliant administrator, a gifted organizer, promoter and fund-raiser, and an inspired leader. He transformed the Banff School from a somewhat idyllic summer school of the arts into a respected international institution, with a growing campus offering programs year-round. Leighton also led the school through the process of gaining its autonomy from the University of Calgary, which had taken over its administration when it achieved its own autonomy in 1966, finally upgrading its status from the Calgary campus of the University of Alberta.

I first met Leighton in the early 1970s, when I was trying to build a supportive environment for filmmaking in Alberta. During those years I was organizing courses for screenwriters and conferences for filmmakers at the centre, and my then-wife, Ruth Bertelsen,[140] was

The Banff Centre Board of Governors, 1983. Standing (left to right): Claude Leblanc, Ralph Scurfield, Harley Hotchkiss, Susanne Palmer, Phillipe de Gaspé Beaubien, Larry Heisey, me. Seated (left to right): Grant Carlyle, Carolyn Tavender, Paul Fleck, John Poole. *Photo: The Banff Centre*

co-director of the Banff Centre writing program. Leighton was and is wonderfully earnest. His enthusiasm inspired staff and students, leading to the realization of many projects unique to Banff. He became a good friend and an essential partner in the creation of the Banff International Television Festival.

The year that Leighton came to Banff was also the year that a Commission on Education, chaired by University of Alberta Professor Walter Worth, launched a study of Alberta's educational needs. It became known as the Worth Commission. Leighton master-minded a plan that envisioned Banff as an autonomous institution with university status. The Worth Commission endorsed the idea, and by the time Peter Lougheed's government took power in August 1971, Leighton knew the ground for the realization of his dream was fertile. With strong encouragement from Jeanne (who had been a summer student at Banff during her university days),

Jeanne and Peter Lougheed cut a cake in the shape of the Jeanne and Peter Lougheed Building at the Banff Centre. *Photo: Fil Fraser*

Peter Lougheed was certainly receptive to the idea. The school was important to Jeanne, and she worked energetically behind the scenes to help it reach its highest potential. All the national arts institutions were in Ontario and Québec, she argued. It was time for Banff to go above and beyond Alberta, to establish a national presence here. It was the same persuasive energy she had brought to raising the professional status of the Alberta Ballet.

In 1977, after a great deal of groundwork, David Leighton was invited to make a presentation to a meeting of the full Alberta Cabinet. It was the first and last time that any outsider was invited to a meeting of Peter Lougheed's full Cabinet. "I thought that when they saw Leighton at the table," a smiling Lougheed told me years later when I interviewed him for this book, "the Cabinet would get the message that I wanted this thing to go ahead." Leighton, with Neil Armstrong and Ted Mills, made a compelling presentation. The result was the Banff Centre Act, establishing the Banff Centre for Continuing Education as an autonomous institution with university status. The object was to provide "to the public the opportunity of access to a broad range of learning experience with emphasis on the fine arts, management studies, language training and environmental training."[141]

I was greatly honoured when Peter Lougheed asked me to serve on the board of governors of the new institution, a post I held from 1980 to 1986. It was the best board I ever worked on, with distinguished Canadians such as Phillipe de Gaspé Beaubien, Larry Heisey, John Poole, Roger Beaulieu, Harley Hotchkiss and Carolyn Tavender, among others, as members. We're called governors *emeriti* now, but when we were there, we were caught up in the excitement of building the centre into one of the most important cultural institutions in Canada and the world. There were energetic discussions about the best way to make Banff an essential stop for the world's great artists. What I enjoyed most were the occasional meetings in which we put the agenda aside, and, at the urging of Québec media baron de Gaspé Beaubien, did a little "blue sky" thinking.

In 1975, a wily promoter, Québec's Serge Losique, became alert to Alberta's astonishing support for the arts. He was scanning all horizons for funds for the Montréal World Film Festival, which he planned to launch the following year. He came, of course, to see Horst Schmid. His pitch, that if Alberta would help fund his festival, he would locate a sidebar event at Banff, was not persuasive to a culture minister who already had the how-can-we-do-this bit in his teeth. Losique was like the sand in the oyster that produces a pearl, the pearl, in this case being the Banff International Television Festival. It wasn't long before Horst was on the phone to me.

"Why would we want to help some guy from down east?" he said. "Let's do it ourselves." We had already successfully launched the Alberta Film Festival, now run annually by AMPIA. Horst, a key player in securing the 1978 Commonwealth Games for Edmonton, wanted to establish a cultural festival as a permanent feature of the games. Part of it was to be the first Commonwealth Games International Film Festival. Unlike the first Alberta festival, organized on short notice in 1974, we wanted the Commonwealth event to be the springboard for an even larger annual Alberta event. We knew how to do it.

Schmid was able to provide funds to kick-start the venture, but now we wanted national participation. Bill Marsden, president of AMPIA at the time, and I went east in search of federal funds. Both the Montréal and Toronto festivals were receiving substantial federal support. We asked Jean Lefebvre, then director of the Film Festivals Bureau in the Department of the Secretary of State, for $50,000. After many presentations and pleas, we came away with $15,000. We were able to proceed with the Commonwealth Games Film Festival only because Horst Schmid was able to come up with $50,000 in lottery funds. He suggested, prudently, that it might make sense to set up a not-for-profit foundation to manage this and future festivals. The result was the New Western Film and Television Foundation.

We put together a strong team to launch the Commonwealth Games event. The officers of the foundation included Bill Marsden as vice-president, Banff Centre Arts Director Neil Armstrong as secretary-treasurer, and Frederik Manter, who was head of the Ottawa-based Canadian Film Institute. The ever-helpful Len Stahl was our executive secretary. I took on the role of president and was happy to be able to persuade Wayne Clarkson (who had launched the successful Toronto International Film Festival) to serve on a consulting basis, as the Commonwealth Games Film Festival director. The founding members of the foundation, led by Jeanne Lougheed, were a cross-section of outstanding, mostly western, Canadians. The members of the foundation (in alphabetical order)

With entertainment columnist Dave Billington at the Banff International Television Festival. *Photo: Banff International Television Festival*

were Charles A. Allard, Edmonton; R. Ronald Brown, Edmonton; Evelyn Cherry, Regina; Milton Fruchtman, Banff; Gunter Henning, Winnipeg; David Leighton, Banff; Andrew Little, MLA, Calgary; Sidney Newman, Toronto; Francoyse Picard, Ottawa; Tom Radford, Edmonton; G.R.A. Rice, Edmonton; Patti Robertson, Vancouver; Vic Rogers, Calgary; Charles N. Ross, Edmonton; John L. Schlosser, Edmonton; Jim Shaw, Edmonton; and Derek Whittal, Calgary.

The first Commonwealth Games International Film Festival was held in Edmonton, July 28 to August 2, 1978, in the five days immediately preceding the sporting events. The Canadian Film and Television Association, for the second time, held its annual convention

With Dinah Shore and David Leighton at the Banff International Television Festival. Peggy Leighton is in the background. *Photo: Banff International Television Festival*

in conjunction with an Alberta festival, with a large number of central Canadian film producers coming to see what we Albertans were up to. We invited filmmakers from every Commonwealth country to submit work on a non-competitive basis. No jury, no prizes. Our objective was to showcase what a world of non-American filmmakers could do.[142] A selection committee chaired by Dr. Jeremiah (Jerry) Ezekiel included, among others, Jim (who later officially changed his name to JR) Shaw, founder of the Shaw Cable empire, and the late Dave Billington, the much-appreciated entertainment writer for the *Edmonton Sun*. Billington, who was later to serve on the selection committee for the Banff Television Festival, is commemorated in the David Billington Award, awarded by AMPIA to distinguished members of the Alberta film community.[143] We received 150 entries from Commonwealth countries around the world: England, Scotland, New Zealand and Australia, of course, but also from India, Sri Lanka, Cyprus, Singapore, Fiji, Papua New

With David Leighton and Carrie Hunter at the Banff International Television Festival. *Photo: Banff International Television Festival*

Guinea, Jamaica, Bermuda, Guyana, Lesotho, Ghana and the Solomon Islands.

The festival was a huge success. Thousands turned out to see the films. Len Stahl made sure that everything ran smoothly, and we ended up with a surplus of some $15,000. Among the international fare the festival offered were the world premiere of Australian Peter Weir's *The Wave;* a powerful Indian production, *The Chess Players;* Britain's *The Naked Civil Servant;* a beautiful Maori film, *Pouihi...A Legend of New Zealand;* and, in the spirit of the Commonwealth Games, a series we created called *The Athlete in Film.* The respected Canadian director Alan King also previewed his new film, made for the CBC, *One Night Stand,* starring Chapelle Jaffe, Brent Carver and Dinah Christie.

There were evening galas at the Princess and Citadel theatres and afternoon screenings at the art gallery and the public library. Horst Schmid threw a gala dinner at Government House for members of

With filmmaker Gil Cardinal at the annual BBQ hosted by the Banff International Television Festival. *Photo: Fil Fraser*

the film community, including those who had come from across the Commonwealth to show their work.

Premier Peter Lougheed introduced my film *Marie Anne* at its Canadian premiere at the Princess Theatre.[144] For the opening night gala, I borrowed a stately Rolls Royce, which had once been owned by Debbie Reynolds, from my friend Jack Cohen, who owns a large Alberta auto parts operation and is a collector of fine cars. With Alan King and Chapelle Jaffe in the back seat, and Andrée Pelletier beside me as I drove, we arrived in high style. Happily, the partisan audience received the film warmly.

The festival's official program boldly invited participants to attend the first annual Banff International Festival of Films for Television at the Banff Centre, August 23 to September 1, 1979. Our conversations with Jean Lefebvre, who was personally supportive, made it clear to us that the federal government, already underwriting the Toronto and Montréal festivals, was not anxious to support another major film festival. Why not, he suggested, launch a television festival. We were reluctant. There was much on television that we didn't think belonged in any celebration of the arts. But we got Lefebvre's point—and came up with the idea of a "films for television" festival. All of the high-quality drama shown on television was shot on film in those days; films for television, we thought, would weed out the "junk," which was almost always shot on videotape.

Somewhere there exists a scrap of paper—we can't remember if it was the back of an envelope, a napkin or a menu—and the financial basis for the now world-famous Banff International Television Festival is written on it. Horst Schmid and I were having lunch in a German restaurant he liked on Edmonton's southside. The Commonwealth Games Festival successfully behind us, it was time to have a serious discussion about funding the Banff event. Horst, as mentioned, was also the minister in charge of allocating funds from the province's successful lottery to various arts, sports and community organizations.

"So," he said, writing the numbers on a scrap of paper, "if we take two percent from the Calgary Stampede and two percent from the Edmonton Exhibition, and, let me see, say one percent from the Historical Foundation, we could give five percent of the lottery money to the festival."

"Every year?" I asked.

"Yes!"

"How much is that?"

"This year, I think—about $250,000."

I wish we could find that piece of history, because, as much as anything, it symbolizes the unprecedented, unorthodox and creative way the Government of Alberta supported arts and culture through the 1970s and early 1980s.

With the New Western Film and Television Foundation in place, it was time to put together a solid structure to run the festival. The first, and for me, the essential element came when David Leighton agreed that the Banff Centre would co-sponsor the festival and that the event would take place at the centre's beautiful facilities on Tunnel Mountain. Together we decided to hire a Banff journalist, Carrie Hunter, to be the first executive director of the festival.

Leighton had worked with her on a number of projects and vouched for her administrative abilities.

I wanted Jerry Ezekiel, assistant director of the Film and Literary Arts Branch of Horst Schmid's Department of Culture, to be an integral part of the festival team. He had done stellar work as chair of the selection committee for the Commonwealth Games festival, and knew more about film than anyone else around. I asked Horst if he would second him to work with us on the festival. He suggested I write him, requesting Ezekiel's services. I asked Jerry if he would write an appropriate letter to the minister, which I would sign, formally requesting his full-time participation in the festival while remaining on the staff (and payroll) of the Department of Culture. Horst received my letter and sent it down the line for reply. It ended up on Jerry's desk. In the fullness of time the reply, written by Jerry and signed by Horst, came back to me, agreeing to my proposal. Jerry and I have since had many a chuckle about the wonderful ways of bureaucracy. He wrote two letters, both signed by others, which changed his life. He has been, ever since, an essential senior member of the festival team. As senior vice-president, he still selects the jury and oversees the selection of films to be entered in competition. In 2002 Jerry invited me to serve as president of the festival's international jury, an honour that, after all these years, surprised and touched me.

From the beginning, the festival was designed to celebrate the artistic best in television, from every part of the planet. We dispatched Carrie Hunter on an international search for films, delegates and jury members. But I took it upon myself to invite Sidney Newman, who started it all, now acknowledging that we *could* make movies in Alberta, to preside over the first Banff festival international jury. To join him, Carrie Hunter recruited American Melville Shavelson, a writer-director-producer with respectable credits, including *My World and Welcome to It* and *Ike*, the story of General Dwight D. Eisenhower; Katsuhiro Kurata, head of international operations for Japan's Nippon Television; Verity Lambert, then with Thames Television where she developed *Rumpole of the Bailey* and *The Naked Civil Servant;* and from France, Jean Louis Bertucelli, the respected director of many films, including *Cliffs of Clay*. That first jury set high standards for those that would follow.

Far from being dominated, as some worried, by American productions, the festival showcased films from all over the world. A respectable number of Canadian productions made the pre-selection cut. There were 200 entries, which Jerry Ezekiel and his team winnowed down to 65 to 70 hours of screen time for Sidney Newman and his jury to watch. They selected a beautiful, sensitive arts film from Italy as the first winner of the Grand Rockie.[145] *Ligabue* was the poignant story of the travails of a brilliant but eccentric Italian painter.

The first purpose of the festival was to celebrate excellence in television production, but the second was to provide an environment in which our filmmakers, Albertan and Canadian, could meet the world. The seminars, workshops and "pitching sessions," and the breakfasts, lunches and dinners are, in many ways, the most useful parts of the festival experience. A third objective, from the beginning just as important to me, was to make room at the event for film students from across the country. We invited film schools across the country to send students, whose Banff expenses would be covered by the festival in exchange for their doing some of the basic grunt work involved in its operation. They were given the opportunity to attend screenings, to mingle with the filmmakers and actors there and, most importantly, to take part in a wide-ranging series of educational seminars that were part of the event.

By the time of the first festival, many of the players in the Canadian film and television community had signed on, none more supportively than the CBC. We had the active participation of English TV head Don MacPherson, Radio Canada's Robert Roy and Vice-president André Lamy, who, from his Ottawa office, gave the green light for full CBC cooperation. I don't think Lamy knew that we would virtually gut the CBC's Calgary operation for equipment to provide much of that first festival's infrastructure. But the Calgary staff was enthusiastic about the event and have played a key role in it ever since. The festival attracted a who's who of the Canadian industry. Ted Kotcheff was there along with such luminaries as the NFB's Donald Brittain, lawyer-producer Michael Levine, critics Jamie Portman, Martin Knelman and Louise Cousineau, a young Michael Hirsh and new CFDC head Michael McCabe. Marcel Ophuls came from France, and the American contingent included producer/agent Hillard Elkins and casting director Mike Fenton. Some 200 delegates from North America, Europe, Britain, Austria, Italy, the Soviet Union and Japan came to Banff to be charmed by the scenery, and by the event. We were inventing a very new wheel; nothing like this had ever been attempted in Canada. We wanted a first-class event, a showcase for the world to see who we were and what we could do. Jeanne and Peter Lougheed and Horst Schmid pulled out all of the stops. The excitement surrounding that first event was unlike anything I have experienced, before or since.

Some of the programs, we knew, would come in on 35mm film, and the Banff Centre had no facility for screening them. Horst Schmid, again, came to the rescue. The Alberta Censor Board, based in Edmonton, was in the process of upgrading its facilities and had a pair of surplus 35mm projectors. It was not long before the projectors were on a truck bound for Banff and, after construction of a concrete platform to support them, they were installed in the centre's Eric Harvie Theatre, where they remain to this day.

That first festival threw the best party the Canadian television community had ever seen. Peter and Jeanne Lougheed hosted a magnificent dinner for all delegates. Joe Clark, newly elected prime minister, was having a Cabinet retreat at the Jasper Park Lodge, 180 miles (288 kilometres) over the mountains north of Banff. He agreed to send David MacDonald, the secretary of state whose portfolio covered the arts, to attend the banquet. We sent a single-engine Cessna tail-dragger to pick him up at the grass strip airport that served Jasper and bring him to the very tricky airport adjacent to the traffic circle just outside the town of Banff. The Banff airport, now closed, is at the base of Cascade Mountain. There were two windsocks, one at each end of the bumpy grass strip. Pilots were encouraged to make sure that the windsocks were both blowing in the same direction before they landed. Those who did not pay attention to the windsocks had been known to end up upside down on the runway, flipped by gusty winds coming around both sides of the mountain. I had flown in and out of the strip a number of times, until the nose wheel of a beautiful, retractable-gear Cessna Cardinal I was flying found a gopher hole, badly pranging the aircraft. It wasn't until years later, when I worked with David MacDonald on other projects, that he told me how much the trip terrified him.

We arranged for a pair of Québec journalists, Connie and Pierre Tadros, publishers of *CineMag*, then the Canadian Motion Picture and TV industry paper, to produce a daily newspaper during the festival. They did a fine job of reporting daily events through the 10 days of the festival, and a daily publication has been an ongoing part of the event ever since. Most of the ads in that first paper came from member companies of AMPIA. The official festival program featured a full-page ad from Fraser Film Associates, announcing that principal photography was about to begin for *Four's a Crowd*, based on W.O. Mitchell's play *Back to Beulah*. It was to be directed by Eric Till, who had come up with the title. Colleen Dewhurst and Carol Kane were in the cast and, with the help of casting director Mike Fenton, I was on the way to landing Susan Sarandon when the project collapsed, partly a victim of the fact that writers are often too close to their own material to write a workable screenplay.

The festival was a critical success, but like my movies, did not do nearly as well financially. I spent a lot of time aggressively fundraising, and while we got a splendid response in Alberta, the rest of Canada was a hard sell. We had two budgets, one based on money in the bank or firmly committed; another, a dream budget, based on what we reasonably thought we could raise. Carrie Hunter, as executive director, controlled the day-to-day spending. I asked her, almost daily, if we were on budget, and she said yes. Years later she admitted to me that she was working on the dream budget, not on the cash budget, expecting that all of the Canadian sources that helped to fund central Canadian festivals would come through. They did not, and the festival ended up with a substantial deficit.

When the numbers came in, I was devastated. I offered to resign, and Mary LeMessurier, Horst's successor as Minister of Culture, accepted. David Leighton took over as president of the foundation and chair of the festival, and he needs to be credited as the major saviour of the event. Every other festival in Canada operated in the red—the Montréal festival has rarely, if ever, met its budget. It would have been shameful to let such a successful initiative die. Again, Jeanne and Peter Lougheed made the critical decision. They

The 2002 jury for the Banff International Television Festival, which I chaired. Left to right: Russell Honeyman, Zimbabwe/Netherlands; me; Deborah Stewart, US; Phillip Jones, UK; Anne Georget, France; Ikeo Masuru, Japan; Glenda Hambly, Australia; and Jerry Ezekiel, Banff Festival senior vice-president. *Photo: Banff International Television Festival*

supported Leighton and Hunter who, with the help of a great many others, brought the festival back to life, not in 1980, but in 1981. In subsequent years the festival has broken records every time it was held. Today, close to 2000 delegates attend every year.

Over the years, the praise for the festival has been gratifying, as the following quotes show:

> It's not just our business to broadcast good television; we're in the business of creating it as well. And we can't think of a better way to do that than supporting the mandate of what we consider the finest gathering of creative talent and broadcasting opportunity in the world here at the Banff Television

Festival.—*Bill Harris, Vice-president, Production, A&E Networks, USA*

The Banff Television Festival has a unique quality: unlike so many of these occasions, everyone was very relaxed, all pretensions were dropped and people were very much themselves.—*Olivia Lichtenstein, Executive Producer, Documentaries and History, BBC, UK*

The Banff Television festival is the best of them because of its purity. It is not a program market in disguise, and it is divorced of global politics. The central issue at Banff is: What are the world's best programs.—*Les Brown, Journalist/author Founder, Television Business International*

In our very difficult business, with more and more satellites operating and the standard of broadcasting inevitably falling—because there isn't enough to go around—it's marvellous to have festivals like Banff which show how very high the peaks are.—*Peter Ustinov*

Ustinov is just one of many world figures who have participated in and been honoured by the festival. A highlight list includes Bob Newhart, *60 Minutes* producer Don Hewitt, Peter Bogdanovitch, Gregory Peck, Ted Turner (he brought his then-wife, Jane Fonda), Dinah Shore, Leslie Nielsen, Walter Cronkite, Bea Arthur, John Candy, Steven Bochco, Jonathan Winters, Tom Jackson, JR Shaw, Steve Allen, Dame Edna (aka Barry Humphries), Channel Four's Sir Michael Grade, Hagood Hardy, Barbara Frum, Lorne Green, Pierre Juneau (after whom the Juno Awards are named), k.d. lang (who had delegates standing on tables at the barbecue), Megan Follows, Joe Clark, David Suzuki and, of course, Jeanne Lougheed, Peter Lougheed and Horst Schmid.

I am grateful for the efforts of all those who picked up the pieces and developed the festival to its present prominence. And most especially to David Leighton, who really saved the festival after its first-year stumble. My successors have treated me with great generosity. I am a lifetime honorary director. At the second festival, in 1981, the directors presented me with a specially commissioned Roy Leadbeater sculpture called *Inspiration*. The inscription reads, "For his dedication as founder of the Banff Television Festival."

In 1984 the festival outgrew the facilities of the Banff Centre, changed its dates from fall to spring and moved to the picturesque Banff Springs Hotel. Today it has the full and generous support of all sectors of the Canadian industry and many key players, including A&E, of the American industry. The governments of Alberta and Canada have continued their support. The Banff International Television Foundation, in addition to operating the festival in Banff, now also manages separate International Congresses of Science and History Producers in countries around the world. The Banff Centre and its sister organization, the Banff International Television Festival, are, and should be, celebrated as two of Canada's national treasures.

Another international event, begun on David Leighton's watch but completed in 1985, was the Banff International Symposium of the Arts. It symbolized, more than anything I can think of, the reach of Leighton's vision. With Pierre Trudeau as honorary president and School of the Arts Director Neil Armstrong as chair, the symposium brought to reality an idea that had first been broached in 1978. It began with plans to celebrate the 50th anniversary of the centre, when the board agreed to proceed with a planning conference involving artists and leaders from a dozen countries representing world constituencies. Neil Armstrong went on a 29-country tour, making sure to include many of the underdeveloped areas of the planet. The result, in April 1985, saw more than 100 artists from 38 different countries spend an intense week at Banff, speaking to their concerns as individual artists, not as representatives of their countries or of any ideology. They were challenged to think about the role of the arts in addressing world issues and crises, and about their role as artists.

The Banff Symposium was unique. "By bringing together from around the world artists and workers for the arts to discuss their role

Paul Fleck with David and Peggy Leighton. *Photo: Fil Fraser*

in mitigating today's world crisis, the symposium asked how artists might come in from the margins of society to society's centre. It asked how the cultural degradation, which is part of the world crisis, can be halted by the action of artists themselves."[146] What was not in doubt was the importance of the arts in world affairs.

"All art," the symposium report asserted, "involves values and value judgements communicated through the art form. ...If artists, by the nature of their work, are placed at the centre of humanity's non-material cultures, and if this area of human activity at present represents an under-used resource in the world's affairs compared with its material culture, it follows that there exists an additional power or influence which could be exerted to mitigate the world's crisis. This is Art Power."[147]

At its final plenary the symposium decided to send a telegram to the secretary-general of the United Nations, recommending an

International Year of the Arts. The message to Javier Perez de Cuellar, read

> In view of the particular significance of the arts in expressing and nurturing human values and needs, and at the request of 119 artists, arts administrators and others concerned for the arts from 38 countries assembled at the International Symposium on the Arts…their unanimous conviction [is] that artists should be enabled to make a fuller contribution to the serious problems which face the world.

It was a richly stimulating gathering. One of the most popular features of the symposium was the nightly open house for participants in a lounge atop Lloyd Hall on the Banff campus. Drinks and conversation flowed freely, and every night the world's great problems were seriously discussed, if not solved. During one of these sessions I struck up a conversation that led to my taking a festival of Canadian films, which I described in the chapter on making movies, to the Soviet Union. Moscow film director Valentin K. Chernykh told me that many well-made films, by himself and by many of his colleagues, had never been released or seen by the public in the Soviet Union. But things were changing. Barely three weeks earlier Mikhail Gorbachev had been elected general-secretary of the Central Committee of the Communist Party of the Soviet Union. The terms *glasnost* and *perestroika* had yet to enter our western consciousness and language, but Chernykh was already hopeful. During one somewhat lubricated conversation he said, "You should come with some films to the Soviet Union." "Sure," I said, "I would love to," not for a minute thinking that anything would come of it, but it led to a tour of Russia in 1987, which I describe in Chapter 8.

Just as important and, as it turned out, more enduring than the International Symposium on the Arts, was the Banff International String Quartet Competition, launched in 1983 as part of the celebration of the centre's 50th anniversary. The event drew entries from all over the world, and from the finest young string players of that generation. The string quartet is, in my view, the most challenging and most rewarding of musical forms. When four musicians play as one, the impact can be transporting. I remember talking, for a CKUA interview, with the winners of that first event. The Colorado Quartet, four young women who named their ensemble after their school, were stunned by their success, already getting advice about how to manage what was sure to be a promising career. "Stay together!" one of their mentors urged them. And they have, becoming internationally celebrated for the depth and intensity of their playing. The winners of the competitions, held every three years, read like a who's who of world string quartets. The Banff International String Quartet Competition is one of the world's leading musical competitions.

Many other noteworthy programs were launched at Banff during the Leighton years. The celebrated author W.O. Mitchell led a writing program that helped to develop some of the best Canadian writers of that generation. And Tom Peacocke headed a drama program that inspired young actors at Banff, as he inspired them at the University of Alberta.

David Leighton, who had contributed so much to Banff, resigned in 1982 to become president of the organizing committee of the 1988 Calgary Olympic Games. He left what he described as "the best job in the world" to meet the irresistible challenge of running the games. He is currently the chair of the Board of Trustees of the National Arts Centre, still exerting a strong, positive influence on the arts in Canada.

Dr. Paul Fleck, who succeeded Leighton, had, like him, been on the faculty of the University of Western Ontario at London, a popular English professor. Later he survived a rocky interval as head of the Ontario College of Art, the Toronto institution famous for its hippie hi-jinks during the '60s and early '70s. Paul Fleck and the Banff Centre were a good match. Building on the outstanding work of Elizabeth Sterling Haynes, Donald Cameron and David Leighton, with a strong infrastructure in place, Fleck concentrated on enhancing and solidifying the centre's arts programs. He and his wife Polly, a poet, became fast friends with my wife Gladys and me, and we still relish the memory of holidays we spent together travelling in France or house-boating on BC's Shushwap lakes. Paul Fleck died, too soon, of cancer in 1992. Tragically, his successor, Graeme

McDonald, also died of cancer less than a decade later, in 2001. The Banff Centre, now in its 70th year, is under the direction of a new president, Mary Hofstetter, who has already demonstrated a strong commitment to the arts, and the centre continues its remarkable development.

When the centre decided it needed a new building to replace Critch Hall, the photography building that had burned down a few years earlier, and to house the developing new media programs, the board decided to name it for the Lougheeds. We all applauded the suggestion that it be named the Jeanne and Peter Lougheed Building. During our July 1985 board meeting, we invited the Lougheeds to lunch to give them the news. We had managed to keep it a secret from them, even from Peter's highly effective radar. The premier was so overcome, Jeanne says, he leaned over and said, "You speak first." He needed a little time to compose himself, one of the few times when he was, albeit briefly, at a loss for words.

By the time we dedicated the building, November 18, 1988, I was off the board, a governor *emeritus* of the centre. A plaque in the lobby of the Eric Harvie Theatre lists all of the governors *emeriti* of the centre. Every now and then I walk by to see if my name is still there, and to remember one the richest periods in my life.

Chapter 10

The Alberta Conundrum

Alberta is a province full of contradictions. Edmonton is university, intellectuals, civil servants and blue-collar workers. Calgary is financial and decision-making executive power, white collars and cowboy boots. Business is more important than culture. Edmonton's river valley has been developed into a series of attractive parks, including large areas left in their natural state. Calgary's Bow and Elbow rivers are lined with homes and highways. The chinook-challenged city to the north, "Redmonton" to many Calgarians, elects Liberals—as I write this the only two, federally, from the province. The southern financial capital, Joe Clark's bravado election victory notwithstanding, is solid for the Alliance. Provincially, the NDP gets elected in Edmonton, never in Calgary. The farther south you go in the province, the more right-wing the politics. Stereotypes abound. The term "redneck Albertan" still sticks and stings. The fact that Jim Keegstra and Aryan Nations leader Terry Long founded communities of support here underlines the contradictions between the north and the south.

The differences, and the rivalry, between Edmonton and Calgary are deeply rooted, often intense and sometimes bitter. If you probe enough, leading Calgarians still retain an underlying resentment that, when the province was formed in 1905, Edmonton became both the provincial capital and the site of the provincial university, unlike neighbouring Saskatchewan, created at the same time as Alberta. There, Regina became the capital, and Saskatoon got the university. (It is interesting to speculate how Alberta might have evolved had government and education been divided between the two major cities.) Heated arguments develop over whether recent provincial governments give more cultural support to Calgary than to Edmonton. An Edmonton entrepreneur I know, a major supporter of the arts, goes red in the face when he talks about how he thinks the government has heavily favoured Calgary in the grants it makes, and has made, to major arts institutions. We work out some of the rivalry in sports: on the ice between the Oilers and Flames, on the gridiron between the Eskimos and Stampeders. The names, if you're into such things, tell you something—friendly Eskimos and Oilers in the north, aggressive Stampeders and Flames to the south. Competitive tension can be healthy, but, in many ways, we live in a province divided.

Jenny Belzberg, whom I first met when she joined the board of governors of the Banff Centre, is one of Calgary's influential women. A current trustee of the National Arts Centre and a long-time supporter of the Calgary Philharmonic Orchestra, she agrees that there are distinct cultural differences between the two cities. Part of the reason, she points out, is that Edmonton has always had a greater ethnic mix compared to Calgary's more dominant Anglo-Saxon majority. In the north, early support for the arts came principally from the interactive mix of ethnic communities, most predominantly from immigrants from the Ukraine, Germany and other central and eastern European countries. They were never the discounted minority in Edmonton that they were in Calgary and, Winnipeg excepted, in other major Canadian centres. One of my favourite pictures, found in the Provincial Archives of Alberta, is of a family on their way to a homestead somewhere in north-central Alberta. They are riding on a covered wagon piled high with all of their worldly goods, pulled by a lone, tired horse. Hanging out the back of the wagon is a piano. In my mind I imagine a pioneer family for whom music was as important as bread on the table and for whom it was important to help set the cultural tone in their adopted land.

Edmonton, the most northerly of Canada's major cities, has a long cold winter—and people have to do something to keep their spirits up. Note that Winnipeg, also devoid of midwinter chinooks, and with a similar ethnic mix, also has a lively theatre community. In Calgary, Vancouver, Toronto and Montréal, it is a lot easier to avoid or ignore the weather.

There's another thing. Part of the reason the arts were late in taking root in Calgary, I would argue, are the ever-present, ever-inviting mountains. You can feel them even when you can't see them. It's so easy to slip out of town and, within a couple of hours, lose yourself in some of the most spectacular scenery in the world. It is a city where it's almost ridiculously easy to be out of town—skiing, hiking, snowmobiling, fishing, boating or otherwise goofing off. The drive into the mountains is itself a treat.

Calgary's late coming to the arts table also has a lot to do with the easy accessibility of the Banff Centre. There was no pressing need to develop cultural facilities in Calgary when Banff was a relatively short drive away. Calgarians love the summer festival, the music, the dance, the theatre offered at the centre. They almost think of Banff as an extension of the city, like the mountains, part of *their* back yard. Canmore, at the entrance to Banff National Park, is close to becoming one of the city's playground communities, where many well-to-do citizens maintain vacation homes. And as the Banff Centre gained international prominence through the 1970s and 1980s, much of its private-sector support, and many of its board members, came from Calgary.

For a time, Calgary was called the largest American city outside of the US, with the major oil companies setting up their Canadian operations in the foothills centre. A large part of the reason for the difference between Edmonton and Calgary may be in just that fact. For years Calgary hosted a substantial, but largely transient, executive and middle management population. People were transferred in and out by the real head offices in Dallas or Houston. The Americans loved and contributed to the romanticism of the "wild west" Calgary Stampede, with its bullriding and chuck wagon races. The city almost felt like home to them. Of course, direct flights could get them stateside in less time than it takes to travel to Toronto or Montréal, and a growing fleet of corporate jets gave top-echelon honchos all the travel options they could want.

As a consequence, it is Calgary's, not Edmonton's, international airport that has become the western hub, the gateway to international travel, leaving the northern facility in an ongoing struggle to stave off feeder status. Direct flights from Edmonton to Europe and to American cities such as Los Angeles, Seattle and San Francisco have mainly become a thing of the past. You go through Calgary, whether you like it or not.

Some of the Americans stayed and have become good citizens. Ted and Lola Rozsa, for example, who came to Calgary from the US in 1949, are a striking example of a transplanted family contributing substantially and creatively to their new community. The family, through the Rozsa Centre Recital Hall, and through substantial contributions to the Calgary Philharmonic and the Calgary Opera, are among the city's leading arts patrons. Ted Rozsa won the 2002 Edmund Bovey Award for leadership support of the arts. But when I'm in Calgary, I still almost feel like I'm in the US. The architecture and the shopping all seem redolent of big-city America.

I'm sure I am not alone in wondering why Alberta's financial and energy capital, the home of its head offices, is Calgary, not Edmonton. Most of the oil is in the north. The discovery that really put Alberta on the financial map was a figurative stone's throw away, on the outskirts of Leduc. And today, the big oil action is even farther north, in Fort McMurray, with Edmonton as its self-proclaimed gateway. Edmonton is the seat of government and the home of the province's major university—if it were also the province's financial capital, it could have been as powerful in the West as Toronto and Montréal are in the East.

Maybe it *was* just about golf.

Peter Lougheed told me the following story, which may or may not be apocryphal. A senior executive of Imperial Oil, the major player in the 1947 Leduc strike, just didn't like Edmonton's Mayfair Golf Club. He preferred a Calgary club with spectacular mountain views and decided to locate the company's western head office in the southern city. Whatever its inspiration, the decision profoundly affected the shape of the province's economy as its base moved from agriculture to energy. Calgary became Alberta's, *and* western Canada's, financial capital. Today only Toronto hosts more national head offices.

It was some time after Edmonton had developed as the province's cultural capital that Calgary decided it too should have a significant cultural infrastructure. I know that this is, to some extent, simplistic. But it's a perception that many of the people I talked with in Calgary's arts community tend to accept. A number of people told me that for a long, long time, getting money for the arts in Calgary was a hard, hard sell. Not that they didn't try—and not that the city did not have a respectable history of amateur theatre, beginning in the 1930s with Betty Mitchell's Workshop 14.

Mitchell, in some ways, was to early theatre in Calgary what Elizabeth Sterling Haynes had been to Edmonton. She has been appropriately recognized in the naming of the Betty Mitchell Theatre in the Calgary Jubilee Auditorium. When William Aberhart's Social Credit government incorporated the fine arts into the province's high school curriculum in 1935, Mitchell became one of the first teachers of high school drama, at Western Canada High School. In 1937 she was appointed chair of the Provincial Committee on Drama for the Alberta Department of Education. Three of her students—Kaye Grieve, Betty Valentine and Frank Glenfield—created Workshop 14, named after the number on the classroom door in which they held rehearsals. Workshop 14, for which Mitchell was a talented director, went on to win many awards in the Dominion Drama Festivals, at the time the hallmark of Canadian theatrical excellence. In 1964 Workshop 14 merged with the Musicians and Actors Club to form MAC 14, renamed Theatre Calgary in 1968 and going on to become Alberta's second professional theatre.

So there were people interested in the arts in Calgary, but their history is a story of struggle. Theatre Calgary, and later Alberta Theatre Projects, produced good work, but for decades they worked out of inadequate facilities, lurching from one financial crisis to another. The Calgary Philharmonic Orchestra, the 30-year-old Opera Calgary and, since its move to the city in 1990, the Alberta Ballet have all made important contributions to the cultural life of Calgary. But while Joe Shoctor was successfully launching the province's first professional theatre in Edmonton and Edmonton added insult to injury by becoming not only the City of Champions, but Festival City as well, dedicated arts supporters in Calgary met with frustration after frustration trying to catch up. They simply could not get serious financial support from their city government, their corporate offices or their citizens.

Sandra LeBlanc, like Jenny Belzberg a dedicated supporter of the arts, recalls meeting after meeting of the Calgary Regional Arts Foundation that she helped found in the mid-60s. Walter Kaasa, newly appointed Cultural Affairs Coordinator in the Manning government, was personally supportive, travelling to Calgary on his own time, but there were few resources available at the provincial level.

Lucille Wagner and Douglas Riske, who later founded Alberta Theatre Projects (ATP), were there too. There is a 1970s letter in the Provincial Archives of Alberta from Jock Osler, then-chair of ATP's Board of Directors, pleading with Peter Lougheed for life support. The theatre, the letter said, was about to go under. The support came through, but the crisis was indicative of how hard it was for Calgary theatre to survive.

What they needed, what they dreamed of, were decent facilities from which they could launch a professional theatre company. "It took 16 years for us to go from dream to reality," Sandra LeBlanc says. The reality is the Calgary EPCOR Centre for the Performing Arts.

As I get on in life, I am learning more and more about the tricks that memory can play. I talked with many Calgarians and heard many, sometimes conflicting, stories about the origins of the

EPCOR Centre for the Performing Arts. It is not clear just when a campaign that had been spinning its wheels for nearly a generation finally found traction. George Crawford, a Calgary lawyer and businessman who had practised with Glenbow Museum founder Eric Harvie, recalls a meeting at the Calgary Ranchmen's Club.[148] People attending the meeting, including himself, he told me, were jealous of Edmonton's progress in the arts, and particularly of the Citadel Theatre.

Jealousy may have been part of the motivation. Civic pride is a more positive expression. The traction may have begun to grab when Peter Lougheed let it be known to the growing number of Calgarians who were lobbying him that, if they could get the private sector to step up to the plate, his government would match their contribution. Many people, with a variety of motivations, worked hard to bring the EPCOR Centre for the Performing Arts into existence.

A team of extraordinary women led the way, three women in particular—Martha Cohen, Sandra LeBlanc, Vera Swanson—whom, having met them, I list in alphabetical order so as not to give any one prominence over the others. They worked together to persuade, to cajole, bully and browbeat the city's affluent citizenry, the city, and provincial and federal governments for their support. Martha Cohen had the fund-raising clout, Sandra LeBlanc had the administrative skills and Vera Swanson had an iron will that never accepted "no" as an answer.

I had known Sandra LeBlanc during my tenure on the board of governors of the Banff Centre, when her physician husband, Claude, was a fellow board member. As I prepared to write this book, Jenny Belzberg invited Martha Cohen to her home, where, over a cup of tea, she told me how she and her colleagues started their fund-raising at home with their husbands. As I drove her home, she told me she still felt a great deal of humility over the naming of the Martha Cohen Theatre in the Performing Arts Centre.

I called Vera Swanson out of the blue. Her late husband, Frank G. Swanson, had been a long-time publisher of the *Calgary Herald*. I found her in the garden of her home in the foothills west of

Calgary. It was just after the huge snowfall that struck the Calgary area in the spring of 2002, but she had cleared a bed adjacent to a south wall and was busy planting the first of her spring annuals. I spent a pleasant hour listening to her account of the challenges they faced in persuading Calgary's elite that the arts were worth supporting. She had been described as the toughest of the three, with a never-take-no-for-an-answer determination to seek out every avenue that might lead to a contribution. She insisted I talk with George Crawford, who had been an early supporter of the project.

With her explicit directions, I drove south to meet Crawford at his ranch near Priddis. There was still enough snow left to make the driving a bit tricky as I followed his truck up a winding road to a beautiful ranch house. Crawford and his wife, in their 80s and in remarkably good health, were gracious in receiving me. While she went out to feed the horses, he poured a drink and confirmed the dedication of Cohen, LeBlanc and Swanson to the arts. They were the key players who literally willed the performing arts centre into existence. After they had winkled all possible support from their husbands and their friends, they attacked the nearly impenetrable corporate head offices. By the time they were finished they had raised $16 million. Harry Cohen, Jack Singer, the Max Bell Foundation, the Carthy Foundation in memory of Mrs. Margaret Mannix and many others made significant contributions.

But it was still a hard sell. Their first objective was to build a facility for theatre. It was only after much discussion, some would say wrangling, that the Calgary Philharmonic Orchestra agreed to come into the scheme, but not as a part owner. They agreed to be a renter of space in what was taking shape as a performing arts centre. The federal and provincial governments promised support, but City Hall was reluctant. Calgary Mayor Rod Sykes flatly refused to support the project. When all attempts at persuasion failed, the women went around him, eventually getting a majority of council members on side. Sykes finally agreed not to stand in their way and physically left the city council chambers when the vote to support the centre was passed.

The budget, faced with the renovation of a block of heritage buildings in downtown Calgary, ballooned to more than $80 million,

Calgary arts fund-raiser Sandra LeBlanc main-streeting with Peter Lougheed. It was on a walk like this that he told her that the projected cost of the Calgary Performing Arts Centre was too high. *Photo: Government of Alberta*

double the cost of Edmonton's Citadel. At one point during a political campaign, Lougheed took Sandra LeBlanc with him on a walk down Calgary's Stephen Avenue Mall. Between main-streeting handshakes, he let her know that, if she wanted continued government support, she would have to cut the budget by $10 million. One of the first things she cut was the pipe organ. Vera Swanson, who subsequently organized the International Organ Festival in Calgary, would have none of it. She went out and single-handedly raised the money to build one of the country's more spectacular pipe organs. But the necessary cuts were made, and in the end, the province kicked in close to $50 million. Far more, some Edmontonians complain, than was offered the Citadel Theatre.

It was by the force of will of a small, determined group that the Centre for the Performing Arts opened its doors on September 15, 1985, just as Peter Lougheed was about to step down as premier.

The centre is the home of Theatre Calgary, Alberta Theatre Projects, One Yellow Rabbit and the Calgary Philharmonic Orchestra, as well as the Calgary International Children's Festival, Vera Swanson's International Organ Festival and the Esther Honens Calgary International Piano Competition. It is a busy place, and Calgary is rightly proud. But getting there was not easy. And the potential demise of the Calgary Philharmonic Orchestra places the centre's operating budget in jeopardy. As I write this, the orchestra has filed for bankruptcy protection. A major supporter of the arts in Calgary told me in May 2003 that she was not optimistic about the long-term survival of the orchestra, and a June concert was cancelled. But the 2003–04 season has been announced.

There are Albertans who dream of bringing the two cities together. The idea of a high-speed rail link joining them still generates periodic waves of support. You could turn them into one market, they argue, perhaps even one community. You could travel downtown to downtown in less time and in considerably more comfort than it takes to drive from Scarborough to Mississauga in Toronto's GTA, or to Bay Street from any of the bedroom communities to which the denizens of that financial capital retreat every night. What a powerhouse the two cities together could create! Though many others disagree with me, I think it is more the Alberta conundrum than economics that gets in the way.

*Please, Lord send me another oil boom
and I promise not to piss this one away.*

—Sign in the office of one-time Alberta oil magnate and
Liberal leader, now Senator Nick Taylor [149]

Chapter 11

Culture Shock II:
The End of an Era

When the lights went down on Alberta's truly golden age of the arts, it felt like we had come to the end of a fairy tale, and that we weren't about to live happily ever after. Budget and program cuts began while Lougheed was still in power. Anyone who remembers the inflation of the early 1980s, when bank interest rates climbed above 20 percent, knew that Alberta's years of open chequebook spending had to end. The impact of the collapse of Alberta's oil economy on the province's economy was devastating.[150] In a startling shift of public perception, Lougheed was actually booed at the Edmonton Coliseum on the night of September 18, 1984, when he was introduced at a hockey game between Team Canada and Sweden.[151]

The first casualty was the International Aid Financial Assistance program in which the province matched money raised by charitable groups to help people in underdeveloped countries. In its first year, 1975–76, the program saw Alberta match $2,301,000 raised by church and community groups with $1,995,626 for a total of $4,296,626. By 1981–82 the government contributed $7,049,819, which with NGO fund-raising of $8,895,773 saw an impressive $15,945,592 given to international aid. But the Department of Culture report for 1982–83 makes no mention of the fund. It had disappeared without a trace.

Through the early 1980s, basic cultural budgets remained relatively stable. In addition, the government made a number of extraordinary grants, including $4 million for Mel Hurtig's *Canadian Encyclopedia*, and $47.3 million towards the construction of the $80.9 million EPCOR Centre for the Performing Arts.

But as the decade passed, the erosion of Department of Culture budgets was a sad tale of belt tightening and changing priorities. From a peak of $80,969,112 in 1979–80 (which included the 75th anniversary celebrations), the annual budget began a painful decline, as the department's annual reports show:

1980–81 $54,769,690
1981–82 $42,218,976
1982–83 $77,733,298, but that included renovations of the Jubilee Auditoria,[152] leaving just $34,471,923 for departmental operations.
1983–84 $50,740,668, but now additional programs were being transferred in from other departments.

In 1987 the department was reorganized as Alberta Culture and Multiculturalism, with budgets stretched to cover programs transferred in from other departments, remaining around the $50-million mark.

What began as a slow fade governed by economic realities became an over-the-waterfall drop in support for the arts. There was a blunt change in attitude when Ralph Klein became the premier in December 1992. The Department of Culture and Multiculturalism disappeared. The new minister, Gary Mar, announced that "Alberta Community Development…was the newest ministry of the provincial government…refocusing its activities from specific recreation and cultural programs to the broader community development perspective."[153] Folded into Community Development were the Alberta Human Rights Commission,[154] the Premier's Council on the Status of Persons with Disabilities,[155] the Alberta Multiculturalism Commission, the Alberta Alcoholism and Drug Abuse Commission (AADAC), the Glenbow Foundation, the Alberta Order of Excellence Awards (the Alberta Achievement Awards disappeared) and the Government House Foundation. Previously separate funding agencies—the Alberta Arts Foundation, which focused on support for the visual arts, and the Alberta Performing Arts Foundation—were folded, along with a handful of other programs, into the new Alberta Foundation for the Arts (AFA). The new foundation also assumed funding for writing and other programs that had had their own envelope under the former Department of Culture. All lost prestige, dollars and clout.

Grumbling by right-wing, rural Alberta MLAs about Lougheed's pragmatic, centrist policies had been sternly held at bay during his regime. But it was no secret that this segment of the electorate was not overjoyed by the red Tory government in Edmonton. Just as there was a dramatic change in mindset when Lougheed took power from the rural-based Social Credit government, attitudes toward the arts took a sharp turn toward the negative when Ralph Klein, "dancing with the ones that brung him,"[156] took power. The changing of the guard came on December 5, 1992, when Ralph Klein and the rural Alberta caucus defeated Nancy Betkowski for the leadership of the Progressive Conservative Party and the premiership of the province. Betkowski, who had been Minister of Education, had a strong urban base, particularly in Edmonton. She was ahead of Klein by 16,393 to 16,292 votes after the first ballot. But with other candidates in the race, she came short of the necessary 50 percent + 1 majority needed to win. The run-off election pitted Betkowski directly against Klein. The rules allowed candidates to sell memberships right up to the last minute of the vote, not in the polling booth, but not very far away, stretching the envelope of democracy in Alberta to new dimensions. Ken Kowalski, MLA for Barrhead Westlock and later Speaker of the House, led a group of rural MLAs that offered to bring in the vote for Klein. And that was it. Rural Albertans turned out to support the populist, right-leaning Klein. He won in a 60–40 landslide.

"Almost immediately," according to Melville L. McMillan and former Lougheed Cabinet member Allan A. Warrack, "the severity of the province's fiscal difficulties emerged to become the focus of attention with a January budget revision announcing an extraordinarily large and unexpectedly high deficit. …The provincial government's response…outlined a plan to eliminate the deficit within four years by cutting expenditures 20 percent without increasing taxes."[157]

The steep slide in arts funding in the name of the deficit was a disaster for the province's artistic and cultural communities. Economies rise and fall and people adjust. The real culture shock was in the change in attitude toward the arts. The winding down— of the matching grant programs, the Alberta Performing Arts Foundation, the Alberta Motion Picture Development Corporation and scores of less visible, but important, arts funding programs— was almost gleeful in its bloody mindedness. The right-wing, given definition and voice by Preston Manning's federal Reform Party, seemed pleased to see the end of such generous spending on *special interest groups*. The Alberta Foundation for the Arts, with its budget frozen since 1988, became the sole source of arts funding. All of its money comes from lotteries.

An *Edmonton Sun* reporter, Paul Bucci, quoted Klein talking about sports funding: "It would be nice to get out of it. I don't know if we ever can. It's just like the arts. I don't know if we ever can. But the less we can spend on these things the better."[158] Klein has never been a supporter or consumer of the arts. In his book *King Ralph*, journalist Don Martin reports that, "The last stage show Colleen [Klein] can recall attending with her husband was *Evita*. The last movie was *E.T.*—in its original release."[159]

George Melnyk, one of the founders of NeWest Press and a former executive director of the Alberta Foundation for the Literary Arts, in an essay in *The Trojan Horse: Alberta and the Future of Canada*, wrote, "On May 26, 1994, the *Calgary Herald* published a cartoon titled 'No Funding for Risqué Art Says Government Minister' in which a character from the 'Purity Panel' looks at an abstract painting—sweat streaming from his face—exclaims in a horrified voice, 'Is that a breast?!!' "[160] As *Edmonton Journal* columnist and author Mark Lisac put it, "The government changed more of its beliefs and operations than at any time since the Conservatives had won their first election in 1971."[161] "As a symbolic act of cost cutting and the creation of a lean and mean Cabinet, Ralph Klein amalgamated ministries in 1993. He closed down Culture as a separate entity,"[162] wrote Melnyk.

The most devastating attacks came in 1994. In both its brutal, unilateral finality and its naked, get-the-message symbolism, the province's move to get out of broadcasting reversed 67 years of public policy. The privatization of ACCESS, Alberta's pioneering educational television network, was made somewhat palatable when CHUM-TV's Moses Znaimer agreed to take over the station and to maintain its educational focus. Television was one thing, but the abrupt and scandalous amputation of funding to Canada's oldest public broadcaster, CKUA, was like taking a meat cleaver to the arts. This was carnage.

The party was over. The attack on the deficit was not at the top of Ralph Klein's agenda. It was the agenda.

For me, the slide, which started during the Lougheed administration, was personal. In 1981, bank interest rates climbed to more than 20 percent. Jack Wynters and I (he was at the time the only other producer making feature films in Alberta) had joined forces to try to mount a production called *4x4*, a chase film through the mountains starring, among others, *M*A*S*H*'s Jamie Farr. We had raised $750,000 of the $2.1 million budget when the arithmetic became depressingly clear. In the best of worlds, the cash flow from a feature film's box office receipts begins two or three years after the film has been completed. Under the then "capital cost allowance," investors in film were allowed to borrow 80 percent of the money, put up 20 percent in cash and write off 100 percent in the current taxation year. The expectation was, of course, that proceeds from the film would pay off the bank loan. Even if the film just broke even, the investors would be way ahead. But suddenly, interest rates for film ventures shot up to the 23 percent to 25 percent range. An Andersen accountant might have found a way, but it was clear to us that even if the film were wildly successful, any return, let alone profits, would be eaten up by the interest. Jack and I did the arithmetic and returned the $750,000 to our investors. When Peter Newman asked Sam Bronfman what, of all of the things in the world, he wished he could have invented, his one word answer was "interest."

It was the end of my involvement in the feature film industry and the beginning of another kind of shock. I declared bankruptcy. My lawyer, former University of Alberta chancellor Louis Desrochers, advised me that there was no shame in bankruptcy. I had done nothing wrong, he told me. The laws were there precisely to protect people and businesses facing changing circumstances beyond their control that destroyed the viability of their enterprises.

I thought that my life was over. But two things that took place during the gloom of that period stunned me. I decided to resign from a number of organizations, including the boards of two provincial government organizations, the Alberta Foundation for the Performing Arts and the Banff Centre. I did not want to embarrass them. I wrote to Minister of Culture Mary LeMessurier tendering my resignation from the Performing Arts Foundation, and to Peter Lougheed, who had appointed me to the Banff Centre Board of Governors. As expected, I received a letter from Mary accepting my resignation. But I was stunned to receive a telephone call from Peter Lougheed telling me, quite firmly, that he would not accept my resignation. There's no shame in bankruptcy, he told me. I want you to stay. And I did, through that term and another.

I was almost as stunned when Tommy Banks, who had been a good friend over the years, scolded me for not having called him when I got into trouble. "Your friends, including me," he said, "would have done what they could to bail you out." I was surprised, and touched. It brought home to me what a loner I had considered myself to be, and had in fact been. The best thing about this period was that this was when I met my wife, Gladys Odegard. I haven't been a loner since.

Now, looking back, I understand that the real legacy of those golden years is the solid foundation that Alberta was able to build under the arts institutions it created. In spite of the cuts, in spite of the changes in attitude, the Edmonton Heritage Festival, the Edmonton Fringe Festival and the Banff International Television

TAX DEFERRAL
INVESTMENT OPPORTUNITY

Public issue: $2,000,000.
200 Film Units at $10,000. Per Film Unit
A Feature Length Motion Picture Entitled

A WILD, RAUNCHY, FUNNY TALE OF THE GREATEST OFF-ROAD 4x4 VEHICLE RACE EVER STAGED

Featuring JAMIE (KLINGER) FARR as "HARD LUCK HARRY"

Executive Producer FIL FRASER   Producer JACK WYNTERS

A feature length motion picture produced so as to be eligible for certification as a certified
Canadian Feature film. Investors will have an opportunity to deduct 100% of the subscription price
from ordinary taxable income in the 1980 taxation year. A film produced with the
participation of the Canadian Film Development Corporation and Famous Players Ltd.

OFFERED BY PROSPECTUS ONLY — for copies of the prospectus please
contact:
4x4 Productions Ltd., Fil Fraser, President.
EDMONTON: 2001, 9918 - 101 Street, Phone: 428-6690
CALGARY: 401-5920 MacLeod Trail, Phone: 252-6660
Rhodes Denton Securities Ltd.
645 Gulf Canada Square
Calgary, Phone: 233-7377
Houston Willoughby of Alberta Ltd.
1837 Toronto Dominion Tower
Edmonton Centre, Phone: 423-5333

Jack Wynters and I thought that this movie would be a winner. Unfortunately, interest rates in the 20 percent plus range made the project impossible to finance. *Photo: from the* Edmonton Journal

Festival remain the largest, most successful events of their kind in the world. The Banff Centre is still one of Canada's most highly respected cultural institutions. The Citadel Theatre complex is still the finest in the land. They, and scores of other events and institutions, are the legacy of the Lougheed years, that magnificent era when Jeanne and Peter Lougheed, Horst Schmid, Les Usher and many, many others, turned Alberta into one of the most exciting parts of Canada.

Epilogue

What Now?

Albertans are not likely to see another era like the one that so enriched us during the Lougheed years. Attitudes by political leaders have changed to the point of being almost unrecognizable from the perspective of those golden years. Funding for the arts has moved from a high rung to the bottom of the priorities ladder.

The North American economy, into which we are now almost fully integrated, follows very different imperatives from those that animated us during the 1970s and 1980s. We seem to be becoming more like the Americans, who leave funding for the arts to the private sector. The difference is, however, that Canadian corporations are less generous than their American counterparts, who enjoy significant tax breaks when they fund the arts. There is no CBC, no

Peter Lewis created this design for the new Edmonton concert hall at the request of its major funder, Francis Winspear, but the board opted for a more conventional design for the facility, which boasts one of the best acoustic environments in the world. *Photo: courtesy Peter Lewis*

Canada Council, no federally funded National Arts Centre in the US. PBS, the closest thing to public broadcasting, continues to plague its viewers with seemingly endless telethons and politically safe entertainment programming. When I attended a PBS convention in the 1970s, station executives were, even then, worried that corporate funding was reducing their ability to deal with serious or controversial subjects. Support for music, children's and nature programs was relatively easy to get. But funding for cutting-edge documentaries was, even then, fading fast. Today it is virtually nonexistent. The kind of boat-rocking programs we see regularly on the CBC are not found on PBS.

While the proliferation of specialty channels in Canada has created new opportunities for documentary, and for a few dramatic filmmakers, those same channels have, in the aggregate, vastly increased the quantity of American programming available to anyone whose TV is attached to a cable or satellite system. The dream of the 500-channel universe may have come true. But the dream is about the past, not the future.

Scanning the offerings on my satellite system sometimes makes me feel that almost every program that has ever been on commercial television is still on. Endless repeats of programs that we watched in the 1960s, 1970s and 1980s populate the dial. Program material from the 1950s keeps turning up in retrospectives. In this environment, Canadian programming, no matter how good, plays second banana.

The momentum created by the Lougheed era has extended beyond its years with the creation of facilities such as the Francis Winspear Centre for Music in Edmonton's city centre, the Timms Centre for Drama on the campus of the University of Alberta and the Rozsa Centre on the campus of the University of Calgary. They were created long after the Lougheed era had ended. But without the strong foundation built then, it is unlikely they could have been realized. The Winspear Centre for Music, according to international trumpet virtuoso Jens Lindeman, is, acoustically, one of the top half-dozen concert halls in the world.

In hindsight, the most valuable innovation of the 1970s was Alberta Culture's program of matching grants. It led to unprecedented support for the arts from private citizens, who knew that they were getting great value when their contributions were matched, dollar for dollar, by the government. The clear role of government was not only to fund the arts, but to encourage the private sector to do so as well.

Is there any likelihood that anything close to the matching grants program of the 1970s will be reinstated in the foreseeable future? I don't think so. Time and attitudes have moved on. But that does not in any way diminish the challenge for people who care about the arts to fight for new ways to make them viable. Yet, we can be thankful that there are still many Albertans who dedicate substantial resources of time and money to supporting the arts.

Alberta Minister of Community Development Gene Zwozdesky has worked hard to broaden government support for the arts. An artist in his own right, he had some success in the 2003 provincial budget, getting a modest increase in funding for the Alberta Foundation for the Arts, the first since the Klein administration came to power. And he persuaded his Cabinet colleagues to restore some of the support that helped build a substantial film industry in the province during the 1980s. Some of the new money, he told me, will be devoted to a study of the economic impact of the arts in Alberta. Anecdotal evidence suggests that more people attend arts events than sports events and that the economic impact of the arts in employment, in tourism and related fields provides more "bang for the buck" than many other forms of government investment. But we need good research, not anecdotes, to prove the case to those who control the purse strings. I can only hope that Zwozdesky succeeds.

The Honourable Lois Hole, lieutenant-governor of Alberta, has announced the creation of the Lieutenant-Governor of Alberta Arts Awards Program. The awards are designed to raise the profile of the arts through the introduction of significant prizes that will have an impact across Canada. They will recognize distinguished contributions from Albertans in all categories of artistic creativity, from senior artists who have created an important body of work, to talented newcomers who have broken new ground, to mavericks who have stretched the envelope, changed or broadened the way we see the arts and ourselves. The awards, up to three in number, will be given biennially, beginning in 2004. Each winner will receive a cash award of $30,000, the largest award for the arts in Alberta and among the largest in Canada. The money will come from a privately funded endowment administered by the Edmonton and Community Foundation and the Calgary Foundation. No taxpayers' dollars are involved. Lieutenant-Governor Hole has appointed a council to advise her office on the design, promotion and implementation of the program, as well as on the selection of recipients for the awards. I am honoured to be a member of that council.

As we struggle toward becoming a more civil society, Alberta's golden era should stand as an example for all of Canada, a template for broadening and enriching the value and quality of our citizenship. Alberta has demonstrated that it can rise to the challenge. I have not given up on the hope that my son, Randall Fraser, who has made a life as a member of the Edmonton arts community, will some day experience a renaissance of government commitment that will rival that of the magnificent '70s.

In spite of its ultra-conservative reputation, Alberta is the place in all of Canada where, over nearly four decades, I have found a happy, supportive home for my serendipitous, richly varied career.

I love this place.

Endnotes

Introduction: An Explosion of the Arts

1   *Edmonton Journal*, October 5, 2002.

2   Fred Klinkhammer, in a submission to the Federal Task Force on Broadcasting Policy (aka Caplan Sauvageau), 1985–86. I was a member of the task force, established in 1985 by the federal Minister of Communications Marcel Masse.

3   There were two half-hours called *The Political Process*, a chronicle of Doug Roche's first campaign. Then there were seven half-hours called *Peoples of Alberta* and about eight five-minute vignettes for ACCESS-TV, *Ghost Towns of Alberta*. There was a documentary about the Winter Cities Showcase, held here in 1988, and a second documentary on the Ice Lantern (sculptures) Festival set up in West Edmonton Mall parking lot by a group from Harbin, China. This film was unofficially the first Canada-China co-production, although they failed to complete the paper work on their side, so it remains unofficial. There was a documentary about engineering for the 100th anniversary of APEGGA, an engineering association, which starred Peter Newman and Joe Shoctor. Looking at old Beta tapes, I see a show called "Consider the Eskimo," which was the second of two programs in a series called *The Competitive Process*.

4   It should be noted that central Canadians seem naturally to assume that, because most Canadians live there, anything generated there is "national." Toronto has the National Ballet, established in 1951, years after the Royal Winnipeg Ballet was established in 1939. Winnipeg received Royal designation in 1953, while the Toronto organization was still struggling. Other examples include the Canadian National Exhibition in Toronto.

5   Editorial, "Future Cloudy for Arts in Alberta…it would be sad to backslide now," *Calgary Herald*, May 26, 1986.

6   *Edmonton Journal*, August 19, 2002.

Chapter 1: Culture Shock: The Changing of the Guard

7   T.C. Byrne, *Alberta's Revolutionary Leaders* (Calgary: Detselig, 1991), 238.

8   A.J. (Alf) Hooke, *30+5: The Incredible Years of Social Credit* (Edmonton: Institute of Applied Art, 1971), 9. Hooke was a former Cabinet minister.

9   Orvis Kennedy, *Principles and Policies of Social Credit—A Free Individual Enterprise Movement Opposed to Socialist and all Other Forms of Statism*. 1951. [pamphlet] n.p. Available at the Legislature Library.

10   Peter C. Newman, *Home Country* (Toronto: McClelland & Stewart, 1973), 198. His statement about the Americans might not seem quite as funny today.

11 Murray's story is chronicled in Jack Gorman, *Père Murray and the Hounds: The Story of Saskatchewan's Notre Dame College* (Sidney, BC: Gray's Publishing, 1977) and in my feature film *The Hounds of Notre Dame.*

12 Both CCFers and Socreds railed against the control of the eastern banks during the Depression years.

13 The legislation establishing the Treasury Branches (now known as ATB Financial) was challenged by the federal government, and the province was forced to make amendments that restricted the areas in which the "Branch" could operate.

14 David G. Wood, *The Lougheed Legacy* (Toronto: Key Porter, 1985), 23.

15 First with Jean Patenaude, now a successful arts film producer, and with Dawn MacDonald, whose company produces religious television programs in Toronto.

16 I met him on my first day in Saskatchewan, when I found myself standing side by side with him at a urinal in Regina's Hotel Saskatchewan.

17 The Co-operative Commonwealth Foundation was the forerunner of the New Democratic Party.

18 Free University North had a brief existence in Edmonton during the late '60s when people with knowledge and expertise volunteered to share their skills. The mantra was "each one teach one." Rochdale was a Toronto experiment in creating an unstructured university, where students learned what they wanted when they wanted.

19 Alan Hustak, *Peter Lougheed: A Biography* (Toronto: McClelland & Stewart, 1979), 78.

20 Aritha van Herk, *Mavericks: An Incorrigible History of Alberta* (Toronto: Viking/Penguin Press, 2001).

21 Byrne, 197.

22 The Mannings, father and son, later published *Political Realignment: A Challenge to Thoughtful Canadians* (Toronto: McClelland & Stewart, 1967).

23 From an account by Jim Edwards. Southern Alberta is quite flat, and the roads may not have a bend in them for many miles.

24 It is not unlikely that Lougheed influenced the departmental evolution. After becoming leader of the Conservative Party in 1965, he had made it clear that he championed a more cultural and multicultural agenda. Lougheed had recruited Edmonton businessman Horst Schmid as his advisor for the "Preservation of the Ethno-Cultural Heritage of Alberta."

25 *Edmonton Journal,* August 7, 1971.

26 Letter from Rudy Michetti to Peter Lougheed, August 28, 1971. Lougheed Papers, Alberta Provincial Museum and Archives.

27 *Time Magazine,* September 13, 1971.

28 *Time Magazine,* September 13, 1971. Blakeney defeated Thatcher (Sask.);

Hatfield defeated Robichaud (N.B.); Regan defeated Smith (N.S.); Bourassa defeated Jean-Jacques Bertrand (Que.); Schreyer defeated Weir (Man.); Lougheed defeated Strom (Alta.).

29 *Edmonton Journal,* August 31, 1971.

30 *Edmonton Journal,* August 31, 1971.

31 *Calgary Herald,* September 28, 1968. History seems to repeat itself whenever any government gets too long in the tooth.

32 Government of Alberta, *Position Paper No. 7: New Directions Position Paper on Alberta's Cultural Heritage,* November 1972.

33 *Edmonton Journal,* David Staples, March 17, 1996.

34 Anna Porter and Marjorie Harris, eds., *Farewell to the 70s* (Toronto: Thomas Nelson, 1979), 54.

Chapter 2: From Agricultural Fairs to Arts Festivals

35 *Alberta Culture Youth and Recreation Annual Report,* 1972.

36 Interview with Walter Kaasa, spring 2003.

37 Jablonski, born in Nazi-occupied Crakow, Poland, in November 1939, came to Edmonton with his family in 1949. He died of cancer in 1999.

38 To paraphrase philosopher Alan Watts's tongue-in-cheek rant, the arts are totally useless—"they serve no purpose beyond themselves." You don't play music to get to the end. "If that were the case the best conductors would be those who conducted the orchestra the fastest. Some would specialize in playing only finales. And, you don't dance to get to a certain spot on the floor. You dance to dance. And you make music for the sheer joy of it."

39 Alberta Legislative Library, Vault 19.

Chapter 3: The Lougheeds

40 *Edmonton Journal,* August 31, 1971.

41 *Time Magazine,* March 13, 1972.

42 When ballet star Karen Kain invited me to watch her in a performance from the offstage wings at Niagara-on-the-Lake, I got a close-up view of how hard members of the National Ballet worked. Karen was slated to play the lead in a movie I tried to make, *The Falcon and the Ballerina.* Unfortunately, the film was never made.

43 See *Alberta Views* magazine, Sept.–Oct. 2002, for a description of Beaulieu.

44 I know that's no easy role. My brother Frank played for several years in the Canadian Football League, most of them with the Ottawa Rough Riders, but later with the Saskatchewan Roughriders, the Eskimos and the Winnipeg Blue Bombers. I often watched from the stands as, in his role as a punt return specialist, much bigger players tried to grind him into the ground. Both he

and Lougheed have had knee problems. Frank, after surgeries, still has a slight limp. Peter, in August 2001, took advantage of new medical technology and had a successful knee replacement.

45   The Lougheeds have four children: Steven, Andrea, Pamela and Joe.

46   *Time Magazine,* March 13, 1972.

47   One of the originals elected with Lougheed in 1967 and a key member of his Cabinet.

48   *Edmonton Journal,* September 30, 1971.

49   When I asked him if it was true that he had had a letter of resignation from every member of his Cabinet in his safe, he gave me that steady, steely-eyed look he gets when he wants to be very clear and replied with a single, almost challenging, word: "Yes." After a cool, deliberate pause, he added, "I thought that was the way it should be." He was once described, because of that look, as the "white laser." (Robert Sheppard in the *Globe and Mail,* February 16, 1985.)

50   The National Energy Program, introduced by the Trudeau government in October 1980, was seen by Lougheed as an attack on the province's ownership of its mineral resources. There ensued a bitter battle that saw Alberta reduce oil exports to eastern Canada. The Mulroney government repealed the program following its 1984 election victory.

51   No one I talked to could remember the words, but according to Alan Hustak the song went something like this:

> I'm the Sheik of Calgary
>
> These sands belong to me
>
> Trudeau says they're for he
>
> Into my tent he'll crawl
>
> Like Algeria did to de Gaulle
>
> The gas we've got today
>
> We don't just fart away
>
> Gas pains don't worry me
>
> Cuz I'm the Sheik of Calgary.

A thin-skinned politician would have been mightily offended.

52   Private correspondence, Jeanne Lougheed's personal files. Poole is a member of the family that built Poole Construction Ltd., now known as PCL, one of Canada's largest construction firms. John Poole's Order of Canada citation recognizes him for his support of the arts.

53   The official version is reflected in correspondence in the Lougheed papers and was reported and commented on in news reports of the day.

54   *Calgary Herald,* May 13, 1976.

55   The unofficial version was told to me by Jeanne Lougheed.

56 See *Edmonton Journal* article by Kathy Kennedy, April 28, 1976.

57 Private correspondence, Jeanne Lougheed's personal files.

58 *Calgary Herald,* May 27, 1976.

59 Lougheed papers, Provincial Archives of Alberta. While the negatives for Karsh portraits are fixed in time, each print, made personally by the artist in his darkroom, is unique. Prints of a particular photograph could vary according to his mood, and presumably according to where the photograph would be used. The artistry is in the Karsh eye, both behind the camera and in the darkroom.

60 Lougheed Papers, Provincial Archives of Alberta.

61 I met Karsh at a dinner thrown by the American Ambassador to Canada Thomas Enders, in honour of film director Frank Capra. Capra is famous for such classic movies as the perennial *It's a Wonderful Life, Mr. Smith Goes to Washington* and *It Happened One Night.* On his 80th birthday, he was being honoured for a lifetime of remarkable films. Following a screening of *It's a Wonderful Life* at the National Arts Centre I, then in the middle of my movie-making years, was invited back to the reception at the ambassador's house, where small tables for two or three had been set up. Miraculously, I thought, I found myself sharing a table with Capra and Yousuf Karsh. Capra, energized by the honours he had received, was proud of his remarkable filmography. "I made all of my films in four weeks," he told me, decrying the huge budgets and virtually open-ended shooting schedules of contemporary films. I was just getting ready to make *Marie Anne* and told him I would follow his example and make it in four weeks. Big mistake. Should have taken five or six; but that's another story. The always gentlemanly Yousuf Karsh asked Capra what he thought of the current crop of movies. "Bullshit!" Capra pounded on the table, his voice rising, "It's all Bullshit! Sex and violence, and no story—*and no story.*"

62 Her daughter Andrea, now a horticulturalist living in Victoria, was a dancer with the Royal Winnipeg Ballet before moving into a career in stage management.

63 Borden was later to make the grant that resulted in the construction of the Sally Borden Building at the Banff Centre.

64 *Edmonton Journal,* October 12, 1985.

Chapter 4: Mr. Alberta Culture: Horst Schmid

65 Hugh Planche, according to Bill Marsden, who worked for him as director of Film Development.

66 Jim Edwards has had an illustrious career as a Member of Parliament and Cabinet minister, as head of Economic Development Edmonton, and as chair of the Board of Governors of the University of Alberta.

67 The Metropolitan Edmonton Educational Television Association (MEETA), forerunner of Alberta's ACCESS Educational Television Network, went on the air March 1, 1970, on Channel 11, a VHF channel available through rabbit ears on any television set. TVOntario went on the air on September 1, on Channel 47, a UHF channel not available on all sets.

68 Kaasa, in charge of cultural development, had become one of the stars of the department. Away from his job, he was an accomplished actor, later recognized by the naming of the Walter Kaasa Theatre in the Edmonton Jubilee Auditorium.

69 In 1991, the Alberta Foundation for the Arts (AFA) replaced the Alberta Art Foundation, the Alberta Foundation for the Performing Arts, the Alberta Foundation for the Literary Arts and the arts and cultural industries grant programs of Alberta Culture and Multiculturalism. http://www.cd.gov.ab.ca/ all_about_us/commissions/arts/act/index.asp

70 The grants allowed them to make ticket prices more accessible and helped to create an audience of 400,000, triggering, according to departmental reports, $4.6 million in production. But that was just the warm-up. In the next fiscal year, $1,280,216 was granted to 18 professional performing arts organizations, leading to budgeted expenditures of $7.4 million. Thirty-seven amateur groups received $92,760 in grants.

71 For a short sketch of Billington's influence on the arts, see endnote 143.

72 Dave Billington, *Edmonton Sun*, June 27, 1985.

73 From a 1965 white paper issued by Pierre LaPorte entitled "A Cultural Development Policy for Quebec," Vol. 1, 22. Laporte held the important post of Minister of Immigration, Manpower and Labour.

74 Reid, now the executive director of the Canadian Music Centre, Prairie Region, was then executive assistant to the co-ordinator of the Festival of the Arts.

75 Daddy Warbucks was a mysterious character in the Depression-era "Little Orphan Annie" comic strip, always turning up at times of crisis with a solution that often included money. He was the quintessential fixer.

76 The term achieved currency in the mid-1990s and is mostly used by the United Nations and others to describe the objectives of non-governmental organizations (NGOs). For example, the Center for Civil Society Studies of the Johns Hopkins Institute for Policy Studies seeks to encourage the development and effective operation of nonprofit, philanthropic or "civil society" organizations.

77 In 1974–75, 29 NGOs had their fund-raising efforts matched in the amount of $996,597, covering 59 projects in 33 countries. In 1975–76, the first year the program was fully operational, 35 NGOs were matched for a total of $1,995.626 for 94 projects in 39 countries. The next year the amount matched was $2,178,133. In 1978–79—254 projects—39 NGOs—70 countries—NGOs raised $4,319,993 for a total of $8,639,993. And in 1979–80,

the Alberta International Assistance Program continued in its position as the largest aid program in Canada directly funded by a province. Forty-seven NGOs supported 245 projects in 66 countries, with a total dollar-for-dollar government contribution of $4,849,967.

78   This quote comes from a letter dated February 22, 1973, from Ernie Jamison, the head of the Censor Board, to Peter Lougheed. Lougheed Papers, Alberta Provincial Museum and Archives.

79   Correspondence files of Premier Peter Lougheed held in the Provincial Archives of Alberta. As with the Jamison letter above, this letter and the protest for the Women of Unifarm are part of the Lougheed Papers that are not available to the general public.

80   Personal recollection of Terry Keiko told to me in an interview, September 25, 2002.

81   Hustak, 186.

82   *Calgary Herald*, May 6, 1978.

83   Ivor Dent, *Getting the Games* ([Alberta]: Ardent Enterprises, 1977).

84   Kathryn Warden in the *Calgary Herald*, May 6, 1978.

85   Heritage Day, which falls on the first Monday in August on Schmid's recommendation, was designated as an official provincial holiday in 1974.

86   While I have been unable to find a source for this description, it is one Horst knows about and enjoys. He has also been called an "overweight dynamo" (John Dodd, *Edmonton Journal*, January 13, 1979) and a "garrulous Bavarian" (Keith Ashwell, *Edmonton Journal*, November 6, 1982)—all of which show that Horst's rotund dimensions were often the subject of "friendly" humour.

Chapter 5: Joe Shoctor: A Theatrical Colossus

87   The early history of theatre in Edmonton has been chronicled by Mary Ross Glenfield, herself one of the pioneers of theatre in Edmonton. In 2001, at the age of 80, she completed a Master of Arts degree in the Department of Drama at the University of Alberta. I am indebted for much of what follows to her MA thesis, *The Growth of Theatre in Edmonton: From the Early 1920s to 1965*, The University of Alberta, 2001.

88   Glenfield, 158.

89   David S.R. Leighton and Peggy Leighton, *Artists, Builders and Dreamers: 50 Years at the Banff School* (Toronto: McClelland & Stewart, c1982), 23.

90   Leighton and Leighton, 43.

91   Ron Hayter, in *The Edmontonian*, May 7–13, 1966, 3.

92   The award-winning movie version, starring Sidney Poitier, has become a classic.

93   Glenfield, 9.

94   According to Tom Peacocke, before launching the Citadel, Joe produced a season

of some six plays at the Strand Theatre, with actors that included Mickey MacDonald and Wally McSween. One of the shows was *My Three Angels*.

95 The grant was doubled to $30,000 the following year.

96 John Neville had already established himself as a distinguished actor on the British stage before immigrating to Canada where Joe Shoctor recruited him as artistic director of the Citadel. He has had a monumental impact on Canadian theatre. From 1973 to 1978, he created performances that saw the Citadel break all records for attendance and full-season subscriptions. He moved to Halifax in 1978 to head the Neptune Theatre in Halifax, where he erased a sizeable deficit. In 1983, he became artistic director of the Stratford Theatre, again bringing in record audiences with productions that were both highly professional and very popular. Neville also developed a parallel career in film with movies such as *The Adventures of Baron Munchausen* and *Sunshine*. He continues to appear in film, on television and on stage.

97 Ashwell once complained in print that the Edmonton CBC dinner-hour show wasn't hosted by "real Canadians." The co-hosts were Francophone Jean Patenaude and me.

98 The Edmonton Space and Science Centre is now called Odyssium.

99 Screenwriter William *(All the President's Men, Butch Cassidy and the Sundance Kid)* Goldman's book, *Adventures in the Screen Trade*, is one of the bibles of Hollywood writing.

100 From a video tribute to Joe Shoctor assembled for a memorial to him, held in his beloved Citadel Theatre, Monday, October 22, 2001.

Chapter 6: Mel Hurtig's Magnificent Gift

101 Much of the material in the chapter is derived from conversations with Mel Hurtig and others in the Alberta publishing industry, and from my own involvement. During the 1970s my then-wife, Ruth Bertelsen, and I operated a publishers' representation business.

102 *Edmonton Journal*, November 10, 2002.

103 The book retailing business is the only one I know in which, if you can't sell the merchandise, you can return it to the manufacturer for full credit. The practice was a key factor in the crisis in publishing in 2000–01, when a large retail chain seemingly over-ordered its supply, and then unexpectedly returned thousands of books to publishers for credit.

104 I have since acquired a copy of the first edition, signed by Hurtig, which I treasure, thanks to Nancy Foulds of Lone Pine Publishing and her aunt, Thelma Dennis.

105 See Mel Hurtig, *At Twilight in the Country: Memoirs of a Canadian Nationalist* (Toronto: Stoddart, 1996), for an account of his battles over the years with bankers.

106 Hurtig, 234.

107 The title of Hurtig's first book as an author. See Mel Hurtig, *The Betrayal of Canada* (Toronto: Stoddart, 1991).

108 A few years earlier, Mazankowski had offered me a position as a CRTC commissioner, which I declined.

109 From a conversation with Allan Shute, September 25, 2002.

Chapter 7: Road to the Fringe

110 Don Blake, *Alberta Trivia* (Edmonton: Lone Pine, rev. ed. 1990), 69.

111 Anne's father, Leslie Green, is an internationally known expert in international terrorism and professor emeritus at the University of Alberta.

112 The name probably came from the fact that the company was the third to offer plays, following the long-standing Walterdale Theatre and the Citadel. Some considered the name to be a snub of the University of Alberta's venerable Studio Theatre, with which Schoenberg had had some disagreements.

113 *Alberta Views*, Jan.–Feb. 2000, 16.

114 James DeFelice, *Canadian Theatre Review*, Winter 1978, 17.

115 Juliani starred, with Andrée Pelletier, in *Marie Anne* and went on to join the small circle of Alberta movie producers with *Latitude 55*, for which I was executive producer.

116 One of the charming aspects of the Fringe is a new name every year. Some are 1982–A Fringe Theatre Event; 1983–Return of the Fringe; 1984–The Fringe Strikes Again; 1985–Home on the Fringe; 1986–Fringe the Fifth; and 1999–The Bride of Frankenfringe.

117 Clive A.F. Padfield, *The Economic Impact of the 1984 Fringe Theatre Festival.* (Unpublished report)

118 David Belke is one of the mainstays of Edmonton theatre, both as a playwright (his *Dreamland Saturday Nights* at the 1998 Edmonton Fringe was the winner of the Sterling Award) and as an actor. He has written 15 produced plays.

119 Edmontonians know that it can snow in any month of the year and are rarely surprised when it does.

120 Fringe Festival Web site, http://www.fringetheatreadventures.ca/

Chapter 8: Making Movies in Alberta

121 Linda Kupecek, *Alberta Views*, January–February, 2000, 16.

122 Dr. Allard (1919–91) was a prominent Edmonton businessman, medical doctor and media mogul. Allard graduated in medicine from the University of Alberta in 1943. He was a surgeon and then chief surgeon at the General Hospital in Edmonton. He established Allarcom Developments, one of the

largest real-estate companies in Canada. He started Allarcom Broadcasting, which in 1987 owned Edmonton's ITV station and western Canada's Super-Channel.

123 The Etrog, named for artist Sorel Etrog who designed it, is the name of the statuette of a roundish woman in dance. It was given to winners of the Canadian Film Awards before the Academy of Canadian Cinema, established in 1979, brought in the Genie Awards.

124 When the legendary Ottawa-based film pioneer Budge Crawley and I tried to mount a sports film about the Smoky River boat race, an elite affair that attracted expensive, high-powered jet boats piloted by such luminaries as Peter Pocklington and Paul Newman, we flew the length of the river in a government-owned Queen Air turboprop. One of the aircraft in the fleet was an ancient twin-engine DC3 airliner, once the workhorse of Trans-Canada Airlines. Crawley produced one of Canada's earlier feature films, *The Luck of Ginger Coffee* (1964) and won Canada's first feature film Oscar for his 1975 production of *The Man Who Skied Down Everest.* Pocklington, who started out in the used-car business, rose to become an industrialist and owner of the Edmonton Oilers. His empire began to collapse after he sold Wayne Gretzky to the Los Angeles Kings.

125 There is some argument about this. The Shipmans were Canadian (Ernie was born in Shipman, now Almonte, Ontario), but they had long since moved to Hollywood.

126 Linda Kupecek, *Alberta Views,* Jan.–Feb., 2000, 16. Linda Kupecek was a Canadian correspondent for *The Hollywood Reporter* for 10 years and appeared as national film columnist on the CBC Newsworld network in 1990. She played a supporting role in *Marie Anne* and had a speaking role in Robert Altman's *McCabe and Mrs. Miller.* She is a graduate of the BFA (Acting) program at the U of A.

127 Most of those programs were taken over by AMPIA—particularly training for the various film crafts. It was AMPIA, for example, that arranged for Albertans to work as apprentices or trainees on some of the Hollywood films that were made in Alberta. Much of this was in the early days of Bill Marsden's presidency, when a very cooperative Chuck Ross was film development officer. Later, when Marsden took on the development officer role himself, he formalized some of the arrangements. Many of the more creative programs were carried on by the Banff Centre and became an integral part of the writing program chaired by W.O. Mitchell and co-directed by Ruth Fraser.

128 Stahl, who is principled, hard working and deeply spiritual, became a close ally as we developed our film industry. He was general secretary to AMPIA and worked with me not only on our first film festival, but also on the launch of both the Commonwealth Games Film Festival and the Banff International Television Festival.

129 Kotcheff is one of many Canadian directors who have moved successfully to Hollywood. His films include *First Blood, North Dallas Forty* and *Fun with Dick and Jane.*

130 *Alberta Film Industry Report,* December 1977.

131 German was the first language of several of the early directors in Hollywood. Some say it was Otto Preminger who had trouble with the word *with.* So instead of saying, "We are recording this scene without sound" the words came out, "We are recording this scene mit out sound." Because of this word corruption, *MOS* means "without sound," and the term has been used in Hollywood ever since.

132 When I reviewed the official *Alberta Film Industry Report* handed to the government on December 1, 1977, I found it made no mention of our five-day stop in Hong Kong. The writers of the report, it seems, were concerned that that part of the trip might have been considered a junket, which to some extent it was. But Hong Kong is not too far off the beaten path when you are travelling from Australia to Canada.

Chapter 9: Cultural Treasures at Banff

133 David S.R. Leighton and Peggy Leighton, *Artists, Builders and Dreamers: 50 Years at the Banff School* (Toronto: McClelland & Stewart, c1982).

134 Leighton and Leighton, p. 27.

135 Moira Day. *Elizabeth Sterling Haynes and the Development of the Alberta Theatre,* PhD thesis, University of Toronto, 1987, 51. Quoted in Glenfield, 9.

136 Ringwood was western Canada's regional dramatist par excellence. Her prairie tragedy, *Still Stands the House* (1938), is one of the most frequently anthologized and performed Canadian plays. A pioneer of western community theatre, she wrote and produced her first stage play, *The Dragons of Kent,* in 1935 when she was registrar of the new Banff School of Fine Arts. She polished her playwriting skills at University of North Carolina drama department, where she wrote numerous folk plays, culminating in *Dark Harvest.* She received the Governor General's Award for outstanding service to Canadian drama (1941) and published the first volume of collected plays in 1982 by a Canadian dramatist. The Gwen Pharis Ringwood Civic Theatre (1971), Williams Lake, BC, is named for her. (Source: *The Canadian Encyclopedia* on-line http://www.thecanadianencyclopedia.com/)

137 This quote is from a tribute by Ringwood that appeared, among other places, in a brochure titled "Remembering Elizabeth," October 1974. It was produced for a special evening in Haynes's honour, chaired by Isadore Gliener and held in conjunction with a production of *Mr. Arcularis,* the proceeds of which initiated the Elizabeth Sterling Haynes Memorial Scholarship Fund at the University of Alberta.

138 And if you'll permit me a rant within the rant, I find it sadly deplorable that in today's world when people or corporations with means make a contribution to the arts, it is usually to a building named after them, or their wives, or their companies. Rarely now do we find buildings or facilities named for artists.

139 Haynes, according to the unpublished doctoral thesis by Mary Ross Glenfield, had been a supporter of the Council for Canadian–Soviet Friendship.

140 My marriage to Ruth was a casualty of, among other things, my bankruptcy resulting from the failure of my film business.

141 Banff Centre Act [2000] R.S.A., c.B-1, s.3.

142 The idea of a film festival not overwhelmed by Hollywood is one of the reasons the Commonwealth Festival continues. Following Edmonton, the festival was held at the Cyprus games.

143 Dave Billington moved to Edmonton in 1973 to join the newly launched *Edmonton Sun* after a stint at the *Montreal Gazette* where he had won two national newspaper awards for critical writing. As the *Sun*'s entertainment columnist, he produced some of the most insightful writing that we had seen about the city's burgeoning cultural life. A genuine film buff, he was a member of the jury of the first Alberta Film Festival and an active participant in the Banff International Television Festival. In recognition of his contributions, AMPIA created the Dave Billington Memorial Award, following his untimely death in 1988. The award was presented to Tom Peacocke in 1989 and to me in 1990.

144 I had unrealistically high hopes for the movie. An earlier preview in Seattle, at the Motion Picture Seminar of the Northwest, had received the longest standing ovation I had ever experienced, and I let myself believe that the magic of the story would overcome the flaws I knew were the result of inadequate pre-production.

145 Michael Prytula of Edmonton designed the perfect, enduring logo for the Banff International Festival of Films for Television. It is an image of 35mm film placed to look like a mountain range. Prytula's designs include the attractive symbol adopted for the XI Commonwealth Games held in Edmonton in 1978. When Len Stahl and I told him what we had in mind, he came up with the design in a matter of days. We paid him somewhere between $1200 and $1500, a terrific bargain by today's standards. I asked sculptor Roy Leadbeater to create a three-dimensional version of the logo in bronze, and he continues to produce the famous Rockies, awarded annually to winners at the festival. Now, like the rest of us, advancing in years, he has signed the copyright over to the festival and arranged for the awards to continue to be produced in perpetuity.

146 The symposium, titled Artists and World Crisis—Co-operation for Action, was held at the Banff Centre, April 5–8, 1985. The report on the symposium can be found in the Paul Fleck Library at the Banff Centre.

147 *Artists and World Crisis—Co-operation for Action*, report of the symposium held at the Banff Centre, April 5–8, 1985, 2.

Chapter 10: The Alberta Conundrum

148 Part of its reputation came from the fact that, for years, women were not admitted.

Chapter 11: Culture Shock: The End of an Era

149 Andrew Nikiforuk, Sheila Pratt and Don Wanagas, *Running on Empty: Alberta After the Boom* (Edmonton, NeWest Press, 1987), 40.

150 Nikiforuk, Pratt and Wanagas, 36–37.

151 Nikiforuk, Pratt and Wanagas, 23–25.

152 This included construction of the Walter Kaasa Theatre in Edmonton and the Betty Mitchell Theatre in Calgary.

153 Department of Community Development, 1992 Annual Report.

154 The commission, when I headed it, was an arm's-length, quasi-judicial body reporting to Cabinet through the Minister of Labour. After the changes, it became a secretariat reporting to an assistant deputy minister.

155 Created by Premier Don Getty after Rick Hanson's successful Man in Motion World Tour.

156 A phrase attributed to Brian Mulroney after he became prime minister in 1984.

157 Gordon Laxer and Trevor Harrison, eds., *The Trojan Horse: Alberta and the Future of Canada* (Montreal: Black Rose Books, 1995), 134.

158 *Edmonton Sun*, October 13, 1994.

159 Don Martin, *King Ralph* (Toronto: Key Porter, 2002), 39.

160 George Melynk, in Laxer and Harrison, 259.

161 Mark Lisac, *The Klein Revolution* (Edmonton: NeWest Press, 1995), 198.

162 George Melynk, in Laxer and Harrison, 238.

Index of Names

About the Cover Illustrator

Edmonton-born artist Toti completed her formal art training at St. Martin's School of Art in London, England.

On returning to Canada, she established herself as a printmaker. Her ongoing commitment to recording the people and places of Edmonton has left a rich legacy of works collected by art lovers across North America and in Europe.

Toti works on commissions and private projects at her studio on Vancouver Island.